FEB 21

God Bless our Home

Una Abrahamson

God Bless our Home

Domestic Life
in Nineteenth Century Canada

by Una Abrahamson

BURNS & MacEACHERN LIMITED

For My Husband and our Children

1867 | 1967

Published on the occasion of the Centennial of Canadian
Confederation and subsidized by the Centennial Commission.

Ouvrage publié à l'occasion du Centenaire de la Confédération
Canadienne, grâce à une subvention de la Commission du Centenaire.

*I acknowledge with gratitude
all who have helped with this book.
I am particularly indebted
to Howard Pain who designed
the book and brought to it not only
his considerable talent as an
artist but also his knowledge of
Canadiana.
To Roy Abrahamson for his
encouragement and criticism.
To the Centennial Commission
whose award helped make the
extensive research possible.*

Preface

This book has grown out of my interest in early housekeeping books. It has been a labour of love to record our history from within the framework of the nineteenth-century home: to go back in time and live for a while under that ornate and reassuring parlour motto — "God Bless Our Home".

The knowledge of this lesser history often explains the larger events, or at least puts them in perspective. Brillat-Savarin said, "Tell me what you eat, and I'll tell you what manner of man you are."

After many years of collecting social and domestic history, so few Canadian books came into my library that I realized whatever such books existed were rare, and most were being destroyed before their content could be collected and interpreted. Thus, a secondary reason for this book: I want my children to have an understanding and a pride in their inheritance, to know and to understand the self-reliance, the courage as well as the joys and tragedies of our recent past.

Domestic books reveal a phase of development in our country which, though recent by historical standards, is fast receding into the mists of time. First-hand witnesses are disappearing. Fewer people are able to recall with any clarity, and without nostalgia, daily life in the nineteenth century.

This distillation of the past is offered as a guide, to give the reader the knowledge and perspective for a journey back in time. Our background as a nation is complex, leaning heavily on the traditions of Great Britain, France and America. Many cross-currents affected the Canadian way of life; everything from the age-old wisdom of the Indians to the inquisitiveness of the Yankee-Canadian. There were frontier attitudes, while in the towns there was an awareness of caste and rank in what was meant to be a casteless society. Life in Canada was kaleidoscopic, always changing, full of anomalies, advanced yet primitive, different from the life of its southern neighbour, different from Europe. It was Canadian.

This is a country of great distances; to the European, one of unbelievably wide rivers; to the pioneer it was a land of silence. The ring of the axe could be heard for miles. There was isolation, and women in particular suffered from lack of social contact. They would pound corn outdoors, at pre-arranged times to make contact with a distant neighbour. Lack of news made settlers generous with their hospitality; lack of neighbours and conversation tended to make them speak in monosyllables.

There were new foods and new experiences. Neither the social rules nor the farming methods were the same as in the homeland. This was a country of bitter winters and burning summers, far more extreme than today. There were persistent outbreaks of disease, hordes of insects, and periodic food shortages. But there were fish and game for the taking, and hunting was no longer an aristocratic privilege.

For many there was a complete upheaval in manners, morals and values, as revolutionary as those of our own changing times. It called for strength of character and firm beliefs for a man to lead his family to an uncleared section. Nor was it easy for a woman to discard the gentilities she had learned in her parents' home. Pioneer life was practical and circumstances bred individualists. They had a sense of humour, sometimes rough and crude but often brilliant and witty. If there is one thing we could learn from our past, it is the ability to laugh at ourselves.

Though nostalgia tends to blur reality, life in nineteenth century Canada was hard for most, and the hardship was compounded by lack of knowledge. That we are here today to read, and I trust enjoy this book, God must have indeed blessed our home.

Una Abrahamson
September, 1966.

"... Any short-comings that may be noticed by our friends, must be excused on the score of the work being wholly Canadian in its execution."
Mrs. C. P. Traill, Canadian Wild Flowers, Montreal, 1869

Contents

	Preface	viii
1	Light on Dark Corners	2
2	Things a Lady Would Like To Know	14
3	Happy Homes	30
4	The Family Adviser	46
5	The Art of Preserving Health	56
6	The New Household Manual	68
7	The Experienced Housekeeper	84
8	Domestic Duties	96
9	The Canadian Haberdashery	110
10	Ladies' Indispensable Assistant	126
11	Treasures of Use and Beauty	136
12	Our Deportment	144
13	The Dinner Question	162
14	Curiosities of Food	174
15	Mother Hubbard's Cupboard	182
16	Youth's Miscellany	202
17	Omnium-Gatherum	220
	Bibliography	229
	Index	233

God Bless our Home

Light on
Dark Corners

CHAPTER ONE

The relationships between men and women in the nineteenth century bring to mind long and delicate courtships, large happy families with proud wise fathers and devoted saintly mothers, all wrapped up in a lace-edged valentine. This was sometimes the case, but in many instances it is the story we have come to believe after reading their literature and leafing through the inherited albums. But this is the expurgated version. There is another side to the coin which reveals the sordidness, the scandals and the widespread vices that flourished. Today we may smile reading the advice cautioning young girls not to come home from their work alone, nor to wander into such public places as dance halls and theatres. We may feel that our times have a new moral standard outmoding other mores, but the nineteenth century was also a time of upheaval. The same problems existed but perhaps on a larger scale in relation to a smaller population. There was illegitimacy, extensive drug addiction, homosexuality, as well as the hypocrisy of the double standard which believed in purity for all but allowed young men to adventure if not caught, while women were isolated at home.

How did it all come about? Up to the early days of the nineteenth century women in the educated classes were venturesome, knowledgeable, cultivated, and they enjoyed personal freedom. All this was gradually curtailed as time passed, while education became more sketchy and the home became a gilded cage. Women became symbols, enjoying greater prestige than ever but no longer participating in daily affairs nor able to discuss the problems of the day with their men. Their interests were restricted to the social world; they

were on a pedestal, adored, revered, but untouched. As a result, every young man of the social classes who conformed to this new attitude was denied the companionship of women of his own background.

Henry Mayhew wrote at mid-century one of the great social works of all time, *London Labour and the London Poor*, describing sordid town life. It would be wishful thinking to believe it was not repeated in this country. The books, the advertisements and the patent medicines to cure unnamed diseases, as well as the thundering from the pulpits, show that under the pompous urbanity of the respectable there were festers. The growth of prostitution and the lack of adequate relationships between the sexes colour the social life and the etiquette of the period. It increases in intensity and depth as the century progresses.

Naturally, as in all generalizations there are exceptions. Most of these social problems were restricted to larger areas of population although the new frontier towns of the west cannot be exempted. Perhaps the strident voices of the temperance leagues, the food reform fanatics and the women's rights groups would not have been so hysterical if women had continued to express their personalities, increased their education and enjoyed the freedoms their ancestors knew; and if men had been able to enjoy their companionship, and life had not been restricted by such severe conventions. It is all like one of their favourite parlour games, Charades, play-acting, a facade, that completely hides a way of life, until you read between the lines of the many books of the period on social life, health, medicine and sex.

The marriages of Canadians have been interesting ever since Louis XIV turned his attention to procreation abroad, sending annually between one hundred and one hundred and fifty "King's girls" to marry Quebec men. The brides came mostly from northern France. The day after marriage the Governor presented the King's dowry, which included such livestock as an ox, a cow, pairs of swine and fowl, as well as two barrels of pickled or salted meat and some money. Canadians were among the first people to have a family allowance. To encourage large families Louis gave money to men married before the age of twenty and girls younger than sixteen, as well as an annual bounty to those families with ten or more living children. Later settlers from countries, where the dowry and the match-maker were important, were astonished to find that young Canadians settled courtships themselves, and even permission from the bride's father was a mere formality.

The choice of a wife was important and her accomplishments and good health were of primary concern to the man settling in the backwoods. In 1842 N. Willis listed her assets: "Her skill is shown in the arts of manu-facturing maple sugar; candle and soap-making; baking; cooking; salting meat and fish; knitting stockings and mittens; spinning woollen yarns; feeding poultry; managing a dairy; and, lastly, in mending and making clothes for herself, her husband and children. These are the occupations of an emigrant's wife; and if a female cannot resolve to enter upon them cheerfully, she should never think of settling in the woods of Canada or New Brunswick".[1]

The chances for marriage for women were excellent, and it was said that any woman should be married within six months of landing. There was some concern that women married too young and this gave rise to an old saying still heard occasionally, "Early wed, early dead". The truth of the maxim can be seen when looking through church registers, family bibles and old burial grounds.

Both men and women enjoyed consulting books on how to choose the right partner, and these books were usually written by "professors" who mixed plain common sense with a lot of mumbo-jumbo. Their books had tremendous sales and were often sold by subscription only, mailed in plain packages. Their words ring with assurance and authority:

What Women Love in Men

"Women love sexual vigor in men, this is human nature. Weakly and delicate fathers have weak and puny children, though the mother may be strong and robust. A weak mother often bears strong children, if the father is physically and sexually vigorous. Consumption is often inherited from fathers, because they furnish the body, yet more women die with it because of female obstructions. Hence women love passion in men, because it endows their offspring with strong functional vigor. All men would be of good size in frame and flesh were it not for the infirmities visited upon them by the indiscretion of parents and ancestors of generations before."

What Men Love in Women

"No weakly, poor-bodied woman can draw a man's love like a strong, well-developed body. A round, plump figure with an overflow of animal life is the woman most commonly sought. A woman with a large pelvis gives her a superior and significant appearance, while a narrow pelvis always indicates weak sexuality. In the female beauty of physical development there is nothing that can equal full breasts. As a face looks bad without a nose, so the female breast, when narrow and flat, produces a bad effect. Small feet and small ankles are very attractive, because they are in harmony with a perfect female form, and men admire perfection. Small feet and ankles indicate modesty and reserve, while large feet and ankles indicate coarseness, physical power, authority and predominance."

How to Tell Disposition and Character

By the nose:
"Flat noses indicate flatness of mind and character, by indicating a poor, low organic structure.
Broad noses indicate large passageways to the lungs, and this, large lungs and vital organs, show great strength of constitution and hearty animal passions."

By stature:
"Tall persons have high heads, and are aspiring, aim high.
Small persons generally have exquisite mentalities."

By laughter:
"Vulgar persons always laugh vulgarly, and refined persons show refinement in their laugh."

By eyes:
"Those who have their eyes half shut are peek-a-boos and eaves-droppers."

By the hair:
"Coarse black hair and skin, and coarse red hair and whiskers, indicate powerful animal passions, together with corresponding strength of character. Abundance of hair and beard signifies virility, and a great amount of character; while a thin beard signifies sterility and a thinly settled upper storey with rooms to let, so that the beard is very significant of character."

"If a man wears his hat well down on the forehead, shading the eyes more or less, he will always keep his own counsel. If criminally inclined will be a very dangerous character."

"Do not marry a man with a low, flat head; for, however, fascinating, genteel, polite, tender, plausible or winning he may be, you will repent the day of your espousal."

"The old rule: 'Never marry a man that does not make his mother a Christmas present every Christmas', is a good one."[2]

With all this counselling it did happen that things went wrong and difficulties arose. It could be that not enough money was given for housekeeping and the way to tackle a parsimonious man was to keep housekeeping books and show them to him, or take him shopping with you. But you were never to leave this to a Saturday night, else the groceries might be delivered so late as to desecrate the Sabbath.

Other ladies had other problems. "Some ladies discover after marriage that they have taken a ninny for a partner, and have not the policy to conceal his defect when in company, but join in the laugh against him, thus making a severe reflection upon their foolish choice, which ought and must be as painful to a thinking woman, in her solitary moments when she comes to review her conduct, as it is to the poor husband at whose peculiar manner and sayings his wife is always ready to turn the shaft of ridicule. Tactics are

necessary when you have a husband of this sort to deal with; and if you do but bring him out, and place him in an important position whenever you can, it will serve very much to counteract the impression that might get abroad, that he was 'non compos mentis' ".[3]

The prevalence of drunkenness made many wives suffer and was doubtless the reason for so many women being in the Temperance movement. Books of advice warned young women of the constant truth that love and persuasion will not wean a drinker from his cups. Men were warned that hell's fires awaited the drunkard who neglected his family. Later, as the Temperance movement grew, prohibition was enacted.

Men were threatened with dire results going on for generations. According to the *Ladies' Companion, Saint John,* 1901: "But should you continue the moderate use of wine in your family, and your children become drunkards thereby, what sad colouring must it give to life's last moments; the thought of leaving behind a family of depraved children to nurture other children equally depraved; thus transmitting the misery you entailed upon them to a remote posterity!" Women continued to be without civil rights and at the mercy of their husbands. "Lastly there are those men we would rather not mention on these pages, and those are the demons in human shape — wife-beaters. But we trust that the public execration of such people, combined with the present more stringent regulations of the law, may prove efficient enough to quell such brutes".

Advice given to men was succinct: they were to become refined, uplifted and interested in things cultural, surely the beginning of the national custom of bored men enjoying the intermissions of concerts and lectures. The advice was there although in advance of its time: "Seek to refine your nature — it is no slander to say that many men have wives much more refined than themselves. This is natural in the inequalities of life. If your wife has the advantage of culture and refinement, and this is quite a common condition, as girls usually have a better chance for education and more leisure for books than boys, do not sink her to your level, but by study and thoughtfulness rise to her plane".[2] For obviously wrong choice in the marriage partner the advice was, "Suffer for your wife, if need be — Christ suffered for the Church".[4] Of divorce there was no question.

The feminine malady of the age seemed to be the "decline", and the victim was said to be suffering from an unhappy love affair. "Our cemeteries receive within the cold shadows of the grave thousands and thousands of victims that annually die from the results of 'broken hearts'. It is no doubt a fact that love troubles cause more disorders of the heart than everything else combined".[2] In actual fact it was more likely than not tuberculosis.

There were a number of books that for want of a better description may be called sex manuals, and they give quite a different picture of this period. These books, if anything, were far franker than books published for decades afterwards and are startling when read in the context of the rigid social barriers and formal etiquette of the time. They not only gave explicit sex instruction but also family planning advice. "It is the fashion of those who marry nowadays to have few children, often none. Of course this is a matter which married people must decide for themselves. Remember that the thousands of preventives which are advertised in papers, private circulars, etc. are not only inefficient, unreliable and worthless, but positively dangerous, and the annual mortality of females in this country from this cause alone is truly horrifying".[2] Women could make in the privacy of their homes "Orange Blossoms" or female suppositories from a mixture of zinc, cocoa butter, henbane and sweet almond oil.

Venereal disease was one of the scourges, running unchecked and inadequately cured since the Renaissance. Men tried to cure themselves with massive doses of mercury and patent medicines purporting to cure. There are countless almanacs with advertisements that drew attention to hidden sores, worries unknown by everyone else, hidden from friends, known only to the victim . . . help would come in a plain package. Commercial contraceptives were known and sold. The most famous had been invented originally to prevent the spread of disease by an English physician named Condon in mid-eighteenth century. He thought he was helping mankind but he little knew that the clergy would denounce him for inventing a new aid to sin. His name was corrupted and lived to become almost a household word. The English called it the "French coat" and the French called it an "English frock coat". His invention was made of sheep gut softened and dressed with almond oil and so it remained until the latter part of the century.

Among the Canadian myth-cures for venereal diseases were water-lily seeds and drinks of wood sorrel or oxalis. One of the reasons that sarsaparilla drinks and teas are featured so much in early cookery and medical books is because it was thought to be an effectual cure.

There is no doubt there were fates worse than death, and vice was well-organized. Sermons, magazines and books are full of items such as these, at that some of the more restrained:

Save the Girls

"The church should turn its face like flint against the public balls. In cities public balls are given every night, and many thoughtless young women mostly daughters of small tradesmen and mechanics or clerks and labourers, are induced to attend just for fun. Scarcely one in a hundred of the girls attending the balls preserve their purity. The public ball is always a resort of vile women who picture to innocent girls the ease and luxury of a harlot's life and offer them all manner of temptations to abandon the path of virtue."[2]

Perhaps nothing gives a more intimate and factual picture of life and manners than to leaf through these books which were read privately by both men and women. Their pomposity fades, they were unsure of themselves and forever seeking advice to become more adept lovers, more attractive and above all more virile.

9

The following excerpts bring into true perspective relations between the sexes in the nineteenth century. They are taken from *Search Lights on Health, Light on Dark Corners; A Complete Sexual Science and a Guide to Purity and Physical Manhood*, published in Toronto in 1894 and sold only by subscription. It should be pointed out that the word "lover" is used in its older sense, generally without sexual connotation. A lover was simply a "beau" in some parts of the country, and a "sweetheart" in other areas.

A Complete Sexual Science
and
A Guide to Purity and Physical Manhood

". . . All men feel much better for going a courting, providing they court purely. Nothing tears the life out of a man more than lust, vulgar thoughts and immoral conduct."

". . . Kissing, fondling and caressing between lovers — this should never be tolerated under any circumstances, unless there is an engagement to justify it, and then only in a sensible and limited way. The girl who allows a young man the privileges of kissing her or putting his arms around her waist before engagement will at once fall in the estimation of the man she has thus gratified and desired to please."

". . . A young woman and a young man had better not be alone together very much *until they are married*. This will be found to prevent a good many troubles. Kisses and caresses are most properly the monopoly of wives. Such indulgences have a direct and powerful physiological effect. Nay, they often lead to the most fatal results."

". . . The true test of virginity is modesty void of any disagreeable familiarity. A sincere Christian faith is one of the best recommendations."

". . . Want of desire may prevail and may be caused by loss of sleep, study, constant thought, mental disturbances, anxiety or the excessive use of tobacco or strong drinks. Get the mind and the physical constitution in proper condition and most all these difficulties will disappear. Ladies should doctor themselves instead of running to their physicians. First, inquire as to what sexual laws have been broken, then by proper restrictions, diet and exercise cure themselves."

". . . A good, long courtship will often cure many difficulties or ills of the sexual organs. Up and at it, dress up, spruce up, and be on the alert. Don't wait too long to get one more perfect than you are; but settle on someone soon. Remember that your unsexed state renders you over-dainty, and easily disgusted. So contemplate their lovable qualities."

". . . Boys who marry young derive but little enjoyment from the connubial state. They are liable to excesses and thereby lose much of the vitality and power of strength and physical endurance."

". . . Statistics show that married men live longer than bachelors. Child-bearing for women is conducive to longevity."

". . . Marriage purifies the complexion, removes blotches from the skin, invigorates the body."

". . . A young couple rushing together in their animal passion soon produce a nervous and irritating condition. Young husbands should wait for an invitation to the banquet and they will be amply repaid by the very pleasure sought. Invitation or permission delights, and possession by force degrades. The true principles are as follows: 'Bride, you owe reciprocity to your husband. Your marriage vows consist in covenanting to cohabit with him to the best of your ability. Fulfill it. He is entitled to your hearty participancy'."

". . . Marrying small waists is attended with consequences scarcely less disastrous than marrying rich and fashionable girls. Small waists indicate small

11

and feeble vital organs, a delicate constitution, sickly offspring, and a short life. Beware of them, therefore, unless you wish your heart broken by the early death of your wife and children."

". . . Can the sexes be produced at will? Queen bees lay female eggs first, and male afterwards. So with hens."

". . . Food and Drink: Coffee drank (*sic*) excessively causes debilitating effect upon the sexual organs. Tobacco: those who suffer any weakness from that source should carefully avoid the weed in all its forms. The papers are full of advertisements of 'LOST MANHOOD RESTORED' etc., but in every case they are worthless or dangerous drugs and certain to lead to some painful malady or death. Eating rye, corn, or Graham bread, oatmeal, cracked wheat, plenty of fruit etc. is a splendid medicine. If that is not sufficient then a physician should be consulted."

". . . Drugs Which Moderate Desire: Among one of the most common domestic remedies is camphor. The safest drug among the domestic remedies is a strong tea made out of hops. Saltpeter, or nitrate of potash, taken in moderate quantities are very good remedies."

One of the most interesting and delightful early marriage counsellors wrote a tiny pocket book about 1840 called the *Etiquette of Marriage*. The author himself remains unknown but the advice in most cases stands the test of time. It mainly deals with the daily behaviour of two people in the privacy of their home, but there are chapters on unhappy marriages, the marriage day, connubial happiness, household economy, bachelors and old maids, and that contentious subject, expenditure. It is from the chapters on "Homely Hints for Husbands and Wives" that the following rules are taken:

Etiquette of Marriage

". . . As the gentlemen only are privileged to make advances, we will commence with them, deeming them the more responsible.

Has that man a call to be a husband who, having wasted his youth in excesses, looks around him at the eleventh hour for 'a virtuous young girl' (such men have the effrontery to be very particular on that point), to make up his damaged constitution, and perpetuate it in their offspring?

Has he any call to be a husband, who adds to his wife's manifold cares that of selecting and providing the household stores, and enquires of her after that, how she spent the surplus shilling of yesterday's appropriation?

Has he any call to be a husband, who leaves his wife to blow out the lamp, and bruise her precious little toes while she is navigating for the bed-post?

Has he any call to be a husband, who sits down on his wife's best bonnet, or puts her shawl over her shoulders upside down, or wrong side out, at the Opera?

Has he any call to be a husband, who goes 'unbeknown' to his wife, to some wretch of a barber, and parts, for a shilling, with a beard which she has coaxed from its infantine sprout to luxuriant, full-grown, magnificent, unsurpassable hirsuteness, and then comes home, to her horrified vision, a pocket edition of Moses?"

Has he any call to be a husband, who kisses his wife only on Saturday night, when he winds up the clock and pays the grocer, and who never notices, day by day, the neat dress, and shining bands of hair arranged to please his stupid milk-and-watership?"

A Word to the Ladies . . .

"Has that woman a call to be a wife, who sits reading the last new novel, while her husband stands before the glass, vainly trying to pin a buttonless shirt-bosom?"

"Has that woman a call to be a wife, who expects her husband to swallow diluted coffee, soapy bread, smoky tea, and watery potatoes, six days out of seven?"

"Has she a call to be a wife, who would take advantage of a moment of conjugal weakness, to extort money or exact a promise?"

"Has she a call to be a wife who values an unrumpled collar or crinoline more than a conjugal kiss?"

REFERENCES
[1] *Canadian Scenery,* N. P. Willis, London, 1842.
[2] *Search Lights on Health, Light on Dark Corners,* B. G. Jefferies, Toronto, 1894.
[3] *A Manual of the Etiquette of Marriage,* Anonymous, London, c. 1840.
[4] *Home and Health,* Anonymous, London, Ontario, 1882.

Things a Lady Would Like to Know

CHAPTER TWO

Weddings, funerals and balls could be considered public occasions because in the early years they were attended by all without waiting for the formality of an invitation. As the country developed, the pattern changed. Social life stratified and invitations did not necessarily include the entire neighbourhood within riding distance. As in the case of dress, manners, and pastimes, generalizations have to be made about social events. Some areas of our country developed quickly, some much more slowly. Development in some places was early and then, after a certain point, progress stopped. Some parts were settled late and yet continued to grow. Some areas were settled by a population concerned with social niceties, while other areas kept a frontier spirit for many years longer, and all this is reflected in the daily life of people. It is impossible to say exactly when certain types of event took place. Roughly one can say that in parts of the Maritimes, the cities of Montreal and Quebec, the "front" along the St. Lawrence were all very sociable and wise in etiquette. But then again, this applies only to those of a certain social and educational background. Not only were there events such as weddings and funerals closely tied to family life, but on the perimeter we have the more public events. The birthday of the monarch, always celebrated with much fervour, and the charivari, perhaps the most typical and the most truly Canadian of all the events. The end of year holidays were gay with a mixture of family celebrations and wider social obligations.

Courting customs varied, but generally the young man involved took to spending evenings at the girl's house, and if his suit was favoured by the parents he was a welcome guest. However, by the turn of the century etiquette books remark that the father's consent was a pure formality since young Canadians took matters into their own hands. Sunday was the great day for courting or "sparking" as it was called thoughout the country. The steps of the church were the common meeting ground and the favoured man asked for the privilege of "seeing her home". During the courting period, the girl would start to make herself a wardrobe and household linen. Later there would be a quilting bee.

On the other hand there are many early stories of quick no-non-

sense weddings. A man living in the backwoods and in need of a wife would hear of a suitable girl. He might travel for days towards her home, asking neighbours about the family as he stopped overnight. There would be a short interview and more than likely the young couple would shortly leave on the return trip. Of course the quick wedding had a long tradition, starting with the young women sent from France to marry the early settlers of Quebec. Many years later it was not uncommon for a young Scotsman to write to his relatives in his former homeland enquiring about a suitable bride. By the 1880's life was more leisurely and ladies perhaps more fickle. In any event they were told how to behave when a "beau" came calling. "A

young lady should not encourage the addresses of a gentleman unless she feels that she can return his affections. It is not always necessary to take a lady's first refusal as absolute. Though a gentleman may repeat his suit with propriety, still it should not be repeated too often nor too long. No lady worthy of a gentleman's regard will say no twice to a suit which she intends ultimately to receive with favour".[1] It was not necessary for a man to be on his knees to "pop the question" — one knee was adequate.

That being settled, it was possible to arrange the wedding. In the early days, delays were often the fate of those wishing to marry because people authorized to perform the ceremony were scarce. When the first settlements were governed by the military, the commanding officer or the chaplain or whoever was delegated to act in his stead could perform a legal marriage ceremony. As military power was relinquished this task was taken over by the magistrates. Before 1798 no ministers but those of the Church of England or Roman Catholic faith were recognized. Later, ordained ministers of the Church of Scotland, Lutherans and Calvinists were also given such powers, but it was not until about 1831 that Methodists and Baptists were recognized. Even so the number of ministers was small and often a wedding party journeyed to find one. When this happened all the young friends would make up a party on horseback or else a wagon would be filled with rough benches or chairs. The girls sat on the men's knees and off the merry party went to find the minister.

In some areas the minister would come to the bride's house, in others the whole party went to the church. When buggies became common it was usual to leave the church with a procession of these carriages led by the bride and groom. The popularity of the pair could be measured by the length of the procession following them. The groom tried to get the fastest horse because whoever was the first to arrive back at the house for the bridal meal won the prize: the chance to kiss the bride first. Small children and younger brothers often stretched ropes across the road and held up the carriage until a donation was given.

Quite often the day ended with a dance, all the furniture being cleared from the centre of the room and pushed to the wall. There was rivalry as to who would have the second dance with the bride, the groom always being allowed the first. Wedding trips were not too common then, this being a luxury enjoyed only by the wealthy. Generally the bride wore to her wedding a good dress which would be useful in her later life, and after the festivities she left in it for her new home

As in the case of most services requiring payment, the marriage fees were usually given to the minister in kind. Sometimes it was a special farm implement or some produce, and even a basket of sausages was known to be given.

When in church for the ceremony, indeed in church for any occasion, "it is considered very bad form to recognize acquaintances by bows and smiles".[1] It was thought to be in excellent taste for the bride and groom to pass down the aisle without looking to the left or right.

The bride, of course, was given a ring, gold if it could be afforded, but there was an interesting fashion around the 1880's. "A jewelled ring has been for many years the sign and symbol of betrothal, but at present a plain gold circlet, with the date of the engagement inscribed within, is generally preferred. The ring is removed by the groom at the altar, passed to the clergyman and used in the ceremony. A jewelled ring is placed upon her hand by the groom on the way home from the church. It stands guard over its precious fellow, and is a confirmation of the first promise".[1]

Shortly after the wedding the bride had to carry out certain social obligations, as soon as she settled in her new home, or if she went away on a wedding trip it was during the week of her return. She spent a week dressed formally to receive her visitors, according to the etiquette of the 1850's and later. The week of formality started on the Sunday the husband and wife made their first appearance at church. The bride wore white gloves as a mark of formality and for the first party after her marriage, usually trimmed her hair with orange blossoms.

Mrs. Traill met a young bride and said, "She seemed very much to dread the ordeal she had yet to pass through—in sitting dressed up for a whole week to receive visitors. Nor did I in the least wonder at her repugnance to go through this trying piece of ceremonial, which is absolutely indispensable in Canada. . . . every person in the same class prepares to pay them a visit of congratulation; and if the town is large, and the parties well known, the making of visits to the bride lasts to the end of the week. The bride, who is often a young girl from sixteen to twenty years of age, is doomed for this period to sit upon a sofa or recline in an easy chair, dressed in the most expensive manner, to receive her guests. She knows that herself, her dress, the furniture of her room, even her cake and wine, will undergo the most minute scrutiny, and be the theme of conversation among all the gossips of the place for the next nine days".[2,3]

A sidelight on the brides of the 1840 period in Upper Canada is revealed by this passage from *Canadian Scenery*. "Although a spry lass as she is termed, is certain of repeated offers, and is sure of being early united in the bonds of matrimony, she may frequently before that event have given birth to one or two children. Our author was in company with a lady who volunteered the information, that 'her Betty' had been two years old at her marriage. The correcter feeling, on this subject, of females from the old country are contemned as ridiculous. Nay, where so little delicacy prevails, and the children are so valuable a possession, the bringing of two or three into the world in this irregular fashion, instead of being a bar to marriage, proves it is said, an additional attraction, making the young lady a species of heiress. After marriage, she makes an active industrious wife, but expects from her husband much deference, and even that he should wink at occasional frailities."

Another interesting sidelight on Canadian marriage customs comes from Joseph Bouchette who wrote in 1831 about weddings in Quebec being followed not by one but by a series of feasts and dances. "The whole bridal cortège in a long string of calèches if in summer, of carrioles in winter, passing from house to house, and each night, for perhaps a fortnight, renewing, with unbated vigour, both the eating and the dancing".[4]

The holding of a Charivari was a typical Canadian custom. Mrs. Moodie thought that it was learned from the French in Lower Canada. Regardless of who originated the custom it was practically national and lasted a very long time. If a wedding took place with the contracting parties having too many former dead spouses, or too great a difference in their ages, or "when two old people, who ought to be thinking of their graves enter for the second or third time into the holy state of wedlock"[5] this was the signal for a charivari. On the wedding night all the young men in the neighbourhood assembled to "charivari" the bride and groom. "For this purpose they disguise themselves, blackening their faces, putting their clothes on hind part before, and wearing horrible masks, with grotesque caps on their heads, adorned with cocks' feathers and bells. They then form a regular body, and proceed to the bridegroom's house, to the sound of tin kettles, horns, and drums, cracked fiddles, and all the discordant instruments they can collect together".[5]

They surrounded the house, serenaded the happy couple and beat upon the door with clubs demanding admittance to drink the bride's health. Generally a donation of money was given to treat the band at the closest tavern. Sometimes the bridegroom refused to entertain the mob and then there was mayhem. Occasionally they managed to break in and seize the bridegroom, "and he may esteem himself a very fortunate man, under such circumstances if he escapes being ridden upon a rail, tarred and feathered, and otherwise maltreated".[5]

"Riding a man upon a rail" was the summary mid-nineteenth century justice meted out by rural people to any who transgressed a local or moral law. The victim was stripped and covered with pitch from the pine, rolled in feathers, then sat astride a rail fence. It was understood he would now leave town. When the first Mormon missionaries travelled in Canada advocating, in those days, plurality of wives and at the same time seeking converts to their religion, they were often dealt with in this primitive way.

Life was short and in any community funerals were frequent. There were the usual customs of friends coming great distances, and the ritual of the particular church. There was also a constant discussion of the cost of funerals and the increasing opulence of the last rites. Cemeteries or churchyards as they were called are only found where there is a population of size to warrant a church building. Those who died in the first periods of settlement or who lived in remote areas were buried on their own land. A traveller of the 1840's mentions, "the way in which graves are scattered up and down Canada is, indeed, one of the most affecting sights as one passes. Very often, riding through old parts of the country, a little paling in the side of a field tells the story of some lonely grave".[6]

The whole neighbourhood came to a funeral. It was a breach of good manners not to go immediately. In the later years invitations to funerals were sent, and again such an invitation could not be refused. By the 1880's, when a funeral was held, the door knob or knocker would be draped with black crape and dull black ribbon bows. If, however, the deceased was young or unmarried, white was the colour. "The usual decorations of the coffin are flowers, tastefully arranged in a beautiful wreath for a child or young person, and a cross for a married person, which are placed upon the coffin. These flowers should be mostly white".[1]

There were no regular undertakers in the pioneer days, and all the work from the laying out of the body, the pall bearing and the grave digging were undertaken by sons, neighbours and friends. Carpenters usually made the coffins and it was customary in some areas for people to select lumber from their own land and set it aside for the making of their coffin. In the same way, clothes might be set aside for the occasion. Early coffins were slightly different in shape, the cover or lid being raised in the centre like a house roof and the upper part on hinges could turn back. As soon as the date for the funeral was fixed one of the men would ride around to notify the people concerned.

The hearse was seldom seen in the towns and never in the country. The coffin was generally carried to the grave or else put on a wagon or sleigh. Pall bearers were chosen from among "the gentlemen of note

H. STONE, Senr.,

THE OLD AND RELIABLE

Undertaking Establishment,

239 YONGE STREET.

—o—

OPEN DAY AND NIGHT.

—o—

N. B.—No connection with the other Undertaking
Establishment of the same name.

in the neighbourhood, who, to the honour of the country, be it spoken, never refuse to act on these mournful occasions".[6] After the funeral the crowd returned to the home for refreshments.

Not only did the neighbours flock to the funeral but many writers mention that Canadians were obsessed with visiting the dying. Whether this was morbid curiosity or a neighbourly feeling of showing concern, it is hard to say. There is one delightful story of the poor soon-to-be-widow sitting huddled by the fire while upstairs there is a great crowd of people. The local doctor comes in and asks her why she is not with her dying husband and she tells him she can't get into the bedroom for the visitors.

Immigrants brought with them their old customs and superstitions. Among these were the "watch over the dead" from northern Britain, and the Irish wake. The custom started because those attending the funeral who came from long distances often had to stay several days, and there was a need to give refreshment. In Canada circumstances were no different, the need was the same and people looked forward to a big funeral with relish. It was a grand social occasion. In Ireland the watching of the body before the funeral had been accompanied by a show of formal grief from time immemorial, and it was brought to Canada. It was called the "keen", and this wild crying for the dead was usual in all Canadian-Irish settlements. Originally the keening was done by the women of the family but gradually they were replaced by professional mourners. The bereaved family would send miles for an old woman recognized as an authority on "raising the keen". The old women sat by the coffin with their kerchief or apron around their heads rocking to and fro, and wailing with an unearthly primitive howl.

Canadians were a superstitious people. This is not surprising, since many were uneducated, settlements were lonely and many of nature's ways were inexplicable. Mists rising from the undrained land looked like ghosts, there were flitting fireflies, and during cold winters it might be impossible to bury the dead for quite a while. No wonder whenever neighbours met around the fireside of an evening the talk was of spirits and ghosts. In 1831, Joseph Bouchette, talking of the people in general, wrote: "It may be said, and perhaps with truth, that the Canadian population are, for the most part, superstitious; but this is a failing to all uneducated persons; and we can hardly consider it a vice, unless it lead to cruel conduct towards one another. We, however, have no duckings of poor old women, no desire to burn witches, &c., superstition, with us, merely multiplies the prayers of the fearful peasant, and occasions a somewhat lavish use of holy water and candles".[4]

In Quebec the children believed that on Good Friday the church bells escaped from the steeples and so they watched the bell towers as the sun set and could almost see the shutters open and the bells go off like swallows. The bells of course flew to Rome to be blessed and returned in time to give the Easter Sunday blessing.

Almanacs were very popular and

so many flooded the country from the United States that towards the end of the century we come across the old yet new publishing story of "Canadian edition" almanacs. Most were put out by patent medicine companies, some by dye makers and other tradesmen, and considering how frequently they were consulted, many have come down to us in excellent condition. They contained weather predictions, the phases of the sun, moon and planets, notable events of the past, cooking hints, how to care for livestock, some rudimentary medical lore as well as some simple jokes. They were important and taken seriously. Pioneers always killed the hogs, plucked the geese and made soap at certain phases of the moon. Not to consult the almanac before sowing grain was foolishness. Medicinal herbs, so important in the lives of the isolated pioneer, were always plucked after consulting the almanac. Soapmaking needed added protections because it was so tricky, and so it was customary to ask God to bless the soapmaker or to wish the soapmakers luck. Even the weaning of the youngest child and the cutting of his long hair was done only when the right zodiac sign appeared.

If there was a death in the family, particularly the head of the house, it was the duty of a son to tap on the bee hive and notify the bees of the master's death. Otherwise it was believed the bees would die too. It was considered unlucky to sell a hive of bees. If a man had more hives or "skips" than he wanted, a neighbour would go and take a hive. He never paid for it in person, but would leave a sum of money or a return gift where it could be easily seen. In the same way a cutting from a garden, or any plant for that matter, was never given or paid for directly since this would result in the plant's death. The person wanting a cutting took it unseen by the owner but left whatever offering thought necessary. Many of these superstitions are not exclusively Canadian, but they were brought here and flourished. They go back in the history of rural life for untold generations, and are at the same time common to many different peoples.

Although the people were superstitious and saw jack o' lanterns everywhere in the dark night (usually the miasma from the marsh), they were at the same time closely attached to the church of their faith. In the early years the circuit riders went from settlement to settlement holding services wherever they could. It was not long before itinerant preachers began to hold religious meetings in scattered school houses. When they came in the evening each person attending brought a candle or a lantern and from this we get the old expression to meet "by early candlelight".

However, nothing in this country was ever quite so alive, so colourful and so commented upon as the churches of Lower Canada with their crowds of parishioners and their metal roofs gleaming in the sunshine. Sunday was the biggest day of the week and a respite from hard drudgery. This quotation comes from 1831 but in many ways it could have been written today: "In Canada, as in all catholic countries, many of the people's enjoyments are connected with their religious ceremonies; the Sunday is to them their day of gaiety: there is then an assemblage of friends and relations; the parish church collects together all whom they know, with whom they have relations of business or pleasure; the young and the old, men and women, clad in their best garments, riding their best horses, driving their gayest calèches, meet there for purposes of business, love, and pleasure. The young habitant, decked out in his most splendid finery, makes his court to the maiden whom he has singled out as the object of his affections: the maiden, exhibiting in her adornment every colour of the rainbow, there hopes to meet *son chevalier*: the bold rider descants upon, and gives evidence of the merits of his unrivalled pacer; (the Canadians are particularly fond of ambling or pacing horses), and in winter the powers of the various horses are tried in sleigh or cariole racing: in short, Sunday is the grand fête—it forms the most pleasurable part of the habitant's life; rob them of their Sunday, you rob them of what, in their eyes, renders life most worthy of possession".[4]

It was not of course, like this in the English settlements, and far from it in a Calvinist area. But from the old diaries and travellers' tales in general, religion, church attendance and the formality of the Sabbath grew with civilization, respectability and the passing of the years. There were other ceremonies of the church, such as the naming of the child (see Chapter XVII for a helpful list of possible names). There were also the perennial bazaars that are still with us, and the lovely fall festival known in Canada as the Harvest Home.

Agricultural fall fairs were held very early in this country and from the 1840's there is mention of ladies from the local church having a display table and selling "pretty toys". Possibly the first charity bazaar, and a highly successful one, was that given under the leadership and patronage of Lady Colborne, wife of the Lieutenant-Governor of Upper Canada in 1830. She introduced this old British money-making custom to York to raise money for her favourite charity—clothing the poor. Her friends and assistants used the substantial proceeds to purchase quantities of red flannel to make undergarments for the less fortunate.

It was obvious that the ladies tried to make as much money as they could and that they felt they could pressure men acquaintances to purchase. So much so that etiquette books felt compelled to add this little reminder: "If you have a table at a fair, use no unladylike means to obtain buyers. Never appear so beggarly as to retain the change, if a larger amount is presented than the price, offer the change promptly, when the gentleman will be at liberty to donate it if he thinks best, and you may accept with thanks. He is under no obligation to make such a donation".

Thanksgiving has until recent years been a moveable feast celebrated not only as an ancient Church festival for the bounty of the harvest but also for a multitude of other reasons. In 1763, Halifax proclaimed a day of Thanksgiving for the Peace of Paris which ceded Canada to Britain. Ontario celebrated a Thanksgiving Day in June 18, 1816, giving thanks for the victory over Napoleon. Many years later there was a Thanksgiving when the Prince of Wales recovered from a serious illness. It was finally settled as a fall festival in 1879, and followed the American ritual of thanks for the harvest. The day often began, as it did in the United States, with a shoot for the men. There is probably a great deal of American influence in this holiday, the official observation of which was spurred by Mrs. Sara Hale, the editor of *Godey's Lady's Book* and the author of a number of books on cooking and manners, all of which had wide circulation in Canada.

When a church group celebrated "Harvest Home", as it was then called, the activity usually took place on a weekday, although in some churches it was traditionally on a Sunday. In any event, the church and altar as well as columns, window ledges and archways were decorated with autumn fruits and vegetables. In some communities the local women placed some of their finest baking in the display. After the Thanksgiving Service there was a community dinner for all; usually pots of beans, meat pies, fruit pies, squash, turnips, home-made pickles and salads. After dinner the older men would go to the rectory for a talk and a smoke. The children played games, the others gossiped and strolled. Sometimes there was a late afternoon service before the neighbours disbanded.

The earliest French settlers started the winter party season on November 25th, and in some areas the tradition continues. "La tire" or the taffy pull is held on the feast day of Saint Catherine, the patron saint of unmarried women, particularly those of twenty-five years and more. The candy is always made from molasses and the cooled syrupy mass is pulled into taffy—a great way to get the men and spinsters together. The original taffy pull was held, it is said, by Marguerite Bourgeoys who founded the Congregation of Notre-Dame, and entertained her young pupils with this delicacy. Other peoples brought with them holiday traditions too; the Scots who went "first footing" on New Year's Eve; the Scandinavians and the Ukrainians who decorate their homes at Christmas with sheaves of wheat and who eat from a table strewn with pieces of hay. Unfortunately, most of these customs have remained regional.

Once the first rude years were passed the tradition of the Christmas tree and decorations spread. It wasn't long before mention is made of home-made garlands of forest greens, with the additions of nuts and apples, cranberries and popped corn. Nuts and apples are old symbols from Europe and quickly became naturalized because of their abundance. It was usual not to preserve cranberries but rather to leave them covered with snow and pick them from beneath their protective blanket as needed.

Christmas, as we know it, is an observance made possible by the abundance of manufactured goods and belongs to this century. However, for the first settlers this was a religious holiday marked by as lavish a dinner as the winter supplies would allow and the retention of such homeland customs as decorating with greens and the ritual of the yule log. It was not until the mid-century that Christmas began to be a special occasion with a decorated tree and gifts, both of which were reserved for children only. German-Canadians had introduced the cooky and the Christmas tree many years earlier, but these customs had not spread outside their districts until Queen Victoria and her husband, by celebrating in this manner, gave impetus to this *gemütlich* custom. Today the cooky tree is growing in favour as a sign of hospitality but we have forgotten its beginnings in the "Dutch" households where wooden pyramids were used to display holiday cookies and gingerbreads, for all to help themselves.

There is no doubt that Sara Hale in her writings gave impetus to the new Christmas customs when in 1868 she described how to decorate a tree. "We are glad to notice that every year the German custom of making Christmas-trees for children is becoming more common among us. Few things give greater delight to the little ones, or link happier recollections with the season and the home. Do not load its green boughs with *sugar candies now 'made to sell'*. You can adorn your Christmas-tree with the healthful gifts of Nature — apples, pears, grapes, nuts, and other fruits that the little ones love. You can add lumps of real sugar, white and clear as crystal, if sweets are indispensable; and there are sugar candies honestly prepared from good sugar, and made beautiful without coloring. Pray do not allow your children to eat 'white earth'."[7]

The tree was a spruce seven feet high securely fixed to a moss-covered plank and ornamented with small wax candles of red, green, yellow and white which were attached to branches by little rims of tin, "in such an order as not to endanger the boughs above them, and cause a general conflagration".[7] Small glass, gilt and coloured balls were hung by strings and the lighter gifts were also suspended from the branches. The books and boxes were put around the base of the tree.

Although in many areas goose or roast pork was the main dish at Christmas dinner, the turkey soon became a favourite, and in the days before the holiday there were many shooting-matches. Pigeons were released from traps and whoever killed the most won a turkey. The food markets at this time of the year were lavish, all the supplies of course, being naturally frozen and often decorated. The following is a mid-century picture of Toronto. It could have been any one of the small towns throughout the country. "The markets at Christmas were usually a greater attraction to many people than they used to be in England. If the weather chanced to be cold, you would see huge files of frozen pigs standing on their four legs in front of the stalls, as if they had been killed when at a gallop; countless sheep hung over-head, with here and there one of their heads carefully gilded, to add splendour to the exhibition. Some deer were almost always noticed at some of the stalls, and it was not unusual to see the carcass of a bear contributing its part to the general show. As to the oxen, they were too fat for my taste, though the butcher seemed proud of them in proportion to their obesity. The market was not confined to a special building, though there was one for the purpose. Long ranges of farmers' wagons, ranged at each side of it, showed similar treasures of frozen pork and mutton, the animals standing entirely at the feet of their owners, who sat among them waiting for purchasers. Frozen geese, ducks, chickens and turkey abounded, and that household was very poor indeed which had not one or other to grace the festival''.[6]

Bill of Fare for Christmas Dinner[8]

Oyster Soup
Roast Turkey   Cranberry Sauce
Mashed and Browned Potatoes
Onions in Cream Sauce
Tomatoes
Chicken Pie
Rice Croquettes
Plum Pudding   Foaming Sauce
Mince Pie
Lemon Tarts
Salted Almonds
Celery
Crackers   Cheese
Fruit
Coffee

New Year's Eve was devoted to dancing, although the Wesleyan Methodists would always "pray the old year out and the new year in". New Year's Day was celebrated lavishly, a happy custom brought from the homelands of all the founding races except the English. However, once in Canada the English too embraced the custom wholeheartedly. Today, unfortunately it survives much emasculated in the official levees and is no longer a tribute to the ladies. Why this custom disappeared is hard to tell, unless the conviviality fell before the increased pressure of the temperance leagues.

It was the custom from the earliest days for all the gentlemen to call upon their friends and especially to exchange greetings with the ladies of the family, who sat in their best clothes ready to receive them. Men called either singly, in couples or in groups of three or four, and came in carriages, sleighs or on foot. The day started at around ten in the morning and continued until nine in the evening. The length of a call was from five to fifteen minutes and if all the gentlemen in a party were not acquainted with all the ladies

introductions were made. But no one could presume on this introduction to further a social acquaintance. Refreshments were provided and offered, but it was not necessary that the callers should always accept. Refreshment would consist of oysters, raw and scalloped, cold meats, salads, fruits, rich cakes, sandwiches, wine, hot tea and coffee. Although in the years before 1860 there was a plentiful supply of liquor, "under the old arrangement Young America was apt to take too much wine and an excess of hot whisky punches, hence big treats on New Years fell into disfavor".[9]

Gentlemen arriving at a house on New Year's Day left calling cards in a basket at the door. To have New Year Greetings or other embellishments printed on the card was vulgar. The men were then ushered into the reception room and invited to remove their overcoats, "but it is optional with them whether they do so or not, it is also optional whether they remove their gloves".[1] It was not customary for a bridegroom to make calls the first year after his marriage. He remained at home with his wife. However, a "gentleman who wishes to drop an inconvenient acquaintance, has only to omit calling up his friend's wife and daughters on New-Year's day, without making a suitable apology for the omission of the usual act of courtesy, and the hint is acknowledged by a direct cut the next time the parties meet in public". The "cut" was a very important part of social life in the etiquette-ridden nineteenth century and we shall consider it further in another chapter.

The ladies, of course, counted the number of calling cards left in their halls and there was keen rivalry to find out who was the most popular. New Year's day served another purpose: it "is the gala day for matchmakers among the ladies. All the country cousins, and young ladies in the matrimonial market, are marshalled and drilled to make the best possible appearance—in short, to put on their most bewitching and fascinating smiles—and we are happy to add that casual acquaintances thus made often end in new friendships, and not unfrequently in closer ties".[9]

The party mood was continued into the new year when "the two or three days succeeding New Years are the ladies' days for calling, to pass the compliments of the season. This custom has now become quite as popular as the New Years calls of the gentlemen. The ladies discuss with each other the number of their gentlemen visitors on New Years, the new faces they have seen, and the matrimonial prospects for the year. It is customary on these occasions to offer wine and other refreshments, and to drink each other's health and prosperity".[9]

In Quebec it was the custom at New Year, as indeed it still is, for all the family to gather at the homestead to be blessed by the head of the family. It is among the French-Canadians that the old tradition of a party on Twelfth Night or Epiphany is continued, although at one time all Europe enjoyed this festival. Generally it was a costume party, the garments being made from a thin silk or muslin called "tiffany", actually a corruption of "Epiphany". A special cake containing a dried pea and a bean was served, the recipients becoming the king and queen of the revels.

Throughout the long winters the men never tired of dinners nor the ladies of dancing, and there were plenty of opportunities for both. Public dances brought about a mixing and a meeting of all classes of society and people drove miles to attend them. Young mothers brought their babies and handed them to any onlooker when asked to dance. "The dance is the amusement of which they are passionately fond. No inn is considered worthy of the name, unless it be provided with a spacious ballroom, which is called into requisition as often as convenience will permit. Intellectual recreations have not hitherto attracted all the attention which they merit. Mr. Talbot, during a residence of five years, never saw above two individuals with books in their hands; and, in one case, it was a medical treatise consulted for health".[3]

Large dances were held in the upstairs ballroom over the driving shed of the local tavern. More formal balls were held by the officers at the local garrison, and there were dances at home. A traveller in 1822 remarked on the passion for dancing in a letter home. "Our scouts informed us, that they had found in the cabin four or five Canadians, dancing to a sleeping fiddler, whose music ceased as soon as they awoke him".[3] Balls were often by subscription, a sum of money enabling a man to attend a winter series of dances. Other balls were given on such public occasions as the birthday of the monarch.

Governor and Mrs. Simcoe gave a ball at Newark (Niagara-on-the-Lake) to honour the birthday of George III and this early Canadian social event has recently been revived to recreate the mixture of pomp and gaiety typical of the end of the eighteenth century. Dances were attended by young and old, and Mrs. Traill says that it was not uncommon to see parents and their grown-up children dancing in the same set in a public ball-room.

Some idea of an early ball in this country can be pictured in the following description of Newark at the beginning of the nineteenth century. In many ways this town was far in advance of the other centres of population. Perhaps being the seat of the first parliament of Upper Canada it drew an official population with strong ties to the English court and emulated its protocol. "At Niagara, as in all parts of Canada, they are much attached to dancing. During winter, there are balls once a fortnight. These entertainments are not like many English Assemblies, mere bread and butter billets, where nothing is to be met with but cold tea and vapid negus, but parties at which the exhausted dancers may recruit with a substantial supper, and extend their diversion beyond the tame limits of eleven, and twelve o'clock, hours at which a company only begins to enter into the spirit of amusement. On my first entering the assembly at Newark, I felt much surprised at the gay appearance which presented itself. Feathers, trinkets, and all the paraphernalia, which distinguish haughty dames of Britain, were visible".[10]

Music was provided by military musicians, local players or a single fiddler, paid from a collection taken during the evening. Small dances were known first as "sprees", later as "hops" and many had a "caller-off" —a master of ceremonies who controlled the movements of the square dances. The early dances include the Soldier's Joy, the Money Musk, Pop Goes the Weasel, Sir Roger, and the similar Virginia Reel. Scottish and Irish reels, the four- and the eight-in-hand, polkas and mazurkas, jigs and hornpipes were popular. It was not until the mid-century that waltzes became common and in 1857 *The Ball-room Guide and Complete Dancing-master,* published at fifty cents, gave instructions for "bows and courtesies", as well as instruction in the quadrille, redowas, the German, the Schottische,

the Galop, the Deux Temps, the Varsovienne, and the Hop.

Ball suppers were elaborate. There was an abundance of food necessary to sustain the dancers until dawn. Directions for a supper, sometimes called "a collation" say: "the table is made as elegant as beautiful china, cut glass and an abundance of flowers can make it. The hot dishes are oysters, stewed, fried, broiled and scalloped, chicken, game, etc., and the cold dishes are such as boned turkey, boeuf à la mode, chicken salad, lobster salad and raw oysters".[1]

Rules to be observed at fashionable dancing parties or sociables in large cities:

"A gentleman should never attempt to step across a lady's train. He should walk around it."

"No gentleman should ever go into the supper-room alone, unless he has seen every lady enter before him."

"When dancing a round dance, a gentleman should never hold a lady's hand behind him, or on his hip, or high in the air, moving her arm as though it were a pump handle, as seen in some of our western cities but should hold it gracefully by his side."

"Draw on your gloves (white or yellow) in the dressing-room and do not be for one moment with them off in the dancing rooms. At supper take them off; nothing is more preposterous than to eat in gloves."

"When an unpractised dancer makes a mistake, we may aprise him of his error; but it would be very impolite to have the air of giving him a lesson."

"Unless a man has a very graceful figure, and can use it with great elegance, it is better for him to walk through the quadrilles, or invent some gliding movement for the occasion."

"The master of the house should see that all the ladies dance. He should take notice particularly of those who seem to serve as 'drapery' to the walls of the ball-room (or 'wall flowers', as the familiar expression is) and should see that they are invited to dance."

"If a lady waltzes with you, beware not to press her waist; you must only lightly touch it with the open palm of your hand, lest you leave a disagreeable impression not only on her *ceinture*, but on her mind."

"Dance quietly, do not kick or caper about nor sway your body, but let your motion be from the hips downward. Do not pride yourself too much on the neatness of your steps, lest you be taken for a dancing master."

"When a lady is standing in a quadrille, though not engaged in dancing, a gentleman not acquainted with her partner should not converse with her."[9]

REFERENCES

[1] *Our Deportment*, John H. Young, Paris, Ont., 1883.

[2] *The Backwoods of Canada*, C. P. Traill, London, 1836.

[3] *Canadian Scenery*, N. P. Willis, London, 1842.

[4] *The British Dominions in North America*, J. Bouchette, London, 1831.

[5] *Roughing it in the Bush*, S. Moodie, Toronto, 1871.

[6] *Adventures in Canada*, John C. Geikie, Philadelphia, n.d.

[7] *Manners*, S. Hale, Boston, 1868.

[8] *The New Galt Cook Book*, Taylor & McNaught, Toronto, 1898.

[9] *Complete Rules of Etiquette*, Anonymous, New York, 1857.

[10] *Canadian Antiquarian & Numismatic Journal*, 3rd series Vol. IX, 1912.

Happy Homes
and a Good Society
All Year Round

CHAPTER THREE

The combination work and pleasure parties known as "bees" were the most typical social events enjoyed by the settlers. Like all happenings in the nineteenth century, they were codified with a strict etiquette: who should come, and those who attended knew exactly what was expected of them. Neighbours for many miles around came without expecting payment, but there was an understanding that each would get back from his host, when he required it, as many days' labour as had been given. This understanding, of course, applied to serious work bees of logging, stumping, house and barn raising. Other bees were more social and less demanding, although in these too, there was a tacit understanding. The lesser bees might be classed as the apple, husking, quilting and even butchering gatherings. Not only were bees the means of clearing land and raising homes and barns quickly, they were also a holiday for the lonely settlers who were often miles from their nearest neighbour. Although a great deal of work was accomplished during the one or two days of meeting, it was also a time of gossip, laughter and exchange of ideas.

Unlike all other early social activities such as dancing or visiting, a bee required an invitation from the host or hostess. A visit was spontaneous on the part of the guests, a bee was not. It was not possible to attend without the invitation, and it was considered a direct slight not to be invited. On the other hand, the rules of etiquette did not require an invitation for a meal, a visit, or even a stay that might last several days.

As soon as a bee was announced, the woman of the house, often helped by her close friends, would start to prepare food for the event. The food was the best and the most abundant that the house could provide, and at logging and raising bees where the work was laborious, whisky was plentiful. The supply of liquor often led to fights and fatalities and some settlers thought the ruckus was hardly worth while. Some tried to keep the event "dry" but a dry bee was a rarity. Generally the men worked until midday and then sat down to a huge meal washed down with lashings of tea and whisky. Mrs. Moodie mentions how she catered for her own logging bee: "Our men worked well until dinner-time, when, after washing in the lake, they all sat down to the rude board which I had prepared for them, loaded with the best fare that could be procured in the bush. Pea-soup, legs of pork, venison, eel, and raspberry pie, garnished with plenty of potatoes, and whiskey to wash them down, besides a large iron kettle of tea".[1] Tea with "all the fixin's" was a treat; the fixings being plenty of sugar and lots of cream plus real tea.

Work would continue until dusk when there would be another meal similar to the mid-day one, plenty of pies, and more liquid refreshment. The day would end with dancing. In communities that did not dance because of religious beliefs, singing as well as forfeit games were played. In any event, whether it was dancing or games it enabled the boys to kiss the girls.

Logging bees were extremely important and brought all the men from miles around. They brought not only their wives to help with the food and to gossip, but also their oxen and all the heavy chain they owned. In a well-organized bee the men were divided into teams which raced against each other to speed up the work. Generally four men and a yoke of oxen made a

gang, and while the race was on the "Grog Boss" would go from team to team with his jug giving out the whisky allowance. When the day's work was over the cut logs would be set on fire and the young people would gather to roast corn, tell ghost stories, and dance. It is hard to believe, but after a full day of heavy work, the partying and dancing could go on until dawn.

The raising bee brought the men together once again to help put up the first home for a new neighbour. This too was often done more quickly because of competing teams. Many men thought it lucky to be the first to straddle the cross-beam of the roof. There was much activity with the whisky bucket, so much so that it was looked on as a necessary evil, an adjunct to settling on the new land. However, these bees were rarely as disorderly as the logging bee.

Another bee at which the men played a major role was the butchering day get-together. Like many bees, it took place in the fall when hogs and cattle were killed and the meat prepared for winter storage. Once again speed was essential. While the men did the slaughtering, skinning and cutting, the women started the rendering of fat for lard, and the preparation of the offal for head cheese and the entrails for sausage-casing. Nothing was wasted; heads became souse or head cheese, hams were made ready for smoking, other pieces of meat went into the pickle barrels and fat not used for cooking went into the soap barrel.

Less laborious and more in the nature of a pleasurable day was the apple-paring bee. "The young folks of both sexes are invited for a given evening in the autumn, and come duly provided with apple-parers, which are ingenious contrivances, by which an apple, stuck on two prongs at one end, is pared by a few turns of the handle at the other. It is astonishing to see how quickly it is done. Nor is the paring all. The little machine makes a final thrust through the heart of the apple, and takes out the core, so as to leave nothing to do but to cut what remains in pieces. The object of all this paring is to get apples enough dried for tarts during the winter, the pieces when cut being threaded in long strings, and hung up till they shrivel and get a leather-like look. When wanted for use, a little boiling makes them swell to their original size again, and brings back their softness. You may imagine how plentiful the fruit must be to make such a liberal use of it possible, as that which you see all through Canada. You can hardly go into any house in the bush, however poor, without having a large bowl of 'apple sass' set before you — that is, of apple boiled in maple sugar".[2]

At an apple bee the boys and girls would sit together, and it was usual for the girls to throw a length of peel over their shoulder to see what initial it formed — it was supposed to denote the name of a future husband. "The young folks make a grand night of it when the bee comes off. The laughing and the frolic is unbounded; some are busy with their sweethearts; some, of a grosser mind, are no less busy with the apples, devouring a large proportion of what they pare; and the whole proceedings, in many cases, wind up with a dance on the barn-floor".[2]

The husking bee was similar and took place when the corn was harvested. The young people gathered in the early evening, boys and girls sitting together and stripping the husk off the ears of corn. Husks were usually kept in front of the workers for later use in mattresses, while the corn cobs were thrown in piles in the centre. Boys finding a coloured kernel were able to kiss the girl of their choice, and it was not uncommon for girls to throw a mis-coloured cob to their sweethearts.

33

More sedate was the quilting bee at which ladies both married and single would congregate in the early afternoon. The women worked quickly and professionally on a quilt to be given to the newest bride-to-be. After the chores of the day were over, the husbands and young men would come to the bee to enjoy the meal, the fun and games, and see the presentation of the quilt. The young girls took charge of the games. The one most enjoyed was the throwing of the quilt over some popular single young man and watching him try to extricate himself. Another kind of horseplay was to throw the man in the quilt and toss him in the air. It was at these womanly meetings that ladies took the opportunity to exchange recipes and medical notes and to write these in their personal notebooks. Occasionally a printed cook-book was owned and passed around for all to copy from.

Similar to a bee was the reception given to the threshing teams at harvest time. Women would help each other turn out tremendous meals and jugs of drink for the hot and thirsty men. In the early days, a threshing team required at least eight men; one to drive the horses, one to cut the bands of the sheaves, one to feed the machine, one to take away the straw and pass it on to three or four more men who pitched it into the mow or onto the straw-stack. Food consisted of the usual hams, pies, tarts and custards, and although the whisky jug was passed at some farms, others drank "Switchel" — a sharp, cold drink of molasses and vinegar — or raspberry vinegar made ice-cold by hanging the jugs in the well.

Travelling and excursions were extremely popular. This was the only means many country people had to find out how their friends and relatives fared. Of course there were excursions organized for the tourists, many coming from England, but a growing number from the States. They enjoyed the Victorian pastime of giving themselves spine chills by shooting rapids, and taking the opportunity to sketch scenery for albums. N. P. Willis in *Canadian Scenery* mentions the tourists and describes an almost unbelievable scene of a storm on a lake. While the men rowed towards the shore the "ladies enlivened us by singing the Canadian Boat-Song, 'Row, brothers, row', etc."

As soon as the farm chores were finished it was usual for the entire family to take off for a visit. No invitation was given or expected. "They are not very social in their daily habits to which, indeed, the almost impassable state of the roads oppose great obstacles; but they are fond of large parties, and, in favorable season, five or six families often unite, and, without any notice, arrive to visit another at the distance of ten or twelve miles. Such an arrival would not always be very opportune in an English household; but, in this land of plenty, the flour-barrel, the pork-tub, and the fowl house, afford at all times materials for meeting such an emergency, and the board is soon spread with a plentiful meal".[3,4]

It is perhaps hard for us to equate the settlers' ideas of food with our own ideas conditioned by a life-time of plenty and a knowledge of food values. To the settler, as to all who work the land, food meant prosperity, pleasure, and turning the back on the old days of want and hunger. Even Mrs. Susanna Moodie who had, at first, so many reservations about life in Canada was greatly impressed by the lavish show of food. "My readers should see a table laid out in a wealthy Canadian farmer's house before they can have any idea of the profusion displayed in the entertainment of two visitors and their young children. Besides venison, pork, chicken, ducks, and fish of several kinds, cooked in a variety of ways, there was a number of pumpkin, raspberry, cherry, and currant pies, with fresh butter and green cheese (as the new cream-cheese is called), maple molasses, preserves, and pickled cucumbers, besides tea and coffee — the latter be it known, I had watched the American woman boiling in the frying-pan. It was a black-looking compound and I did not attempt to discuss its merits".[1]

Although visiting was completely spontaneous, some notice was required if the intended guests were to be specially honoured or the party was to be a large one. When the hostess made her preparations ahead of time, this was known as "going to trouble", and woe betide the luckless guest who did not do justice to the victuals or pushed his chair away from the table too soon. Early visitors noted that it was customary in Canada to offer cheese with apple pie, and that the main dinner plate was ranged with several little glass dishes for preserves, honey and the inevitable apple sauce.

Picnics were a favourite pastime and were either pot-luck affairs with all the participating ladies bringing a basket suitably decorated, or else magnificent productions requiring careful catering and planning. The famous Isabella Beeton was the first to detail such an elaborate outing. "A Picnic for 40 persons: A joint of cold roast beef, a joint of cold boiled beef, 2 ribs of lamb, 2 shoulders of lamb, 4 roast fowls, 2 roast ducks, 1 ham, 1 tongue, 2 veal-and-ham pies, 2 pigeon pies, 6 medium-sized lobsters, 1 piece of collared calf's head, 18 lettuces, 6 baskets of salad, 6 cucumbers. Stewed fruit well sweetened, and put into glass bottles well-corked; 3 or 4 dozen plain pastry biscuits to eat with stewed fruit, 2 dozen fruit turnovers, 4 dozen cheese cakes, 2 cold cabinet puddings in moulds, 2 blanc-manges in moulds, a few jam puffs, 1 large cold plum-pudding (this must be good), a few baskets of fresh fruit, 3 dozen plain biscuits, a piece of cheese, 6 lbs. of butter (this of course, includes the butter for tea)."

The list continues with bread, cakes and cookies of all kinds and ends with half a pound of tea — "coffee not suitable for a picnic, being difficult to make".[5] Hostesses apparently forgot things at that time too, and a list of "things not to be forgot" includes wine glasses, "milk if this last named article cannot be obtained in the neighbourhood and 3 cork screws". These latter were essential because the beverage list suggests: "3 dozen quart bottles of ale, packed in hampers; ginger-beer, soda-water, and lemonade, of each 2 dozen bottles; 6 bottles of sherry, 6 bottles of claret, champagne à discretion, and any other light wine that may be preferred, 2 bottles of brandy. Water can usually be obtained, so it is useless to take it".[5]

Favourite excuses for picnics included the occasion of horse races, well organized before the turn of the nineteenth century, and whenever Parade Day was called. For a number of years at the beginning of the century, all grown men were required to join the militia in Upper Canada unless they were certificated Mennonites, Quakers or Tunkers, in which case they paid an exemption fee. Parades were usually ludicrous, with each man his own tailor, and weapons ran the gamut from umbrellas to hoes. However the food was lavish and the beverages flowed.

Everyone went and everyone participated in the social events. There was no distinction on public occasions between classes, sex, marital status or even age. Indeed, the period could well have been called the age of "togetherness".

Those in the backwoods had to make their own social occasions, but wherever there was a small town or a settlement there were many things to do and see throughout the nineteenth century. The local inn generally had a large upstairs ballroom that was used for lectures and political meetings. These were held in the winter when farmers were free from chores and the roads were passable. Tempers could run high, but it was a thoroughly enjoyable occasion for, as the writer of *Adventures in Canada* said, "all Canadians are politicians".

Warmly dressed in blanket coats or buffalo robes and wearing all manner of boots and moccasins, people drove for miles to the inn. "The sleighs were ranged, some under the shed of the village tavern, other along the sides of the street, the horses looking like nondescript animals, from the skins and coverlets thrown over them to protect them from the cold. The 'bar' of the tavern was the great attraction to many, and its great blazing fire, on which a cartload of wood glowed with exhilarating heat, to others. Every one on entering, after desperate stamping and scraping, to get the snow from the feet, and careful brushing of the legs with a broom, to leave as little as possible for melting, made straight to it, holding up each foot by turns to get it dried, as far as might be. There was no pretence at showing deference to any one; a laborer had no hesitation in taking the only vacant seat, though his employer were left standing. 'Treating' and being 'treated' went on with great spirit at the bar, mutual strangers asking each other to drink as readily as if they had been old friends. Wine-glasses were not to be seen, but, instead, tumblers were set out, and 'a glass was left to mean what any one chose to pour into them' (*sic*). We stayed for a time to listen to the speeches, which were delivered from a small balcony before the window of the tavern, but were very uninteresting to me, at least, though the crowd stood patiently in the snow to hear them".[2]

The tavern and the hall of the Mechanics' Institute were used for the constant procession of travelling theatrical groups, when the town did not boast a theatre of its own. Winter evenings were filled with lecturers coming from England, from France and from the United States. Their talks ranged from mesmerism to the new electricity, spiritualism, photography, as well as musicales and sessions of phrenology. The latter was perhaps the most popular fad of the nineteenth century. It claimed to be a science capable of assessing its subject's abilities and personality by means of an external examination of the bumps of the skull. Many books of the period give charts showing the bumps and their attributes for those who wished to try this in the privacy of their own parlour. Even medical men employed this examination to diagnose patients, and travelling professors of phrenology always had a full house. This "science" of course, was given impetus when Queen Victoria and the Prince Consort had their heir examined from time to time in an effort to find out why the young prince would not follow his father's precepts.

Popular too were the Saints' Day processions and the Orange walks which have survived to this day, and the travelling menageries and circuses that have become a legend. It was always a holiday when the circus came, heralded weeks in advance by garish posters in the taverns. Usually there were two shows a day. By our present-day standards admission was high — often 50 cents a person, but the crowds came nevertheless. Barnum was a household name to several generations, and tiny General Tom Thumb was the darling of all. His story and picture appear on post-cards, cans, advertisements, trade cards and on all kinds of products, as did Jumbo the beloved elephant, another star of the period. Contemporary writers mention that the Indians enjoyed the travelling circus almost as much as riding in trains.

Agricultural fairs began very early and were, of course, the means to spread new ideas on husbandry, to improve stock, to introduce the machines that were gradually appearing and to offer honest competition, exactly as they do now. There were flower shows, seed competitions and exhibitions, displays of spinning, weaving, blankets, shawls, carpeting and counterpanes. There was livestock and "pedlars with Yankee notions" as well as medicine men.

One of the first industries, and one that was included in exports, was cheese-making. Fairs always had a huge wheel of cheese on display, made of the finest milk obtainable. A fair in 1853 had a cheese weighing seven hundredweight, "not made of 'double skimmed sky-blue', but of milk of the richest quality, which, from its size and appearance, might have feasted all the rats and mice in the province for the next twelve months".[6] Canada is probably the only country to have had a poet who devoted his talents to her famous cheeses. James McIntyre of Ingersoll, Ontario, in the 1880's tells of a monster wheel that eventually went to London where it astounded all, as indeed it must have since there was no refrigeration:

"To prove the wealth that here abounds,
One cheese weighed eight thousand pounds,
Had it been hung in air at noon
Folks would have thought it was the moon,
It sailed with triumph o'er the seas,
'Twas hailed with welcome, queen of cheese."[7]

From giant cheese it is natural to turn to the general store, which occupied a unique place in the social life of the last century. It was the village club, sometimes the post office, always the centre for gossip and conjecture. Apart from the local justice of the peace, or "squire" as he was called in some areas, the storekeeper was the most important man in town. He was the merchant and the banker of the area, he was consulted on farming, trading and land transactions. A man of consequence, he often became a magistrate, local commissioner and a member of the provincial government.

His store was a focal point of the people's lives, supplying them with the small luxuries they could afford as well as the necessities which the farm could not produce. He took produce in exchange for factory-made articles, and at his discretion gave credit. Often he quietly carried debts when harvests were poor. When sending home an order of groceries it was customary for him to tuck in the bags a few penny candies for the children.

He sold almost everything: "Hiram's store has nothing very remarkable about it that we can discover, unless it be that it is a trifle dingier and more close-smelling than are the generality of American village stores in the winter, when doors are closed, windows pasted over, and stoves fired-up until they glow again. It is a shop of some twenty feet by thirty, having a couple of doors at the opposite ends, one leading into the office, the other into the store-room, where the more bulky articles, barrels of flour and pork, kegs of nails, and tins of paint and varnish are kept until wanted. On either side of the store is a counter having apparently a 'double debt to pay', being at one and the same time the table upon which Hiram displays his merchandise, and the divan upon which his customers perch themselves when the half dozen chairs are appropriated. Hiram's being a 'general store', it would be hard to say what he sells and what he does not. Of the two it would be easier, we imagine, to enumerate the articles which he does not sell, than those which he has in store; for he is a grocery, drapery, ironmongery, confectionery, and a hundred other businesses combined. He sells dresses, pickled-herrings, and lollipops; ribbons, prayer-books, and axes; edgings, petroleum, and crockery ware; patent medicines, ready-made clothes, Yankee notions, and, as he would express it, a 'heap of other fixin's too numerous to reckon'. In the centre of the store is a stove, and round the stove the more well-to-do of Hiram's visitors are seated. It is the dress-circle of the establishment, the counters being the gallery. Of the half dozen individuals seated around the stove four are chewing tobacco, or spruce-gum, the two others, not being chewers perhaps, are amusing themselves by whittling."[8]

Evenings, when the chores were done, were often passed dancing, singing, playing games and giving forfeits. Canadians were a most musical people. It was said if three Canadians got together, two would dance while one would fiddle. The earliest settlers brought with them the songs, ballads and games belonging to their past, and because of the tenuous communications with the mother-country these games continued for many years, although long outmoded in Europe. They all reflect a way of life going far back into history. In fact, many French songs of this country are based on those of France in the Middle Ages and have a flavour of the troubadour, recalling towns the habitant had never seen. A folk lore collection of 1883 mentions Canadians singing:

"Entre Paris et Saint-Denis
Il s'élève une danse;
Toutes les dames de la ville
Sont alentour qui dansent".[9]

On the other hand, some old tunes had later words added to commemorate more recent events. It is said that "Un Canadien Errant" is one of these, the words being written by an exile of the 1837 Rebellion.

These songs and dances were more than just an evening of fun. These pastimes were older than Canada and the games which we in our sophistication feel belong to childhood were played by adults including those of marriageable age, and in some areas by the middle-aged and the prosperous business man as well as the carefree young girl. The pioneers continued a heritage that mentions the maids of Elizabeth I playing tag, and Froissart talks of the French court playing childhood games. As in all folk lore, there was a common heritage, and whether the song or game was in French, German or English they are similar and recognizable. Some were danced in a circle around one in the centre who finally chose a partner; others make fun of the miller whose honesty was always in dispute; some games ended with a forfeit, others with a kiss.

Kissing games were known in Colonial America and in the early settlements of Canada. The mention of much kissing in early records does not mean impropriety, but rather the continuation of an old social custom that had become outmoded in the former homeland. Kissing games recall that etiquette up to the end of the eighteenth century permitted a lady to so honour a gentleman, even on first introduction. Because dancing often went against the religious conscience of a community, an evening might be spent playing games, rounds or forfeits, all adding up to the same thing — a pleasant way to relax and a chance for the younger people to meet, not entirely unsupervised.

There were many amusements to keep the youngsters busy after a full day's work. In the springtime there was the fun of the taffy-on-the-snow at the maple sugaring, when hot syrup would be poured on to pans of clean white snow. As sugar became more plentiful there were evening taffy pulls,

Our Valentine

MLE

Andlis 10,2 the

ell edby still fear

Lest in the air

prin tedon my

timen ortro uble F

A ing may D part

thi swill till 's M brace

T his D Clara tion do spurn

Or LLL des shall

O as £1,000 ken inret

Con 2 B myv al N tine

G. Guyon

fondant- and fudge-making sessions. By the turn of the century, one accomplishment necessary for a young woman was knowing how to make good chocolate fudge.

There were sleigh rides, the idea being for girl and boy to be tossed out together into the snow bank. Hay rides were similar. At skating parties the non-athletic ladies might be pushed over the ice sitting in a chair on runners.

There was much concern with self-improvement and this started the popular Spelling School or Bee. Much as small-fry sport is now closely watched by parents, so the progress of the Spelling School was noted by all parents, teachers and proud villagers. At a set date the boys and girls from different school sections would meet on a winter evening for a match. Generally there were two teams, each headed by a captain, who fielded his spellers with great skill according to their proficiency. Sometimes the members of the team tossed hard-to-spell words at their opponents, sometimes a chairman was appointed to call the play. In any event, crowds gathered for the contest and there was much rivalry between school districts.

A local pastime more strenuous than the Spelling School rivalry was the constant feats of strength between rival villages. Most common was the challenge to fight or wrestle, and the local champion would be pointed out with pride. As time passed these contests became less brutal and rivalries were turned to team games or ploughing matches. Eye-gouging became an event of the past, belonging to the brutal early years.

The Singing School was another winter occupation. The master was usually a young farmer or man from a closeby town with a reasonably good voice—preferably a strong one. Sometimes he had knowledge of an instrument, and a fiddle or piano might be used, but generally the classes were conducted with a pitch pipe or tuning fork. Unless he had a strong personality, the music master had a hard time keeping his pupils under control. The evenings provided pleasure but rarely great musical results.

The teacher was a busy man, driving his cutter across country three or four nights a week and occasionally giving private lessons here and there. At the end of the session it was usual for the Singing School to give an evening of singing, dancing and other entertainment to raise money to present to the master. Although pupils paid for lessons the fees alone were rarely sufficient to pay him. In the early days pupils going to Singing School, which might be held in a home, in the school-house or in a hall, had to bring their own lighting. They brought candles, candlesticks and lanterns and it was usual for the girls to vie with each other as to who could bring the prettiest candlestick.

A summer treat was the Camp or Open Air Meeting. These were public assemblies held in clearings in nearby woods and people would come for miles to attend a session. Some were purely religious, others were sponsored by the Temperance Societies, many had bands, and all drew large crowds. Boards provided the seating and there was a raised platform for the speakers. Temperance meetings were extremely popular from mid-century onwards. Almost everyone went to them, for most of the people living in the country had become rigid teetotallers. "There are poor drunkards enough, after all, but it is a wonder there are no more, when whiskey is only a shilling or eighteenpence a gallon".[2] Many camp meetings were organized by zealous, untiring Methodists and lasted from one to two weeks. People attending tented on the grounds, bringing their own provisions or means of buying food. Often there was communal eating at the camp site.

Some writers have suggested that these meetings were licentious, but the evidence seems to be otherwise. These were lonely unsophisticated people, and in the course of their spiritual outpourings there were some in the huge crowd who became hysterical.

Meetings were held every hour of the day and there was stirring oratory from the assembled preachers. Some of the audience, after listening for an hour or two, would be overcome by "the power" as it was termed, and would then lie prostrate on the ground. As one sermon ended another would begin.

Mrs. Moodie went to a camp meeting and recalls, "Towards the middle of his discourse, the speaker wrought himself up into such a religious fury that it became infectious, and cries and groans resounded on all sides; and the prayers poured out by repentant sinners for mercy and pardon were heart-rending. The speaker at length became speechless from exhaustion, and stopping suddenly in the midst of his too eloquent harangue, he tied a red cotton handkerchief round his head, and hastily descended the steps, and disappeared in the tent provided for the accommodation of the ministers. His place was instantly supplied by a tall, dark, melancholy looking man, who, improving upon his reverend brother's suggestions, drew such an awful picture of the torments endured by the damned, that several women fainted, while others were shrieking in violent hysterics".[6] It was a fine way to spend a lazy summer day.

Of all the outdoor activities that impressed the visitors and settlers from Europe, perhaps it was the hunting and fishing that was mentioned most in early travellers' accounts. It was all so abundant, before too many had indiscriminately thinned wild life beyond recognition, that many a lazy remittance man loafed his time away pot-shotting when he should have been clearing land. A super-abundance of birds, many of which were comparatively tame, made shooting easy to anyone who had a gun and ammunition. In Europe the finest hunting and fishing had always been reserved for the rich and noble; here a man shot for his larder and to keep his family clothed. But he could shoot for sport if that was his desire, and he could shoot without anyone gainsaying him.

There was so much slaughter that entire species disappeared eventually. Some have remained only because of the strict conservation of recent years. "The flocks of wild pigeons that come in the spring are wonderful. They fly together in bodies of many thousands, perching, as close as they can settle, on the trees when they alight, or covering the ground over large spaces when feeding. The first tidings of their approach is the signal for every available gun to be brought into requisition, at once to procure a supply of fresh food, and to protect the crops on the fields, which the pigeons would utterly destroy if they were allowed".[2]

Eventually the passenger pigeon became extinct—it was a relatively friendly bird unafraid of people. Even the sound of guns did not at first frighten them. At one time they were so numerous that the sky darkened when they were in flight, and tree branches cracked under their roosting weight. When used in pies and stews only the breast meat was taken, the rest was discarded.

Similar shooting parties were organized from time to time to clear given areas of wild life, to protect the crops and occasionally to provide fresh meat. Squirrels were cooked with corn and root vegetables to make the well-liked Brunswick Stew. Later in the fall, coon hunting was organized and eventually specially reared and trained dogs were used. "The raccoons, usually called 'coons', were a great nuisance when the corn was getting ripe. We used to hunt them by torchlight, the torches being strips of hickory bark, or lumps of fat pine. We could have done nothing, however, without the help of our dogs, who tracked them to the trees in which they had taken refuge, and then we shot them by the help of the lights, amidst prodigious excitement and commotion. The Weirs close to us, got skins enough one autumn to make fine robes for their sleigh. I never knew but one man who had eaten raccoon and he was no wiser than he needed to be. Meeting him one day after a hunt, in which he had got a large raccoon for his share, he stopped me to speak of it thus—'Great raccoon that—there was a pint of oil in him—it made a most beautiful shortcake'. I wished him joy of his taste".[2]

Coon fat was often rendered in the settlements to help eke out the candles, and this practice was carried on well towards the end of the century as new areas in the west were pioneered. The oil was usually poured into a saucer or cup-like container, much like a Betty lamp, with a twist of rag for the wick.

Fishing at night using lights was an occupation learned from the Indians. A lantern or cresset was fixed in the bow of the canoe and a knot of pitch-pine was lit to give a bright clear light both over and into the water. "Only very still nights would do, for if there was any ripple the fish could not be seen. The quantity of fish that some can get in a night's spearing is often wonderful. In some parts of Canada there was higher game than in our waters—the salmon-trout, and the 'maskelonge', a corruption of the French words 'masque' and 'longue', a kind of pike with a projecting snout, whence its name, offering a prize of which we could not boast. The Indians in some districts live to a great extent on the fish they get in this way".[2] It is interesting that from the earliest times visitors noted that the cleaning of fish was never among the chores a Canadian woman would undertake.

The Indians knew how to fish through the ice, sitting with infinite patience until a catch was made. In later times small portable huts or wind screens were erected, but the first settlers found it a cold occupation. "Suddenly the head and shoulders of an Indian, raised from the edge of the buffalo skin, for such it was, dissipated any alarm. Going up to him, I found he was employed in fishing, and partly for protection, partly to keep the fish from being alarmed, had completely covered himself with the hide which so attracted my attention. He had cut a hole through the two-feet-thick ice about a foot square, and sat with a bait hanging from one hand, while in the other he held a short spear to transfix any deluded victim which it might

43

tempt to its destruction. The bait was an artificial fish of white wood, with leaden eyes and tin fins, and about eight or nine inches in length. He seemed rather annoyed at my disturbing him; but on my giving him a small ball of twine I happened to have with me, we became good enough friends, and after a few minutes I left him".[2]

The long-lasting thick ice provided other sport for many months. There were long afternoons of skating when "School-boys made for it as soon as they got free; the clerks and shopmen were down the instant the shutters were up and the door fastened; even ladies crowded to it, either to skate with the assistance of some gentlemen, or to see the crowd, or to be pushed along in chairs mounted on runners. The games of different kinds played between large numbers were very exciting. Scotchmen with their 'curling', others with balls, battering them hither and thither, in desperate efforts to carry them to a particular boundary. Then there were the ice-boats gliding along in every direction, with the loads of well-dressed people reclining on them, and their huge sail swelling overhead. These contrivances were new to me, though I had been so long in Canada".[2]

Wit and Humour, 1881[10]

"Query: What is the best line to lead a man with? Answer: Crinoline."

"The right man in the right place is a husband at home in the evening."

"Some girls are like old muskets—they use a good deal of powder, but do not go off."

"A young lady says the reason she carries a parasol is that the sun is of the masculine gender and she cannot withstand his ardent glance."

REFERENCES
[1] *Roughing it in the Bush,* S. Moodie, Toronto, 1871.
[2] *Adventures in Canada,* John C. Geikie, Philadelphia, n.d.
[3] *The Backwoods of Canada,* C. P. Traill, London, 1836.
[4] *Canadian Scenery,* N. P. Willis, London, 1842.
[5] *Household Management,* I. Beeton, London, 1861.
[6] *Life in the Clearings,* S. Moodie, London, 1853.
[7] *Poems,* J. McIntyre, Ingersoll, Ontario, 1889.
[8] *The Gentleman Immigrant,* W. Stamer, London, 1874.
[9] *Games and Songs of American Children,* W. Newall, New York, 1883.
[10] *Mother Hubbard's Cupboard,* Anonymous, Hamilton, Ontario, 1881.

The Family Adviser

Medicine was primitive and was usually part of the housewives' duty. It did not matter whether the patient was living in the Maritimes, Canada West, the newly-opened western lands or London or New York, medical knowledge had advanced little since the sixteenth century. In *Pen Pictures of Upper Canada,* (1905) Michael Sherck did say that medical knowledge had leaped forward at such a rate towards the latter part of the nineteenth century that he doubted if the twentieth century could bring more advances.

There were many misconceptions and areas of ignorance, not only in curing disease, but in basic knowledge of the human body. The beliefs of the Middle Ages continued. It was thought that the body had humours, and food and drugs were grouped according to their action on these humours. There was a reliance on remedies going back to antiquity; some were tinged with witchcraft. On the other hand many remedies were not only ingenious, they were effective. Although there was ignorance of how the cure was effected, it didn't matter. There was deep faith. Today, some of these cures have been modernized a little and in many parts of the country they are being used with probably the same chances of success. Reading some of this medical lore we can only marvel at our ancestors' fortitude and come to the conclusion that only the fittest survived.

New settlements were lucky to have a doctor within riding distance. Most families were without professional advice and the diagnosing, curing and dosing were done by the women, helped by neighbours and by the local Indian herbal cures. Women received their knowledge in childhood from their mothers, and this was reinforced by the many books and almanacs published as time passed. Because illness was prevalent and often serious, most cookbooks devoted chapters to curing, arranging sick rooms, the care and comfort of invalids as well as the special cooking required. This was necessary in view of the normal diet of fried pickled pork, fried cakes, root vegetables, strong pickles and hot breads.

Early settlers from Europe found some local plants familiar, while discovering new ones from the Indian medicine men. Families brought with them slips of favourite garden and medicinal plants to grow in their new homes and many such plants have now become naturalized.

The collecting and tracing of home medical knowledge is fascinating. Like all other subjects pertaining to the home, writers copied each other for more than a hundred years, and no matter where the book was published, the same ideas turn up usually expressed in the same words. Early arrivals in the New England States travelled with Elizabethan herbals and a number of them found their way into Canada. Among the most quoted and popular books of the nineteenth century are: *Domestic Medicine* by Dr. William Buchan, first published in Dublin in mid-eighteenth century but current for some one hundred years; *Mackenzie's Five Thousand Receipts*, a do-it-yourself compendium that appeared around 1829 and was popular for some fifty years; and *The Family Adviser* by Dr. Henry Wilkins, which made its first appearance at the beginning of the nineteenth century but continued in many editions with influence until mid-century.

The diseases reflect the changes taking place in the development of the country. Apart from epidemic children's diseases, home accidents and colds, there were serious outbreaks of cholera and typhoid throughout the century, usually following waves of newly arrived immigrants and shortly after further forest areas were cleared. Because of the lack of medical knowledge and effective public health measures, these waves of pestilence occurred and recurred until they had run their course. The lack of drainage, the open sewage, and the overwhelming of quarantine facilities aggravated the epidemics and helped spread them across the country.

In 1832, cholera was thought to be caused by fresh fruits and vegetables and in many areas of North America these were banned from sale. So great were fear and superstition that it was enough to stand near a barrow of fruit to feel contaminated. Dr. Wilkins reflected this thinking when he wrote: "Cantilopes, and watermellons, (like peaches), finally overthrow the digestive powers completely; so that the evacuations of them does not produce speedy relief. They should be abandoned before such an event".[1]

There were innumerable guide books issued to help immigrants settle in Canada, advice was offered on goods to bring, clothes to wear and the changes to be faced. An undated pamphlet from about 1840 gave the following advice:

"Immigrants on their arrival, they ought to abstain from eating new potatoes, green peas, unripe fruit &c., or use in moderation; for many, on their first arrival are afflicted with dysentery, which, I am confident, is occasioned by greediness with which they devour vegetables of every kind, after being confined for a few weeks to the use of salt provisions. Fever and ague are common complaints all over America, but seldom fatal. They generally make their appearance in new settlements, in four or five years after we have commenced clearing land, rage for one or two years, and then almost wholly disappear. They are probably to be attributed to the foul vapours arising from the decayed stumps and roots of trees and other vegetable substances. Intermittant and other fevers are common in the neighbourhood of large marshes and stagnant pools. Emigrants ought to avoid such places."[2]

There was a heavy reliance on cures to be effected with common household supplies or herbs and plants growing around the house. Later, by mid-century, drug houses were established, although Toronto had good apothecary shops in the 1830's. Home drying and curing of plants became less important, but recipes changed very little. Illness was tackled with cupping or blistering and bloodletting, holdovers from previous times. Patients were bled for nearly every illness from headaches to pregnancy. Cool drinks and fresh air were forbidden the invalid. It was believed that cold water would cause immediate death. There are records of men believed dead from the cholera and removed to the outhouse where the cool air brought them back to consciousness.

Doctors were not only handicapped by lack of progress in medical knowledge, but they were also in competition with local herbalists and wise women. Because of fear, distance, and lack of money, doctors were called only in dire emergencies, and usually too late. This unfortunately did not enhance their reputation, and it did not prevent them from fighting among themselves both privately and publicly. Nor did it stop them from giving testimonials to all manner of patented nostrums without regard for professional ethics. The clergy were also given to writing long and glowing testimonials for blood purifiers, vermifuges and boil cures.

Medicine was not far advanced when the ubiquitous Dr. Chase, who sold excellent advice as well as his own brands of medicine had this to say about his brother doctors striving for newer cures:

"Many persons will stick up their noses at these 'Old Grandmother' prescriptions (but I tell many 'Upstart Physicians'), that our grandmothers are carrying more information out of this world by their deaths than will ever be possessed by this class of 'sniffers'."[3]

Early travellers and settlers were faced with the problems of scurvy from the salt meat diet that continued all winter. There was also the danger of bites from rabid animals, wolves, wild cats and other disturbed animals wandering in packs where clearings were made. Snakes were more common than today and rattlesnake bites were frequent. The problem of rabies did not belong to the backwoods only. Sick animals, particularly dogs, were a menace in the towns

and villages throughout the century until a cure was discovered.

We know that they were unable to cure rabies victims and with our hindsight their efforts seem pathetic, strange and even amusing. In 1765, Mrs. Hannah Glasse quoted a famous medical cure of that period in her cook-book. It was attributed to a Dr. Meade and it was in use for some one hundred and fifty years.

A Certain Cure
For the Bite of a Mad Dog

"Let the patient be blooded at the arm nine or ten ounces. Take of the herbs called in Latin, lichen cinerus terrestris; in English, ash-coloured ground liver-wort, cleaned, dried and powdered, half an ounce.

Of black pepper powdered, two drachms. Mix this well together, and divide the powder into four dozes, one of which must be taken every morning fasting, for four mornings successively, in half a pint of cow's milk warm. After these four dozes are taken, the patient must go into the cold bath, or a cold spring or river every morning fasting for a month. He must be dipt all over, but not to stay in (with his head above water) longer than half a minute, if the water be very cold. After this he must go in three times a week for a fortnight longer."[4]

Some years later, in 1845, a different approach was tried:

Hydrophobia

"Take oyster-shells, wash them clean, put them upon a bed of live coals, and keep them there till they are thoroughly calcined, or burnt; then reduce them to fine powder, and sift it through a fine sieve. Take three table-spoonfuls of this powder, or lime, add a sufficiency of egg to give it the consistency of soft dough, — fry it in a little fresh butter, or olive oil. Let the patient eat this cake in the morning and abstain from food or drink at least six hours. This dose repeated for three mornings in succession, is, in all cases, sufficient."[5]

It was also said that draughts of vinegar would help and as late as 1883 it was thought that keeping the wound open with a few beans and covering with linseed poultice constituted a cure.

To Cure Rattlesnake Bites

"Chew and swallow, or drink dissolved in water, alum, the size of a hickory nut. Put thoroughwort leaves pounded on and keep wetting them with water. If the person is very sick, black or purple, let him drink a little of the juice. Renew the application after two hours." [6]

In 1898, the *Galt Cookbook*[7] recommended mucilage for insect bites as well as burns and cuts of all kinds.

It was a time when tuberculosis was not understood and lung hemorrhages were common. One way of stopping them was frequent doses of dry salt, but towards the turn of the century they threw one or two teaspoons of chloroform into the patient's mouth.

Cuts were very frequent in workshops and in the home as well as on the farm. The ways of staunching blood were exceedingly curious:

"If the wound bleeds very fast, and there is no physician at hand, cover it with the scrapings of sole-leather, scraped like coarse lint."[8]

In 1845 soot was applied to ease the bleeding and lessen the pain.[5]

"For a slight cut there is nothing better to control the hemorrhage than common unglazed brown wrapping paper, such as issued by marketmen and grocers."[9]

In 1889, they used the dust from black tea.[10]

During the century the most usual household cure, and one that is still continued in some districts today, was the web of a spider spread over the cut. Nose bleeds were cured with two radical suggestions, one of which was to tie a string tightly around the little finger, another was to pour cold water from a height on the back of the neck. The vigorous motion of the jaws, as if masticating, was also said to stop the flow.

The poor lighting as well as lack of knowledge and general neglect led to eye problems. For many years spectacles would be purchased from the pedlar; later, a selection might be stocked at the general store. The sufferer would try on pair after pair until the surrounding world became a little clearer. It was not uncommon for a pair of glasses to be shared among members of the family.

Of knowledge there was little, but cures were many. Motes were removed either with a loop of horsehair or else with two or three flaxseeds placed under the eyelid.

The tears combining with the flax formed a glutinous substance which would envelope any foreign body. In the early days of railroading, travellers were told to pack at least a dozen seeds in their baggage.

Sore and Weak Eyes
"Take white vitriol, one ounce; sugar of lead, one ounce; gunpowder, two ounces; put into one quart of lime water; let it settle twenty-four hours, and it is then fit for use."[6]

For Inflamed or Weak Eyes
"Half fill a bottle with common rock salt; add the best of French brandy till all but full. Shake it, let it settle, and bathe the outside of the eye with a soft linen cloth on going to bed and occasionally through the day. This will be found a good application for pains and bruises generally.[11]

Another salve in use was the tea of wild violets. The sufferer not only applied the liquid to the sore eyes but drank the tea several times a day.

To Relieve Asthma
"Take the root of skunk cabbage, and boil it until very strong, then strain off the liquor; to which add, one table-spoonful of garlic juice to one pint of the liquor, and simmer them together. Dose, one table-spoonful, three times a day."[6]

A lady writes that "sufferers from asthma should get a muskrat skin and wear it over their lungs, with the fur side next to the body. It will bring certain relief."[9]

50

To Remove Worms

"Honey and milk is very good for worms, so is strong salt water, likewise powdered sage and molasses taken freely."[8]

"Take tobacco leaves, pound them up with honey, and lay them on the belly of the child, or grown person, at the same time administering a dose of some good physic; or take garden parsley; make into a tea; and let the patient drink freely of it; or take the scales that fall around the blacksmith's anvil, powder them fine, and put them in some sweetened rum. Shake them when you take them, and give a tea-spoonful three times a day."[6]

Ringworm

"Boil three figs of tobacco in a pint of urine, add one gill of vinegar, and one gill of lye; rub this wash on frequently."[6]

All ulcers, cankers and sores were known as cancers and treated herbally with local Indian remedies. These usually consisted of washes of corn cob ashes, or potions made from boiling the bark of red or white oak or the roots of the pitch-pine. Sores were by no means the only skin diseases. Eczema was common and was still known by the old name of Salt Rheum. It was treated with either a lotion of sweet fern or a paste of creosote and lard.

Vaccination was known but was not universally practised although Dr. Jenner had been honoured even by the Chiefs of the Five Nations with a belt of wampum. There were periodic epidemics of smallpox and scarred faces were quite common. It is no wonder when we read that as late as the 1880's the following advice was being followed:

To Cure Smallpox

"The worst case of small pox can be cured in three days simply by the use of cream of tartar. One ounce of cream of tartar dissolved in a pint of water, drank at intervals when cold, is a certain, never failing remedy. It has cured thousands, never leaves a mark, never causes blindness, and avoids tedious lingering."[12]

The following prevention of face pitting comes from a handwritten manuscript book of the same period:

To Prevent the Face from Pitting

"When the preceeding fever is at its height, and just before the eruption appears, rub the chest thoroughly with croton oil and tartar emetic ointment. A full eruption on the part of the body is thus secured, and the disease is also prevented from attacking the internal organs "

Warts and boils are old scourges, tackled with aids ranging from willow ashes mixed with strong vinegar to milkweed juice. Although in 1882 a number of books mention wetting the pustule with five or ten cents of cinnamon three times a day. Poultices of ginger and flour were used on boils when the century was young. Later the favorite was Isaiah 38:21; "Go thou and do likewise". Some favored using the skin of a boiled egg. "Peel it carefully, wet and apply to the part affected".

51

For years shoes were made by itinerant shoemakers. Both shoes in a pair were the same: it was many years before there was a left and a right shoe. No wonder there were corns. The corn cures were all weird and wonderful, but since they were all somewhat astringent likely there was some merit in them.

To Cure Corns

"A corn may be extracted from the feet by binding on half a raw cranberry, with the cut side of the fruit upon the feet."[8]

"Use a salve made of equal parts roasted onions and soft soap, apply it hot."[5]

"Wet the corn every morning with saliva, and paste on them young peach leaves."[5]

"Take a lemon and cut off a piece, then nick it so as to let in the toe with the pulp next the corn, tie this on at night, so that it cannot move, he will find next morning that, with a blunt knife, the corn will come away to a great extent."[3]

To Cure Bunions

"Let fall a stream of very warm water from a teakettle, at the highest elevation from which the patient can bear the water to fall directly on the apex of the swelling; continue this once a day for a short time and a cure will be effected, providing you desist from wearing short shoes. The greater the elevation of the kettle, the more effectual the remedy."[9]

The cold winters, the oven-like temperatures around the fireplace and the cold bedrooms led to colds, coughs and chilblains. Beds were warmed with warming pans, pottery bottles, hot bricks, and eventually the rubber bottle. In 1829 the best way to avoid the chilblain was to massage the feet thoroughly before retiring, provided, of course, the feet were clean enough to take advantage of this massage. Feet were also bound in the white skin from suet, sometimes bathed in hot water and then rubbed with butter, "the size of a walnut with plenty of salt worked in".[8]

Chilblains

"If the sinews have been drawn up by disease or accident, rub with an ointment made from the common ground-worms, which boys dig to bait fishes, rubbed on with the hand, it is said to be excellent."[8]

Sore throats came in for similarly homely treatments, the most common being the wrapping of the warm sock straight from the foot around the neck with the internal dose of loaf sugar and hot brandy. Scraped horseradish cooked in a sugar syrup was another cough remedy and so were slices of salt pork covered with red pepper and wrapped around the throat. Pork was always a favourite and as late as 1887 salt pork or fat bacon simmered in hot vinegar was recommended as the sure cure when applied to a sore throat, unless one gargled with a mixture of sulphuric acid and glycerin. The growth of the various "fads" is reflected in an 1856 cure which simply suggests that a daily wash in cold water would prevent swollen glands, quinsy and sore throats. Some people mixed herbs in straight Holland gin and took tremendous doses, while others sniffed lemon juice up into the nostrils. Others wrapped themselves in snuff-sprinkled scarves while some favoured a rubbing with bear or goose grease.

Remedy for a Cough
"The following medicine for a cough has performed such extraordinary cures in private practice, that the possessor is induced to publish it for the benefit of society — Take six ounces of Italian or roll liquorice cut into small pieces, and put into an earthen jar with about one gill of the best vinegar; simmer together until the liquorice is dissolved; then add two ounces of the oil of almonds, and half an ounce of the tincture of opium, stir the whole well together, and it is fit for use. Take two tea spoonfuls when going to bed, and the same quantity whenever the cough is troublesome."[13]

Rheumatic aches were taken care of with a lotion made of saltpetre, vinegar and new rum, although in the 1880's a draught of Canadian balsam in water taken after meals was said to be efficacious. In the 1890's cucumber juice was used as a wash, or the pain was ironed away by placing a flannel soaked in vinegar over the ache and applying a hot iron. Pains in the jaws and teeth were checked with kerosene, cayenne pepper, alcohol, oil of cloves, opium or chickweed juice. Earaches were helped with a hot onion popped in, or a hot brick applied to the side of the head, or a hot clove of garlic put on the sore part. Some even tried puffing tobacco juice into the ear.

Cure for an Earache
"Soak the feet in warm water; roast an onion and put the heart of it into the ear; heat a brick and wrap it up, and apply to the side of the head. When the feet are taken from the water, bind roasted onions on them.[5]

"Roast a piece of lean mutton. squeeze out the juice and drop it into the ear as hot as it can be borne."[14]

Cure for Deafness
"Take a strong glass bottle, and fill it nearly full of pure clarified honey; insert the bottle into the centre of a loaf of unbaked bread, first taking care to stop it tightly, and bake the whole thoroughly in an oven. Pour a small quantity of the honey thus treated in your ears, and protect them from the action of the external air by the use of cotton."[5]

"Take ants' eggs and onion juice, mix, and drop into the ear; or drop into the ear at night, six or eight drops of warm chamber lye."[6]

Although headaches and particularly "megrims" were being tackled by the health faddist by dropping icy cold water from a great height onto the victim, the most usual cure was a mustard plaster on the back of the neck or a stiff drink of raw rum or gin, anywhere up to half a glass.

To Cure a Nervous Headache

The Medical Record is authority for the statement that "nervous headaches may be cured by the simple act of walking backward ten minutes. It is well to get in a long narrow room where the windows are high and walk slowly, placing first the ball of the feet on the floor, and then the heel. Besides curing the headache, this exercise promotes a graceful carriage."[15]

In the middle years it was felt that consumption could be avoided by right thinking and living. When this failed, there were doses of pitch pine boiled in brandy and sweetened with sugar or tar, egg yolks and wine to be taken three times a day. Tuberculosis was also known as Phthisic. In 1850 the cure was a mixture of hen's fat and skunk cabbage juice to be taken three times a day.

Swellings, bumps and bruises as well as lockjaw were treated with hot poultices, always made of household supplies. These ranged from hot stewed white beans to mixtures of rye or wheat bran and vinegar, and brown wrapping paper was particularly saved for this occasion. The poultice for lockjaw was hot Indian meal wetted with warm lye.

In the days before the tetanus serum, lockjaw was fatal. Nevertheless there were ingenious attempts to cure this disease. As late as 1894, a mixture of chopped boiled onions and raw salt pork was said to be good for injuries from rusty tools. For some sixty years the rind of salt pork was advocated, while an alternative cure reads:

"Nothing is better than ear-wax to prevent the painful effects from a wound by a nail, skewer &c. It should be put on as soon as possible."[8]

There were the diseases peculiar to women, known collectively as "Female Obstructions", and in most cases the early Indian remedy of strong snakeroot tea was the cure. Urinary difficulties could be cured if pumpkin seeds were soaked in gin and the liquour taken, three glassesful a day. The most common ailment of ladies was hysterics. The tight corsetting could not have helped much but the usual advice was a mild purgative and visits in pleasant society.

To Restore from a Stroke of Lightning

"Shower with cold water for two hours; if the patient does not show signs of life, put salt in the water, and continue to shower one hour longer."[9]

Lame Feet

"Take one pint of urine, one tablespoonful of fine salt and one fig of tobacco; simmer strong, and apply it as a wash, as hot as can be borne every night; and when about to commence bathing the feet take one tea spoonful of the tincture of guaiacum; and in using the wash, if it should cause nausea, take one more tea-spoonful of the tincture, and cease bathing."[14]

Piles

"Roast, pulverize and mix the sole of an old shoe with lard or ox marrow, and apply it."[14]
"Take of sulphur one ounce, hog's fat four ounces, strong tobacco-

54

juice half a pint, and simmer them together into an ointment; and apply it."

For a Caked Breast
"Bake large potatoes, put two or more in a woolen stocking, crush them soft and apply as hot as can be borne."[16]

Cure for Stammering
"Impediments in the speech may be cured, where there is no malformation of the organs of articulation, by perseverance for three or four months in the simple remedy of reading aloud with the teeth closed, for at least two hours in the course of each day."[17]

To Prevent Inconvenience from Perspiration of the Hands
"Ladies who work lace or embroidery sometimes suffer inconvenience from the perspiration on their hands, which may be remedied by rubbing the hands frequently with a little dry wheaten bran."[17]

The Use of Tar-water in Expanding the Lungs of Public Speakers, &c.
"It has been found by the experience of many, that drinking tar-water very much deterges and opens the lungs, and thereby gives a very sensibly greater ease in speaking. A quart of tar is to be stirred six minutes in a gallon of water; but if there be somewhat less tar, it may do as well, especially at first, to try how it sits on the stomach. Take about one-fourth of a pint, at four times a day, at a due distance from meals. Begin taking it in the spring for about fourteen days, and continue it for a greater length of time, as occasion may require."[17]

REFERENCES
[1] *The Family Adviser*, H. Wilkins, New York, 1833.
[2] *Chambers's Information for the People*, Edinburgh, n.d.
[3] *Dr. Chase's Recipes*, A. W. Chase, London, Ontario, 1868.
[4] *The Art of Cookery Made Plain and Easy*, H. Glasse, London, 1765.
[5] *The New England Housekeeper*, S. A. Howland, Montpelier, 1845.
[6] *Ladies' Indispensable Assistant*, Anonymous, New York, 1851.
[7] *The New Galt Cook Book*, Taylor and McNaught, Toronto, 1898.
[8] *The American Frugal Housewife*, L. Child, New York, 1838.
[9] *The Every-Day Cook Book*, E. Neill, New York, 1884.
[10] *House and Home*, M. Harland, Philadelphia, 1889.
[11] *Mrs. Clarke's Cookery Book*, A. Clarke, Toronto, 1883.
[12] *The Peerless Cookbook*, Anonymous, Montreal, n.d.
[13] *The Cook Not Mad*, Anonymous, Kingston, Ontario, 1831.
[14] *The Improved Housewife*, A. L. Webster, Boston, 1856.
[15] *Search Lights on Health*, B. G. Jefferis, Toronto, 1894.
[16] *Mother Hubbard's Cupboard*, Anonymous, Hamilton, Ontario, 1881.
[17] *New Household Receipt Book*, S. Hale, London, 1854.

The Art of Preserving Health

Perhaps not the most fatal, but certainly the most discomforting and widespread illness of the age was dyspepsia, to give it its contemporary name. So widespread was indigestion that it could be called the disease of the North American continent. Dr. Chase in 1868 gives a very good summing up of some of the reasons for this malady:

"In the good old days of corn bread and crust coffee, there was but little trouble with Dyspepsia; but since the days of fashionable intemperance, both in eating and drinking, such as spirituous liquors, wines, beers, also tea and coffee, hot bread or biscuit, high seasoned food, overloading the stomach at meals, and constant eating and drinking between meals, bolting food, as called, that is, swallowing it without properly chewing, exces-sive venery, want of out-door exercise, with great anxiety of mind as to how the means can be made to continue the same indulgences, &c., all have a tendency to debilitate the stomach, and bring on or cause Dyspepsia."[1]

National indigestion not only brought about the food reform movement as well as the food faddists, but also a spate of cook-books devoted to these new principles of diet, using unbolted flour, fresh fruit, cereals, and fewer pies. The more conventional writers continued with the old-style food, but added pages of cures.

"A quantity of old cheese is the best thing to eat, when distracted by eating too much fruit, or oppressed with any kind of food. Physicians have given it in cases of extreme danger."[2]

"Mix two table-spoonfuls of West Indian rum; molasses, hog's fat, wine each one gill, mix all together, and take it at discretion."[3]

"For the Heart-ache or Heart-burn: For the one keep a conscience void of offence: (says a lady, the remedy cannot apply when a wife has a drunken husband) for the other chew magnesia or chalk, or drink a tumbler of cold water."[4]

"One quart hickory ashes, six ounces soot, one gallon boiling water, mix and stir frequently. At the end of twenty-four hours pour off the clear liquor. Take a teacupful three times a day."[5]

Cholera and dysentery were the two great decimators of the age. Against these ills they had no cure and indeed, there was very little knowledge as to the cause, let alone the prevention. As late as 1897 it was thought the cholera was the result of eating excessively indigestible foods such as unripe fruit, uncooked vegetables and the imbibing of intoxicating drinks.

Certain Cures for Cholera Morbus
"Black or green tea, steeped in boiling milk, seasoned with nutmeg, and best loaf sugar, is excellent for the dysentery. Flannel wet with brandy, powdered with cayenne pepper, and laid upon the bowels, affords great relief in cases of extreme distress. A spoonful of ashes stirred in cider is good to prevent sickness at the stomach. Physicians frequently order it in cases of choleramorbus."[2]

"Take of cherry-rum and brandy, each half a pint, half a pound of loaf sugar, two ounces of essence of peppermint. Dose, one spoonful two or three times a day. Bleeding from the arm, with the patient in an upright position, to (the point of) fainting will often cut short the disease at once."[3]

"I have heard of typhus fever in which all hope was gone, and yet the patients recovered by yeast being given by the wine-glassful every three hours."[4]

"Procure a lump of mutton suet fresh from the sheep, as large as a coffee-cup, and a lump of loaf-sugar one-third as large; put the suet in an earthen bowl, and lay the sugar on it; set it before the fire, where the heat will gradually melt the sugar and suet together in a mass. There must be no heat under the dish, or the suet will melt faster than it should. For an adult a dose is one teaspoonful every hour of the brown sediment in the bowl. This rule has cured cases of this disease given over by the physician."[5]

The ailments of childhood were many and unavoidable. There is probably no way of knowing how many small children died from croup, cholera, diphtheria and whooping cough. Certainly family bibles, church records and private papers are evidence of the appalling dangers of the first five years of life. There was no real progress in pediatrics throughout the period. The whooping cough victim was dressed in flannel and treated with strong mustard plasters and cold baths. Sometimes the doctor recommended a change of scenery, so the child and his contagion were removed to another house some miles away. Medical men of the period were all against the much older method of giving the child a great fright in order to effect a cure.

Whooping Cough Cure
"Two wine-glasses of vinegar, two of honey, two of water, and one onion sliced. Simmer one hour. Dose three tea-spoonfuls night and morning for a child eight years old."[6]

"External Application: sweet oil and brandy simmered with one onion sliced, and anoint the spine, chest and soles of the feet night and morning."

Diphtheria was tackled with the fumes from slaking lime and the general cure-all for scarlet fever was to coat the child's body with lard. Mothers who preferred some medicine usually made the following:

For the Scarlet Fever
"Take an onion, cut it in halves; cut out a portion of the centre, and into the cavity put a spoonful of saffron; put the pieces together, then wrap in a cloth and bake in an oven until the onion is cooked so that the juice will run freely, then squeeze out all the juice, and give the patient a spoonful, at the same time rubbing the chest and throat with goose grease or rancid bacon if there is any cough or soreness of the throat."[5]

There was a wide use of opium, laudanum and spirits to cure practically every illness. What happened, of course, was that the pain was dulled. Medicines were usually a mixture of bitter herbs and roots, many of them based on age-old Indian lore, and there were of course no flavoured syrups for children. In fact, the philosophy was that the worse it tasted the quicker the cure. It was also the age of regular dosings of castor oil, as well as sulphur and molasses. Mothers often boiled the former with milk and sugar. When the mixture was cold it was said that a child could not detect the oil. For adults there was the 1899 gourmet touch:

Castor Oil
"The flavour of castor-oil may be changed to a delightful one of fresh oyster, if the patient will drink a large glass of water poured from a vessel in which nails have been allowed to rust."[7]

For the child who would not be fooled and refused to take physic, an English doctor invented a special spoon that was available in Canada by mid-century. It was advertised in drug-house catalogues as "a kind of spoon which shuts up, so that medicine, if disagreeable may be carried to the throat without touching the tongue or mouth, and they are also so stout that a dose of castor oil may be crammed down an unruly urchin's throat, whether he will or no, and that without danger of harm. They are perfectly irresistible, stand biting, and all manner of resistance".

Domestic Medicine
"Infantile Croup: Simmer garlics in pig's feet oil, or lard, rub it on the throat and stomach freely, and

BITTER MEDICINES MAY HAVE GOOD EFFECT. 59

bind the garlics on the feet; or most excellent, bathe the feet in warm water immediately, rubbing well; give a teaspoonful of skunk's oil if you have it or pig's feet oil; apply a thick paste of Scotch snuff, moistened with sweet oil."[4]

"Leeches should immediately be applied to the upper part of the breast-bone near the neck: it is often difficult to stop bleeding when applied to the neck itself, as there is nothing to make pressure on."[3]

"*The Humours*: make a tea of equal parts saffron and Seneca snakeroot and drink half a pint a day."[3]

"*Rupture*: Rub on angle-worm ointment, morning and evening, make a plaster of the yolk of three eggs, mixed with a gill of brandy, simmer together, and use it as a plaster; at the same time drink freely of white oak bark tea and keep up your rupture with a good truss."[3]

"*St. Vitus' Dance*: Pour cold water, from the height of four or five feet on the patient's head, three or four times a day; at the same time, take of ether one ounce, oil of lavender one drachm, mix well and rub on the wrist and back of the neck a tea-spoonful night and morning."[3]

"*Diabetes*: In one quart of proof brandy, one ounce of spruce gum, and half an ounce of ginger. Dose, from one tablespoonful to half a wine-glassful, three times a day."[3]

"*Dropsy*: Some very serious cases can be cured by eating lemons, the patient should commence by eating one lemon a day, and increasing it until ten or fifteen are eaten."[8]

"*Poison Ivy*: The shop water of a blacksmith's trough is a sure cure."[9]

"*Gravel*: A gentleman says he was relieved of this complaint, of a number of years' standing, by sweetening his tea with half honey and half sugar."[6]

"*Sunstroke*: Put cold bandages to the head, wet and salty ones on the back of the neck, dry salt behind the ears and mustard plasters to the calves and soles. This is an effectual remedy."[7]

"*Travel Sickness*: Take a sheet of writing-paper, large enough to cover both the chest and stomach, and put it on under the clothing, next to the person. If one sheet is not large enough paste the edges of two or three together, for the chest and stomach must be well-covered. Wear the paper thus as long as you are traveling, and change it every day if your journey is a long one. Those who have tried it say it is the perfect defence."[10]

Not only were medicines concocted at home, but salves and ointments were made from common household supplies, the base being soap or linseed oil. Purges were also home-made and were taken regularly in rather startling amounts. The continual purging, the heavy meals and the constant preoccupation with the bowels kept the housekeeper busy finding newer and more effective cathartics.

RECEIPTS FOR ALL KINDS OF LINIMENT.

BARRELL'S INDIAN LINIMENT.

1 qt. alcohol,
1 oz. tincture of capsicum,
½ oz. oil of origanum,
½ oz. oil of sassafras.
½ oz. oil of pennyroyal.
½ oz. oil of hemlock.
Mix.

Figs and Senna
"One pound of best figs, one ounce of senna; the senna to be pounded and made fine as possible; the figs to be chopped fine; to be well incorporated together; a very little molasses to be added, to make it of a right consistency. This is a very gentle cathartic. To be taken in pieces as large as a chestnut."[6]

Family Salve
"Scrape yellow bar soap firm, mix with it, brown sugar, working them smooth with a knife. It is a good salve for old sores, for such as have bad flesh; and for general use."[4]

Universal Cure-All
"Rubbing this composition on, and in the vicinity of the parts affected, will be found to be very efficacious in the liver complaints, consumption, broken breasts, sore or weak eyes, burns (rubbing it around, but not on the sore, or the eyes), bilious or cramp colic, stoppages in the bowels (mixed with goose-oil, and then giving a little physic), chilblains, and by taking one or two tea-spoonfuls in a little sweetened tea, it will cure pains in the side, and stomach, and in short, it will be found efficacious in almost every kind of disease. The recipe is as follows: Take of the oil of lavender half an ounce; sulph. ether three ounces, alcohol, one ounce, and laudanum two drachms: mix all well together, and it is fit for use."[3]

Indian Blood Purifier
"14 oz Sassaprilla (sic) roots, 8 ozs Burdock Root, 8 ozs White Ash Bark, 8 ozs Tag Alder Bark, 6 ozs Moose Wood Bark, 8 ozs Thoroughwort, 2 ozs Lobelia, if green, if dry 1 oz, 2 Tablespoons of Balm Gilead buds, 2 ozs Butternut Bark. Use green barks and roots if to be had. Cover with water boil 6 hours strain and boil to one gallon, add 2 lbs loaf sugar, one pt. rum. Dose 2 table spoons before eating 3 times a day. Boil in a brass kettle."[11]

Toad Ointment
"Toad Ointment for sprains, strains, lame-back, rheumatism, caked breasts, caked udders &c. Good sized live toads, 4 in number, put into boiling water and cook very soft; take them out and boil the water down to ½ pint, and add fresh

churned butter 1 lb and simmer together, at the last add tincture of arnica 2 ozs. This was obtained from an old Physician, who thought more of it than any other prescription in his possession. Some persons might think it hard on toads, but you could not kill them quicker in any other way."[1]

Liquor of all kinds was one of the great curses of pioneer life. From the beginning of the first settlements until late in the nineteenth century, intoxication increased steadily. In the early years the philosophy was one of detachment with the knowledge that to drink too much was foolish. Soon it became the exception to be moderate. Logging, barn-raising and harvesting were all occasions for heavy drinking although as time passed and accident statistics became alarming, many tried to make these more temperate occasions. The majority abided by the tradition of a "Grog Boss" at every bee with jugs strategically placed in the fields during the harvest. Going to market and the return was one long round of drinks for many farmers, while the patient team and wife waited outside the tavern.

There are many reasons for the growth of excessive drinking: liquor was cheap and plentiful. Although legislation was brought in early to control liquor it was often flouted, and many a general store had a free drink ready for steady customers. Spirits helped counteract the cold, the hard life, the loneliness and the boredom. It was easy to obtain, particularly once milling was established and grain could be exchanged for liquor. The quick warmth spirits generated was thought to be good in cases of illness, and most medicines were based on rum or gin.

From mid-century onwards more people began to be aware of this problem, and at this point temperance became confused with prohibition, letting loose a flood of literature on the North American scene. In many areas where the Temperance movement was strong, social life revolved around prayer and camp meetings, militant marches and crusades. The movement collected some sincere and fervent people deeply concerned with this problem, but it also managed to collect the usual lunatic fringe, which in the end proved a decided liability. The movement was not short of money and was able to enter the publishing field as well as compete with the arch-enemy, the tavern, by setting up temperance hotels. These, unfortunately, generally turned out to be rather isolated and extremely dreary.

Dr. Chase was never one to sit back and remain silent. Here is a temperance pledge he published in London, Ontario: 1868[1]

"A pledge I make, no wine to take;
Nor brandy red, that turns the head,
Not Whisky hot, that makes the sot;
Nor fiery rum, that ruins home,
Nor will I sin, by drinking gin;
Hard cider too, will never do;
No lager beer, my heart to cheer;
Nor sparkling ale, my face to pale.
To quench my thirst I'll always bring,
Cold water from the well or spring;
So here I pledge perpetual hate,
To all that can intoxicate."[1]

Those who were addicted sometimes tried to cure themselves. This was often done, say the later books, by eating an orange every morning half an hour before breakfast. There were those who needed a more serious remedy, and for many years this was the most printed:

In Cases of Apparent Death from Drinking Rum
"The head to be elevated, the neck cloth loosened, and cold applied to the head by ice, or cold water. Cupping and leeching are necessary, and the feet and legs are to be kept hot with bricks or water. Some warm water, acidulated with any acid, may be forced into the stomach, by a prepared syringe, and, if possible, the rum extracted by a stomach pump."[12]

Doctors were also aware of the troubles that could beset a temperance man who drank too much cold water on a hot summer day:

"Symptoms: The patient, seen after taking a full drink of water from the pump, when his body is very hot and sweating, begins to feel a dizziness and breathlessness, and then soon falls to the earth speechless. Paste up warnings and notices on pumps, in sultry weather: directions to persons to cool their faces and hands before drinking. This notice might be improved two ways: first by having a plate representing a widow and children following their deceased husband and father, borne from a pump. Secondly, by tolling a bell for persons that die at the pumps in the hot season. This is the more requisite, because many cannot read the directions."[12]

Although men smoked, it was many years before this habit was socially acceptable. Even then those who had social pretensions usually had special clothes as well as special rooms for this. Those who wished to give up smoking were told to chew coarsely ground gentian root and swallow the juice.

The growth of manufacturing together with the emergence of advertising brought about the heyday of the patent medicine industry. During the latter part of the nineteenth century there was no control over what went into a medicine nor what claims were made for it. Once legislation was enacted it did not take long for many of the more flamboyant claims together with the nostrum to disappear. It was without a doubt the great period of "buyer beware". The advertisements speak for themselves:

The Great Shoshonees Remedy
"Invigorator and Renovator of the system. It is essentially beneficial to all, and permanently cures in a very large majority of diseases arising from impurities of the blood, such as Scrofula, Anemia, in each of its varied forms; Erysipelas, Salt Rheum, Canker, Scald Head, Pimples, Blotches, Eruptions, Ulcers, Old Sores or Fever Sores, Diseases of the Liver and Kidneys, Dyspepsia, Bronchitis, Rheumatism, Neuralgia, Headaches of all kinds, Female Weaknesses, Pains in the back, and above all for that 'all-gone' feeling so prevalent among those of sedentary habits and general Langour and Debility from whatever cause, either from undue exposure, neglected colds, and even to the second stage of Consumption

63

itself. It will expel all Scrofulous and Unhealthy Humours from the body, and cure Scrofula in all its stages from the smallest pustule to the most desperate case, after all other available medicines have failed. As a Summer restorative it stands unrivalled, enabling the system to bear up against the constant drain to which it is subjected by high pressure. 25 cents a box."[13]

There was also a large business in the bottling of tonic and spa waters; some of them, particularly those of St. Catharines, Ontario, went to export markets in the United States. Testimonials to the effect of these waters were given unstintingly by all the leading medical men as well as some of the more prominent churchmen. The latter were certainly not shy in giving references for patent medicines and allowing their names and addresses to be quoted.

There was a great fascination with electricity as a new form of power. Many lotions and even belts were described as "electric" to increase their selling power. Electric oils were said in the 1880's to prevent children contracting diphtheria, while "Edison's Electric Belt" prevented everything from costiveness, weak lungs, and sick headaches to female weakness. Prices were high, advertising extensive and customers many. The wearing of a piece of galvanized metal has not entirely died out. There are still some who put their faith in this scientific wonder of eighty years ago.

Cookery for the Sick
"*To make chicken water*: Take a cock, or large fowl, flay it, then bruise it with a hammer, and put it into a gallon of water, with a crust of bread. Let it boil half away, and strain it off."[14]

"*Dr. Radcliff's restorative pork jelly*: Take a leg of well-fed pork, just as cut up, beat it, and break the bone. Set it over a gentle fire, with three gallons of water, and simmer to one. Let half an ounce of mace, and the same of nutmegs, stew in it. Strain through a fine sieve. When cold, take off the fat. Give a chocolate-cup the first and last thing, and at noon, putting salt to taste."[15] (This recipe first appeared in North America in 1823; it was then nearly a hundred years old and continued to be reprinted for some sixty more years.)

"*Eggs for sickness*: An egg divided, and the yelk (*sic*) and white beaten separately, then mixed with a glass of wine, will afford two very wholesome draughts, and prove lighter than when taken together. Eggs very little boiled or poached, taken in small quantity convey much nourishment; the yelk only, when dressed, should be eaten by invalids."[16]

"*Panada*: Take common hard cracker, or in its stead, a slice of old (but not sour) bread, grate it fine, and boil it with a pint of water to a jelly; sweeten it, and add a little nutmeg, and some wine, if the patient is not feverish."[12]

"*Stewed prunes*: Stew them very gently in a small quantity of water, till the stones slip out. Physicians consider them safe nourishment in fevers."[2]

"*Luncheon for an invalid*: Put bread crumbs and red currant, or any other jelly, alternately into a tumbler, and when nearly half full, fill it up with milk."[17]

"*Cakes for the sick*: Sponge cakes and simple cookies, are the best cakes for an invalid. Rich plum cakes should be avoided."[5]

"*Apple toddy*: Boil a large juicy pippin in a quart of water, and when it has been broken to pieces strain off the water. While it is boiling-hot, add a glass of fine old whiskey, a little lemon-juice, and sweeten to taste. Take hot at bed-time for influenza."[18]

Edison's Electric Absorbent Belt

The combination of the great curative principles—electricity and absorption, the two greatest remedial agents known, for the cure of disease without medicine. The Wonder of the Nineteenth century. The mild and continuous current of electricity and the absorbing qualities as furnished by the Belt render it truly the wonder of the age. See pamphlet. Price, No. 1, $1.50; No. 2, $1.75; No. 3, $2.00. For sale by all Druggists.

How Much Medicine to Take as a Dose.

HOLD THE VIAL IN ONE HAND AND THE CORK IN THE OTHER.

How Much Medicine to Take as a Dose.

NAME OF DRUG.	DOSE.	NAME OF DRUG	DOSE.
Aloes................	3 to 15 grains.	Syrup of Sarsaparilla ..	1 to 4 teasp'fuls.
Anise Oil	5 to 15 drops.	" Seneka	1 to 2 teasp'fuls.
AquaAmmonia(dilute)	10 to 30 drops.	" Rhubarb.......	1 to 2 teasp'fuls.
Balsam Copaiba.............	10 to 40 drops.	Tannic Acid...............	1 to 5 grains.
Balsam of Fir............. .	3 to 10 drops.	Tinct. of Aconite Root	1 to 5 drops.
Bismuth	5 to 40 grains.	" Aloes.........	1 to 8 teasp'fuls.
Bromide of Potassium.	5 to 40 grains.	" Asafœtida.....	½ to 1 teasp'ful.
Buchu Leaves	20 to 40 grains.	" Belladona	10 to 30 drops.
Calomel (as alterative)	1-12 to 1 grain.	" Bloodroot......	¼ to ½ teasp'ful.
Castor Oil	1 to 8 teasp'fuls.	" Columbo.......	1 to 2 teasp'fuls.
Citrate of Iron	2 to 5 grains.	" Camphor	5 to 60 drops.
Citrate Iron & Quinine	3 to 8 grains.	" Cayenne......	10 to 60 drops.
Cream of Tartar............	½ to 3 teasp'fuls.	" Castor	½ to 1 teasp'ful.
Dover's Powder...........	5 to 10 grains.	" Catechu	½ to 2 teasp'fuls.
Elecampane.................	20 to 60 grains	" Cinch. Comp.	½ to 4 teasp'fuls.
Epsom Salts................	¼ to 1 ounce.	" Colchicum....	10 to 20 drops.
Gallic Acid.	5 to 10 grains.	" Digitalis......	5 to 20 drops.
Iodide of Potassium.....	2 to 10 grains.	" Ginger.......	¼ to 1 teasp'ful.
Kino	10 to 30 grains.	" Gentian Com	½ to 2 teasp'fuls.
Mandrake.................	5 to 20 grains.	" Guaiac	½ to 1 teasp'ful.
Mercury with Chalk ...	2 to 8 grains.	" Kino	½ to 2 teasp'fuls.
Morphine.................	⅛ to ¼ grain.	" Lobelia... ...	¼ to 1 teasp'ful.
Muriate of Ammonia ..	5 to 20 grains.	" Muriate Iron	10 to 30 drops.
Opium	½ to 2 grains.	" Myrrh........	½ to 1 teasp'ful.
Paregoric........	1 teaspoonful	" Nux Vomica	5 to 10 drops.
Peppermint Essence....	5 to 30 drops.	" Opium	
Pepsin	1 to 5 grains.	" (Laudanum)	10 to 25 drops.
Quinine.................... .	1 to 10 grains.	" Rhubarb	1 to 4 teasp'fuls.
Rochelle Salts........... .	⅛ to 1 ounce.	" " & Senna	1 to 4 teasp'fuls.
Rhubarb.................	5 to 30 grains.	" Tolu......	½ to 1 teasp'ful.
Saltpetre	5 to 20 grains.	" Valerian.......	½ to 2 teasp'fuls.
Santonin	2 to 5 grains.	Turpentine	4 to 10 drops.
Syrup of Squills........	½ to 1 teasp'ful.	Wine Ipecac (Diaph.)..	10 to 30 drops.
" Iodide of Iron	15 to 30 drops.	" " (Emetic).	2 to 8 teasp'fuls.
" Senna.........	1 to 6 teasp'fuls.	" Colchicum Root	10 to 30 drops.

Children should take from ⅛ to ¾ of a dose, according to age. Or divide the age of the child at its next birthday by 24 and take that fractional part of a dose for an adult.

"*Onion gruel*: Is excellent for a cold. Slice down a few onions and boil them in a pint of new milk, stir in a sprinkle of oatmeal and a very little salt, boil till the onions are quite tender, then sup rapidly and go to bed."[19]

"*For very weak invalids*: Six fresh eggs, shells unbroken cover with the juice of twelve lemons. Let digest four days, then remove all pieces of skin or undissolved shell, after which pour over one pint of rum and beat thoroughly; melt in a little water one pound of rock candy, and add after cooling, then bottle, and use a few spoonfuls. It will be found excellent and very nourishing."[20]

Venereal Disease

"As many country gentlemen, with a large number of hands, have frequently need of information on this disease; and those country practitioners who have not resided in cities, where the disease abounds, are often at a loss, the author concluded to add this disease as the last one, so that those who have no need may cut it out of the book more readily.

"The patient must instantly abandon (besides his evil practices) all spirituous liquors, and use a vegetable diet, and but little exercise. He ought to have plenty of barley water, or elm tea, and cold drinks. He should take a dose of salts immediately and repeat it the third day. . . . Rubbing on some mercurial ointment might be both useful and prudent."[12]

REFERENCES

[1] *Dr. Chase's Recipes*, A. W. Chase, London, Ontario, 1868.

[2] *The American Frugal Housewife*, L. Child, New York, 1838.

[3] *The Ladies' Indispensable Assistant*, Anonymous, New York, 1851.

[4] *The Improved Housewife*, A. L. Webster, Boston, 1856.

[5] *The Housekeeper's Encyclopedia*, E. Haskell, New York, 1869.

[6] *The New England Economical Housekeeper*, E. A. Howland, Montpelier, 1845.

[7] *The White House Cook Book*, Zieman and Gillette, Toronto, 1899.

[8] *The Household Guide*, B. G. Jefferis, Toronto, 1894.

[9] *The Economical Cook Book*, J. Warren, New York, n.d.

[10] *Search Lights on Health*, B. G. Jefferis, Toronto, 1894.

[11] *Manuscript Notebook*, Anonymous, Markham, Ontario, 1890.

[12] *Family Adviser*, H. Wilkins, New York, 1833.

[13] *Drug House Almanac*, Anonymous, Markham, Ontario, 1885.

[14] *The Art of Cookery Made Plain and Easy*, H. Glasse, London, 1765.

[15] *The Experienced American Housekeeper*, Anonymous, New York, 1823.

[16] *The Cook Not Mad*, Anonymous, Kingston, Ontario, 1831.

[17] *The Ladies' New Book of Cookery*, S. Hale, New York, 1852.

[18] *Commonsense in the Household*, M. Harland, New York, 1871.

[19] *Every-Day Cook Book*, E. Neill, New York, 1884.

[20] *The New Galt Cook Book*, Taylor and McNaught, Toronto, 1898.

[21] *The Home Cook Book*, Anonymous, Toronto, 1877.

The New
Household Manual

That plumbing was almost non-existent does not mean that Canada was not developing, but rather that she shared the lack of this amenity with the rest of the western world. For most of the population indoor plumbing, running water and sinks with traps to avoid fumes were more or less a novelty. The walk outdoors in a cold climate was bracing. For the less hardy considerable thought was given to this aspect of public health. The constant mention of open running sewers in the towns, and the continuing outbreaks of cholera indicate that drainage for the most part was the same as in the Middle Ages.

In 1869 Miss Catherine Beecher wrote *The American Woman's Home or Domestic Science*, largely a reprint somewhat updated of an earlier work of 1849, in which she discussed household plumbing at length. She included sketches to show how a kitchen sink, a bathtub and the house range could be connected to give hot running water. In much of her writing Miss Beecher broke new frontiers and was understandably popular in this country as well as in the United States.

She redesigned houses, particularly kitchens and storerooms, to be more efficient in view of the lack of servants in North America. Her kitchen designs, as we shall read, were followed for some seventy years. She advocated special training for girls in "domestic science" and may thus be considered the founder of the Home Economics profession. On the other hand she was vehement in her stand against votes for women.

On the question of indoor plumbing she did not guess correctly. "The water-closets must have the latest improvements for safe discharge, and there will be no trouble. They cost no more than an out-door building, and save from the most disagreeable house-labor. A great improvement, called earth-closets, will probably take the place of water-closets to some extent; though at present the water is more convenient. The discharge of earth is effected by an ordinary pull-up similar to that used in the water-closet, or (in the self-acting apparatus) by the rising of the seat when the weight of the person is removed. The vault or pan under the seat is so arranged that the accumulation may be removed at pleasure".[1]

Miss Beecher gives diagrams for the home handy-man to build one of his own and then quotes a Mr. Waring who runs an earth-closet company: "I have in constant use in a room in my house an earth-closet commode; and even when the pan is entirely full, with the accumulation of a week's use, visitors examining it invariably say, with some purpose, 'You don't mean that this particular one has been used' ".[1]

Supplies needed for this contrivance were enormous but nevertheless a great future was seen: "the earth commode and closet, if used by six persons daily will require, on an average, about one hundred weight of earth per week. This may be dried for family use in a drawer made to fit under the kitchen range, and which may be filled with earth one morning and left until the next".[1] In colder climates, it was suggested that piles of earth should be brought into the kitchen yard well before the winter. The earth of course, was often dried in that range drawer, and reused, as often as six or seven times, said Miss Beecher.

At first there was no way of disposing of water used for washing other than to heave it from the back door. Hence the dry sinks in use. Later it became usual to have a pipe from the kitchen sink leading to the back of the house so that the water could run away. This, of course, is more complicated than it sounds and traps were needed to take away the smells. In 1831, *The Cook Not Mad* gave directions "To prevent bad smells in sinks, &c. There is generally a close conductor attached to the spout of the sink. In this conductor let a well fitted trap door, or damper made of tin, sheet iron or wood be inserted, having the arbours or bearings so far on one side of the centre as to cause it to shut off itself after letting the liquid through. Checks should be placed under the heavy end of the trap so as to keep it horizontal to the pitch of the conductor when in a quiescent state. Any common house joiner or similar mechanik would sufficiently understand from this description how to put one in".[2]

Gradually the large open fireplace of the settler's first home gave way to the iron box stove, and the range-stove that was inserted into the old open hearth. The huge logs were replaced by smaller more manageable pieces of wood. Later, coal was used in some areas and finally, by the end of the century, there were gas stoves. In the beginning, cooking and heating were one and the same, the earlier houses having just the open hearth. Although quarters were often crowded the family was warmer in the well-built log or prairie sod house than in the more fashionable stone houses. Later, with the building of upper stories, heat holes were cut into rooms in the upper floors

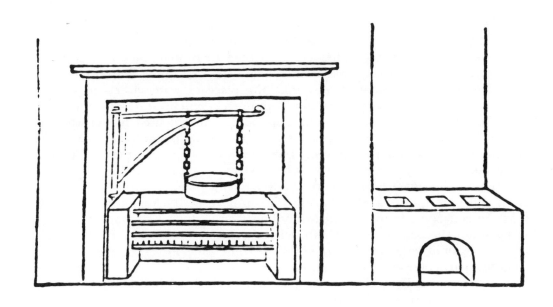

and they were warmed by expansion and rising of the warm air. Nevertheless it was cold, and it is common to read of the water in the bedroom pitchers freezing over during the night. Even the pump when it was indoors in the kitchen would freeze if not covered with its own blanket.

Describing the houses of Lower Canada in 1831, Joseph Bouchette said, "In summer from being low, they are uncomfortably warm, and in winter, by the aid of a stove, they are rendered uninhabitable by a European. The excessive heat in which the Canadian lives within doors is sufficient to kill anyone, not from his infancy accustomed to that temperature. Without doors, however, the habitant bears with ease the piercing cold of the winter blasts, — when any one, not a Canadian, would be compelled to take every possible precaution against this painful influence, he passes with impunity and without pain from his house, in which the temperature is above ninety degrees of Fahrenheit, into the open air, oftentimes twenty-five or thirty degrees below zero".[3]

Early stove foundries existed in Normandale on Lake Erie and in the Province of Quebec. Many were imported from France and the United States. Some settlers, particularly those from Mennonite communities in the United States, brought stoves with them and never did use an open fireplace. The United States did a tremendous export business in cast-iron stoves, many of them going to the United Kingdom. That country was no pace-

setter in home equipment, although many immigrants from the British Isles brought with them coal grates which were utterly useless in Canada for many years.

For the greater part of the nineteenth century there was an overlap of open hearths, box stoves and kitchen ranges for cooking. All the cook-book writers until around the 1880's chose to ignore the newer stoves and continued to call for brisk fires and the use of reflector ovens and spits. As late as 1871 the debate about the modern stove went on, writers taking the old-fashioned view, leaving women to experiment on their own. In *Common-sense in the Household*, Marion Harland wrote "in this day of ranges and cooking-stoves, I think I am speaking within bounds when I assume that not one in fifty uses a spit, or even a tin kitchen for such a purpose"[4] (roasting meat and fowls). However, she took no chances, and like so many other experts, gave all her recipes for both those with stoves and those using a brisk fire.

Ovens of course had to be tested before they could be used. Some put flour or paper in to note the time of browning and the degree of charring. But this was not always the answer: it depended on the dampness of the flour and the type of paper.

Mrs. Webster in 1856 favoured this method: "For pies, cakes and white bread, the heat of the oven should be such, that you can hold your hand and arm in while you count forty; for brown bread, meats, beans, Indian puddings, and pumpkin pies, it should be heated, so that you can only hold it in while you count twenty".[5] Ovens had to be seasoned when first used; that is heated and cooled several times before the first baking could take place. Miss Beecher thought that an oven that had its roof brushed with a wet broom was less likely to char the baking. In many areas women baked their bread on large wet cabbage leaves or corn husks. Baking was inserted and removed from the oven with a long wooden paddle known as a peel. Particularly in Quebec, and later in parts of the west, the baking oven was a little beehive building on its own, built away from the house. Other homes had separate baking ovens built beside the fireplace.

The kitchen itself was a crowded busy place, normally on the ground floor. In the towns, however, there was a tendency to build that Victorian horror, the basement kitchen. In 1849, Miss Beecher started the campaign against this. "A kitchen should always, if possible, be entirely above-ground, and well lighted. It should have a large sink, with a drain running underground, so that all may be kept sweet and clean. If flowers and shrubs be cultivated around the doors and windows, and the yard near them be kept well turfed, it will add very much to their agreeable appearance. The walls should often be cleaned and white-washed, to promote a neat look and pure air".[6]

In her later book Miss Beecher redesigned the kitchen. She did away with the centre work table and the large dresser or cupboard for pots, pans and dishes. Instead, she suggested cupboards hung on the walls and beneath them, at table height, flat counter working space with drawers and cupboards underneath. This kitchen is very similar to our own, the only flaw in the design was that the range was in a separate room.

Many work tables have come down to us as prized antiques. They were used for everything from making cakes to sausage stuffing, and were washed down with strong solutions of lye and water. Work tables in some areas settled by those of German heritage have the interesting variation of tops that can be unpegged so that the complete scrubbing and airing can take place outdoors.

Kitchen floors were painted, although the first floors were planks, log ends or even soil. At mid-century the oilcloth covering came into style. Oilcloth was the forerunner of linoleum and the thrifty housewife could make her own. "Buy cheap tow cloth, and fit it to the size and shape of the kitchen. Then have it stretched, and nailed to the south side of the barn, and, with a brush, cover it with a coat of thin rye paste. When this is dry, put on a coat of yellow paint, and let it dry for a fortnight. It is safest first to try the paint, and see if it dries well, as some paint never will dry. Then put on a second coat, and at the end of another fortnight, a third coat. Then let it hang two months, and it will last uninjured for many years. The longer the paint is left to dry, the better. If varnished, it will last much longer".[6]

Just about every kitchen kept the family gun over the fireplace to prevent rust. Broken pewter spoons were melted down for bullets. Well into the twentieth century a goose or turkey wing was hung beside a fireplace to sweep the ashes away. Some farm houses also had a dinner horn to call the hired hands to the table.

It was the lack of reliable domestic servants that encouraged the invention of so many kitchen gadgets and helped make North American kitchens the pacesetters for the world. The early servants included Irish immigrant girls coming from poverty-stricken homes. They needed extensive and intensive training to fit into middle-class homes, and their intractability brought another round of domestic books. Some books were actually written as a question and answer catechism so that the girls could learn some of the basic requirements by rote. Many such books were published in London by the Church of England.[7]

For a period, slaves were owned in some parts of Canada. Early newspapers carry advertisements for runaway slaves who came here as part of the chattels brought by some of the Loyalists. Among the first actions of Governor Simcoe was to forbid the further importation of slaves. Other servants came here with agreement to repay passage money from Europe, but of course once here they vanished, as did the agreement. Wages were low. An 1872 manuscript book from London, Ontario, has an entry which reads: "Bridget Gow came as cook for $7 per month, September 17, 1877; Mary Simpson came as a nurse at $5 per month, Friday November 28, 1879".

On the west coast Japanese servants, particularly housemen, were employed towards the end of the century. In an age when a large number of servants were needed by even the more modest middle-class homes, this lack of help in North America was so unusual that it was a topic of letters, conversation and articles. It was so newsworthy that society magazines in England constantly ran stories of how Canadian women managed to run their homes without help.[8]

The Gentleman Immigrant examines this question of servants and household equipment more fully. It is interesting to note how old some of these "modern" appliances, such as washers and beaters, really are. "The Mickeys and Biddys of the Canadas and United States have been of this much service: they have by their impudence and ignorance sharpened the inventive faculties of the Yankee. Driven to desperation by bad servants, the American bethought him how he could dispense with their assistance; and the result has been hundreds of labour-saving machines, which else had never been invented. My wife says that for new-fangled inventions I am a very Yankee; and she is right. I never hear of an improved plough, or harrow, or cultivator, without going and having a look at it. I am always glad to see the pedlar of Yankee notions, and ready to overhaul his wares. Has he an improved washing and wringing machine, I buy it. My wife tells me the one we have will do well enough. My answer is, this will do better; it saves soap and labour, and will be sure to pay for itself in time. Is it an improved potato-peeler he has for sale — a cucumber slicer — an egg beater — I invest".[9]

Many of the ladies did not feel quite this eager and had to be sold on progress. Mrs. Harland wrote, "I take it for granted that you are too intelligent to share in the vulgar prejudice against labour-saving machines. A raisin-seeder costs a trifle in comparison with the time and patience required to stone the fruit the old way. A good egg-beater is a treasure. So with farina-kettles, syllabub churns, apple-corers, potato-peelers and slicers, clothes-wringers and sprinklers and the like. Most of these are made of tin — are therefore cheap and easily kept clean".[4]

From about mid-century onwards scales became necessary in the kitchen when both authors and cooks became more aware of accurate measurements. They tended to rely less on "handfuls, pinches or butter as big as walnuts". Another reason for the scales was the greater varieties of goods available at stores and the frequent miscalculation of the storekeeper, in his favour.

The can opener is a surprisingly early gadget and was certainly in use from mid-century onwards. Canned foods had been known to both the British and the French from the beginning of the century. Inventors were spurred on by Napoleon offering a large reward to find the answer to feeding an army fresh food while on the march. The French came up with bottling and sealing in glass, and a chef named Appert collected the prize. Meanwhile, the British led by Peter Durand were working on tin containers. These early cans were costly, until 1847, when a cheap stamping process was invented in the United States.

Soon thereafter, Canada was canning fish, mostly lobster, and by 1848 was even engaged in an export business. Salmon canning came towards the end of the century. A British ship arriving on the west coast with a hold of whisky and gin, would load up for the return voyage with a shipment of canned salmon. In the early days, cans were in different shapes, many being flat as well as oval. Sizes were halves and pounds for salmon, but east coast lobster, then being so cheap and plentiful, was in two and four pound cans.

The earliest household gadgets and kitchen appliances were of iron and

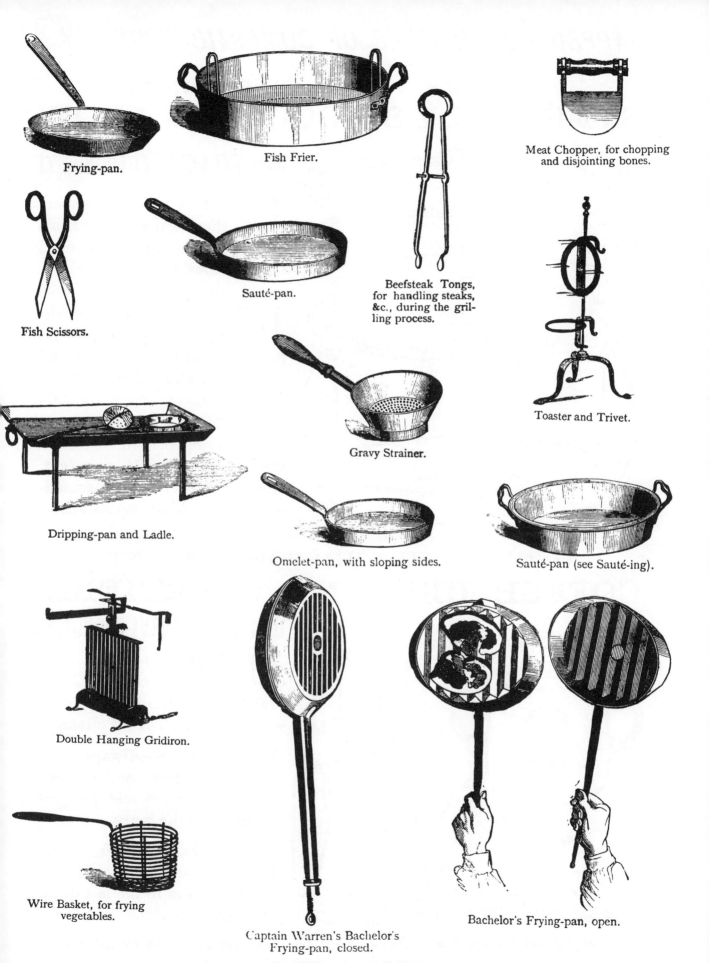

Frying-pan.

Fish Frier.

Meat Chopper, for chopping and disjointing bones.

Fish Scissors.

Sauté-pan.

Beefsteak Tongs, for handling steaks, &c., during the grilling process.

Toaster and Trivet.

Gravy Strainer.

Dripping-pan and Ladle.

Omelet-pan, with sloping sides.

Sauté-pan (see Sauté-ing).

Double Hanging Gridiron.

Wire Basket, for frying vegetables.

Captain Warren's Bachelor's Frying-pan, closed.

Bachelor's Frying-pan, open.

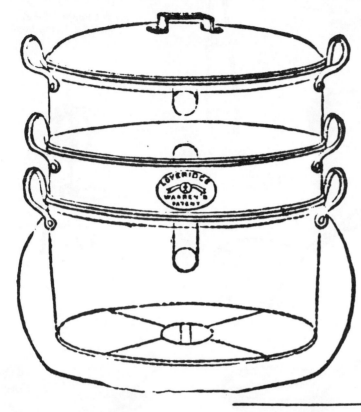

wood. Later, tin and crockery became available. Frypans and skillets for use on the open hearth had very long handles, and like the soup and bean pots, small legs were often attached to keep them above the ashes. Frypans with feet were sometimes called "spiders". Brooms were home-made from splints, or were simply bunches of twigs tied to the end of a stick. Broom-making was one of the industries undertaken by the Indians and Yankee pedlars brought most other kitchen tools to the door.

Small bundles of fine birch twiglets or smooth hickory rods were used to beat and whisk eggs before the invention of the wire whisk and the Dover beater. Surprisingly enough, cookie presses have been known by a variety of names including "squirts" and "syringes" since the seventeenth century and undoubtedly they were used here to make some of the funnel-cakes and fancy cookies enjoyed by those of German ancestry. Early French cook-books give detailed instructions for making cookies, icing decorations and confectionery with this gun.

In very primitive settlements, gourds were used as spoons and dippers but more commonly utensils were of wood, pewter, iron and silver. Later there was silverplate, and the Scottish were fond of horn spoons, especially to spoon up porridge. There were waffle irons and toasters as well as griddles, or "girdles" as the Scotswomen called them, all made of iron. The griddle was a heavy sheet with a bale handle for hanging on the crane over the fire. And of course, there were corkscrews and both bottle openers and cappers. Outside the kitchen door there was usually a mud-scraper of one shape or another.

Metal jacks and spits were used to roast meat over an open hearth; the finer ones had clock-work devices and were self-rotating. A primitive spit was a hemp rope fastened to the ceiling in front of the fire, twisting back and forth itself. There were jelly moulds, pudding bags, jelly bags and a variety of pie plates and cake "hoops", as the early pans were called. There were food grinders called "hoppers", flour sifters of various kinds and eventually in the last years of the century, metal measuring-cups. Flour sifting was important, since in those days flour was damp, lumpy and packed into rough sacks; the sifter retained all the foreign matter. There was a multitude more of gadgets, from sausage stuffers to crumpet rings, as can be seen in the Kitchen List on page 221.

Jelly moulds were made of metal as well as pottery and some are marvellous examples of the tinsmith and potter's art. Although jelly moulds were used throughout the eighteenth century, hot puddings were boiled in cotton cloths. This of course meant cautioning the housewife to wash the cloth clean and to remove all vestiges of home-made soap or earlier puddings. In 1852, changes took place. "Modern taste is in favour of puddings boiled in moulds, but, they are seldom or ever so light as those which are tied in cloths only. Where appearance is the first consideration, we would recommend the use of the moulds, of course".[10]

As early as the beginning of the century, writers were recommending rounded pots for easier cleaning. In 1829, the best-selling Dr. Kitchiner wrote, "let the covers of your boiling pots fit close, not only to prevent

unnecessary evaporation of water, but to prevent the escape of nutritive matter".[11] Tightly fitting lids were doubly important when cooking over the open fire to prevent food from having a smoky flavour.

There were skimmers and ladles of all shapes and sizes, and even egg separators for cooks who could not juggle the yolk from the white. There were muffin and roll pans as well as angel-cake and jelly-cake pans. The latter were the forebears of the layer cake and were often fluted. Perhaps the most important piece of equipment for many years was the dough box. It was developed so that the bread dough could rise free from draughts. This was most important in early homes, especially when the yeast was home made and far more temperamental than the commercial varieties with which we are familiar. For the second rising the bread dough was often placed in woven baskets. Among the Pennsylvania Dutch the basket was conical. When the dough had risen sufficiently it was upended on to the wooden shovel or peel and placed in the oven.

Sometimes adjacent to the house, other times in a basement beneath were the store rooms, most necessary in days of bulk buying of such staples as sugar, flour, tea and coffee. Sugar had to be kept in a very dry place and the cones were stored on slatted shelves. Ice was used quite early, many farmers cutting and storing their own ice. Canadians did not export ice to the extent that the Americans did. In 1842, *Canadian Scenery* mentions, "the butter regularly comes to table with a fine thick transparent piece of ice upon it; large pieces are generally floating in the water jugs at dinner, or in your chambers; and it is often handed round on plates, in small dishes, to be used at dinner".[12]

There was soon a flourishing trade in ice. It was stored in containers, either in the store-room or on the back porch, where it could be serviced without the iceman coming into the house, and possibly enticing the cook's helpers away. These iceboxes were known as refrigerators and were patented in the United States at the beginning of the nineteenth century.

In 1849 Miss Beecher once again comes through with plans for the handy man, when she describes the ideal storeroom or cellar. "A cellar should often be whitewashed, to keep it sweet. It should have a drain to keep it perfectly dry, as standing water in a cellar is a sure cause of disease in a family. It is very dangerous to leave decayed vegetables in a cellar. The following articles are desirable in a cellar; a safe, or movable chest, with sides of wire or perforated tin, in which cold meats, cream, and other articles should be kept; (if ants be troublesome, set the legs in tin cups of water); a refrigerator, or a large wooden-box, on feet with a lining of tin or zinc, and a space between the bottom for ice, a drain to carry off the water, and also moveable shelves and partitions. In this articles are kept cool. It should be cleaned once a week. Filtering jars to purify water should also be kept in the cellar. Fish and cabbages in a cellar are apt to scent a house, and give a bad taste to other articles".[6]

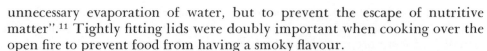

Miss Beecher may have been satisfied with a once a week cleaning of the "refrigerator" but Mrs. Lincoln who wrote the original *Boston Cooking School* book , in 1883 decided that this appliance "must be examined daily

and kept thoroughly clean. If a suitable brush cannot be had, a long stiff wire with a bit of cloth on the end should be used to clean the drain pipe. Pour boiling washing-soda water through it every other day, and do not forget to wash off the slime that adheres to the water pan. Fish, onions, cheese, any strong vegetables, lemons, or meat not perfectly sweet, should not be kept in the same ice-box with milk or butter".[13]

For those who did not wish to bother with an ice-box, there was the old-fashioned but still popular "salting in the snow". In 1852, women were told to "take a large clean tub, cover the bottom 3 or 4 inches thick with clean snow, then lay in pieces of fresh meat and cover each layer with 2 or 3 inches of snow taking particular care to fill snow into every crevice between the pieces and around the edges of the tub. Fowls must be filled inside with snow. The last layer must be snow, pressed down tight, then cover tub and keep in a cold place — the colder the better".[10]

Although the kitchen and storerooms were whitewashed, the remainder of the house was painted in bright colours, or wall-papered with papers printed either in Canada or imported. Occasionally walls as well as floors were stencilled. Paint was usually home made, often with a base of skim milk and pigment, a forerunner of the calcimine washes popular in the depression thirties of this century.

Some Canadians decorated both parlour and tavern walls with glass chains made as whimsies by the skilled glass-makers of the period. Many were of coloured glass and a great many vanished when the bar-room became too noisy and the arguments rough. As the years went by the bright clear colours of the primitive paints on furniture, walls and floors disappeared and an over-all gloom took their place. This made the lady writers take pen in hand and rush into print urging their readers to good commonsense; some of their suggestions are still timely. "Don't make your rooms or stair-case gloomy. Furnish them for light, and let them have it. Daylight is cheap. If your rooms are dark, all the effects of furniture, pictures, walls, and carpets is lost. If you have beautiful things, make them useful. The fashion of having a nice parlour, and then shutting it up all but three or four days in the year when you have company; spending your own life in a small room, shabbily furnished, or an unhealthy basement, to save your things, is the meanest possibly economy".[6]

Then as now, the magazines and housekeeping books tried to help those on a slim income to make the most of it. For those who could not afford elaborate screens to cover the fireplace in summer there were how-to arrangements of feathers, paper lace, as well as crystallized leaves and ferns. Stools from old barrels were being made by 1860; for those really short of cash "paper curtains pasted on old cotton are good for chambers", and "cheap footstools, made of a square plank, covered with tow-cloth, stuffed, and then covered with carpeting, with worsted handles, look very well".[1]

In 1849, the shopping pages told women that it is poor economy to buy cheap carpets and "in selecting colours, avoid those in which there are any black threads; as they are always rotten. The most tasteful carpets, are those, which are made of various shades of the same colour, or of all shades of only buff, or salmon and green, or all shades of green, or of brown. All very dark shades should be brown or green, but not black".[6]

It was the age of the house plant. They grew everywhere and anywhere, around the windows and over to the picture, around the frame and onto the next portrait, like a green and ever-growing octopus. Driftwood was brought indoors, not small bits for lamps, but huge pieces that could support a fish bowl or another potted plant. There were little stumps for kittens to flex their claws, the top padded with velvet, so puss could sit.

And there were the hanging baskets in doorways. The *New Household Manual*, New Brunswick, 1901, had a new approach to a beautiful hanging basket. "Produce a large-sized turnip or carrot; trim off a portion of the root end, and scrape out the inside, leaving a pretty thick rind all around; fill the inside with earth, and plant therein a morning glory or some other clinging vine. Suspend the vegetable with cords, stalk downward, and in a short time the vines will twine around the cords, and the turnip or carrot sprouting from below, will put forth leaves and stems that will turn upwards and curl gracefully around the base".[14]

At first there was no time and no energy to spare for gardening. But as families prospered, flowers and shrubs were grown, and a big trade in seeds developed with England. Many immigrants brought flower seeds and even cuttings from favourite roses and lilacs. Some not only rooted and survived but escaped from their gardens. Even today, old moss and cabbage roses can be found flourishing far from their original home. Beautiful and

D O G   R O S E.
ROSA CANINA.

specific gardening books were available for those who had money to spend and could read. One of the earliest and most colourful mail order publications was the seed catalogue. Gardens had red and yellow lilies; Sweet William; lunaria or honesty, sometimes called silver dollars; pinks; hollyhocks; love-in-a-mist. There were herbs for cooking and medicine, quinces for jams, pie plant (rhubarb) for tarts as well as currants and raspberries. Melons and cucumbers grew so readily in the ditches and along the edges of fields that immigrants were fascinated and wrote letters to their families telling them of these culinary monsters.

Joseph Bouchette leaves us a vivid picture of a farm woman in her garden in 1831. "[The houses] are generally surrounded by a scrambling sort of garden, in which the beautiful neatness of an English garden will be sought for in vain. The fence is formed of coarse pieces of split wood; the walks are but tracks traced of necessity, and without any reference to order, and the whole, though it yields abundance and comfort, yet adds little to the beauty of the scene. It is almost entirely under the management of the women, who, using in place of a spade a species of heavy hoe, called a *pioche*, may be seen labouring with laudable industry during the parching days of summer, each in the little plot of ground she designates her garden, careless of the burning influences of the sun, and ignorant that in other countries the toil she undergoes is deemed beyond the reach of female strength. In the United States of America, at least in the northern and eastern states, such a sight is never seen: there the women take little or no part in the out-door work of the farm, and seldom appear abroad without a sun-bonnet, to shade their beauty from the scorching rays of the sun".[3]

REFERENCES

[1] *American Woman's Home*, Beecher and Stowe, New York, 1869.
[2] *The Cook Not Mad*, Anonymous, Kingston, Ontario, 1831.
[3] *The British Dominions in North America*, J. Bouchette, London, 1831.
[4] *Commonsense in the Household*, M. Harland, New York, 1871.
[5] *The Improved Housewife*, A. L. Webster, Boston, 1856.
[6] *A Treatise on Domestic Economy*, Beecher, New York, 1849.
[7] *The Finchley Manual of Industry*, Anonymous, London, 1855.
[8] *The Woman at Home*, A. Swan, London, 1903.
[9] *The Gentleman Immigrant*, W. Stamer, London, 1874.
[10] *The Ladies' New Book of Cookery*, S. Hale, New York, 1852.
[11] *The Housekeeper's Oracle*, W. Kitchiner, London, 1829.
[12] *Canadian Scenery*, N. P. Willis, London, 1842.
[13] *Boston Cook Book*, D. A. Lincoln, Boston, 1883.
[14] *The New Household Manual*, R. Morrow, Saint John, N.B., 1901.

The Experienced
Housekeeper

Pioneer women knew a vast amount of household lore, some of it little removed from witchcraft and a lot of it highly impractical and doomed to failure. But they all had faith and perseverance. Much of the domestic knowledge had been passed from woman to woman almost unaltered for several hundred years and, crossing the ocean, it took root again in North America. Primitive living conditions and the need to rely on her own resources made the housewife mistress of many trades. As soon as frontier living ended, however, she was only too pleased to pass along chores such as soap- and candle-making, yarn dying and fulling, to professional tradesmen. Household knowledge had to cover every contingency, from clothes catching fire, removing grease spots from the best broadcloth to eliminating the ever-present household pests. Housewives worked from dawn to night, but were always prepared to leave chores to go to bees or a dance.

Most early homes were simple, with one or two rooms, so that a minimum of house cleaning was needed. Nothing was wasted and there was no garbage disposal problem. In fact the most used maxim was: "Eat it up, wear it out, make it do, or go without."

The passing of time brought more comfortable living and the homes grew bigger. The log dwelling became complex with the addition of bedrooms, storerooms, cellars and parlours. This brought a desire for more knowledge; housework was now with us and the question was, would it ever be completed? A never-ending treadmill started, a frenzy set in, and from this chain reaction we have barely recovered even today.

There were chores for every day, apart from the Lord's Day, and for every season of the year. All had to be done well if the woman was to hold her head high and face the neighbours. She was always ready to learn and to seek advice, whether from almanacs, household books or magazines. Writers on household affairs contradicted, argued, plagiarized each other, but women were ready to try anything provided there was an authority behind the advice. These quaint household books picture life as it was only a short time ago, yet within recent memory all this lore has virtually vanished without trace.

The focal point of the home was the kitchen and its fireplace, necessary not only as a source of warmth but the centre for cooking and family life. As the years passed the size of the hearth gradually diminished, partly because of the increasing cost of fuel but also because of the increasing number of iron cooking stoves. Fires were watched constantly so that they would never die completely. If the fire died and the kitchen became cold the bread dough set to rise overnight would be a loss. Because of the scarcity of flour, the difficulties of getting to a miller and the shortage of food, this could be a tragedy. Usually one of the children slept in a settle bed near the fire to see it didn't die, or to give the alarm if the fire should suddenly flare during the night. Before the household went to sleep a primitive damper in the form of a huge log was often rolled into the fireplace.

As the iron range took over, complications set in. It was no more a question of collecting the ashes and adding fresh fuel; the iron monster required a complete cleaning both inside and out and a final polishing with home-made blacking before breakfast could be cooked. The general method given in most cookbooks was to "remove the covers and brush the soot free from the top of the oven into the fire-box then clean out the grate; and if the stove have conveniences for so doing sift the ashes, save all the old coal and cinders. Put in shavings or loose rolls of paper, then fine pine kindlings, arranged crosswise, and a layer of hard wood leaving plenty of air space between the pieces. Be sure the wood comes out to catch the end of the fire-box. Put on the covers; and if the stove needs cleaning, moisten some pulverized stove polish with water, and rub the stove

with a paint brush dipped in the polish. When all blackened, rub with a dry polishing brush until nearly dry. Open the direct draught and oven damper, and light the paper, as a slight heat facilitates the process of polishing. When the wood is thoroughly kindled, fill the fire-box with coal even with the top of the oven. Brush up the hearth and floor, empty the tea kettle and fill with fresh water. Watch the fire and push the coal down as the wood burns away, and add enough more coal to keep it even with the top of the fire-bricks".[1] This was how the morning began in 1883. After all that it was time to cook a meat and potato breakfast.

There were different fuels for fires depending on the period, location, state of the settlement and tradition. The buying and storing of fuel was an art and so was the setting up of the wood pile. Housewives were told to mix green and dry wood and so make the wood pile last longer. Economical women did not buy loads in which there were many crookéd sticks and they learned to calculate and measure the contents of a load in order not to be cheated. Wood was split and piled under cover before winter, each type in a separate pile: green, dry, kindling, chips, charcoal (for the irons), and a bin for ashes. When wood was burned the ashes were saved for soapmaking and only a slattern would let ashes and firewood be mixed in the woodshed.

As wood became more expensive, and the house owner no longer cut his own, the large open hearths of the beginning of the century were modernized and made smaller. By 1849 the following advice was given:

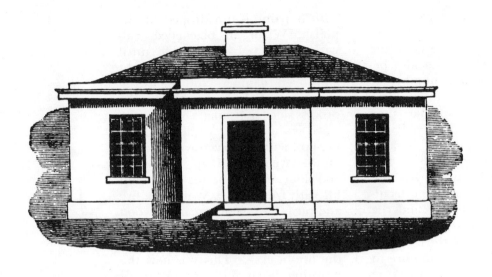

Ground-plan.

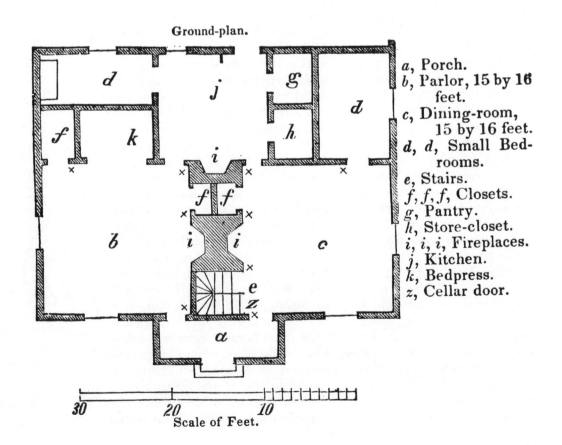

a, Porch.
b, Parlor, 15 by 16
    feet.
c, Dining-room,
    15 by 16 feet.
d, d, Small Bed-
    rooms.
e, Stairs.
f, f, f, Closets.
g, Pantry.
h, Store-closet.
i, i, i, Fireplaces.
j, Kitchen.
k, Bedpress.
z, Cellar door.

30   20   10

Scale of Feet.

"A shallow fire place saves wood and gives out more heat than a deeper one. A false back of brick, may be put upon a deep fireplace. Hooks, for holding up the shovel and tongs, a hearth-brush and bellows, and brass knobs to hang them on, should be furnished to every fireplace. Steel furniture is more genteel and more easily kept in order than that made of brass".[2] The bellows were often put in a holder made of woollen cloth and covered with old silk, that was often suitably embroidered.

From time to time the new-fangled cooking and heating stoves cracked and first-aid was necessary. A cement of ashes, salt and water was plastered on the cold stove, heating turned this mixture almost as hard as iron. Rust was prevented by rubbing the stoves with fat or oil and then polishing to a high shine.

No matter whether it was an open fire or a box heater, lighting the fire was often difficult, and if the fire did not catch, everything had to be raked out and the chore started once again. To prevent this the ingenious medical man, Dr. Chase, designed fire kindlers that could be made at home.

To Make Very Nice Fire Kindlers
"Take resin any quantity, melt it, putting in for each pound being used, from two to three ozs. of tallow, and when all is hot stir in pine saw-dust to make it very thick and, while yet hot, spread it out about 1 inch thick upon boards which have fine saw-dust sprinkled upon them to prevent it from sticking. When cold break into lumps about 1 inch square."[3]

Enterprising households were advised to cut this mixture into neat squares and sell them to their less frugal neighbours.

If the fire remained dull, there was nothing for it but to try the favourite remedy of all pioneers: sprinkle a little powdered nitre on the fire, or throw on some burning fluid or lamp oil. This was the moment to stand back and to be sure that the family knew how to handle a fire. Householders were told to have a lantern ready in case of sudden alarm, and all the valuables in one handy place. Two buckets of water left in the kitchen where they would not freeze was considered good insurance. Salt thrown into the water was believed to increase the flame-quenching power and muddy water was even better than clean for this purpose. In the province of Quebec metal-covered roofs were early attempts at fire-proofing, and in some places the law required a ladder to be kept on the roof.

There was a constant danger of clothes bursting into flame and mothers were told to dress themselves and the young children in woollen clothes rather than cotton. Dresses continued to go up in smoke and possibly the most gratuitous advice ever offered was "Children and families should be informed, that as flame tends upwards, it is extremely improper for them to stand upright in case their clothes take fire".[4]

One final word on fire-making; the housekeeper with the delicate touch remembered that the noise of making a fire in a sick-room was disturbing, so she arranged for each piece of fuel to be carefully wrapped in a paper bag.

In many homes towards the end of the century there was a pause for family prayers at which all members of the house were present. After prayers it was time for the dish-washing ritual, unless of course it was winter and the pump had frozen. "If there is reason to expect extreme cold, throw a horse blanket over your pump; a frozen pump is a comfortless preparation for a winter's breakfast".[5] Dish-washing was often done by the ladies of the house sitting at the dining-room table with small bowls of water. This was done to ensure the safety of the fine china and silver. Crockery was washed by the "help" at the kitchen sink. "No item of domestic labour is so frequently done in a negligent manner as this. A full supply of conveniences will do much toward a remedy of this evil. A swab made of strips of linen, tied to a stick, is useful to wash nice dishes. Two or three towels and three dish-clothes should be used, two large tin tubs painted on the outside should be provided; one for washing, and one for rinsing, also, a large old waiter (tray), on which to drain the dishes, a soap-dish, with hard soap, and a fork with which to use it should also be furnished".[2]

For many years there was little concern with household hygiene. Dishes were cleaned and floors were swept as necessary. By the later years of the century a new school of domestic writers busied themselves with ignorant servants and young over-worked housewives.

Death in a Kitchen Dishcloth
"If they are black and stiff and smell like a barnyard, it is enough; throw them in the fire, and henceforth and forever wash your dishes with cloths that are white, cloths you can see through, and see if you ever have that disease again. There are sometimes other causes, but I have smelled a whole house full of typhoid fever in one 'dishrag'. Therefore I say to every housekeeper, keep your dishcloths clean. You may only brush and comb your head on Sundays, you need not wear a collar unless you go from home — but you must wash your dishcloths".[6]

Domestic writers might hold a variety of views, but on one thing they were unanimous: every woman must have a regular schedule for every day of the week, and every moment of the day. This was not the time for the relaxed homemaker. These general directions were given almost a hundred years ago: "If you wash on Monday, bake on Tuesday, iron Wednesday, clean Thursday, mend Friday, and bake Saturday, of course, you will be somewhat governed by the peculiar situation of the family; but it will be found to be a good plan to have a routine for everyday. If you keep but one servant, it will be found more convenient to wash Tuesday, putting the clothes in soak Monday. There can be a nice cold dinner prepared for washing day, and the same can be arranged for ironing day".[7]

A suggested wash-day dinner was: "Chicken Pie; Celery; Hot Baked Potatoes; Cake soaked in Wine, served with Cold Custard".[7] A few years later, the ladies of Toronto published a cookbook, some of which they took from this earlier publication, but they elaborated on wash-day meals and suggested the following would keep husbands happy.

Raw Oysters with Lemon and
Crackers
Cold Veal with Jelly
Potato Chips
Bread and Butter
Cherry Pie with Cheese[8]

General house-cleaning instructions varied little with the passing of time. A late eighteenth century book with some circulation in Canada gave implicit instructions: "ALWAYS when you sweep a room, throw a little wet sand all over it, and that will gather up all the slew and dust, prevent it from rising, clean the boards, and save the bedding, pictures, and all other furniture from dust and dirt".[9] One hundred years later the genteel touch shows itself with the admonition to shake dusting cloths only out of the back windows.

The Art of Housekeeping
"To clean carpets: wash, dry and chop potatoes, spread them on one side of the room, sweep across the carpet."[5]

"To clean free-stone hearths: keep them stain-free and dark by rubbing with lamp-oil once in a while, this does very well in a large, dirty family; for the hearth looks very clean, and is not liable to show grease spots."[5]

Everyday chores paled beside the semi-annual seasonal cleaning. The editor of *The New Household Manual* and *The Ladies' Companion*, New Brunswick, wrote at the turn of the century:

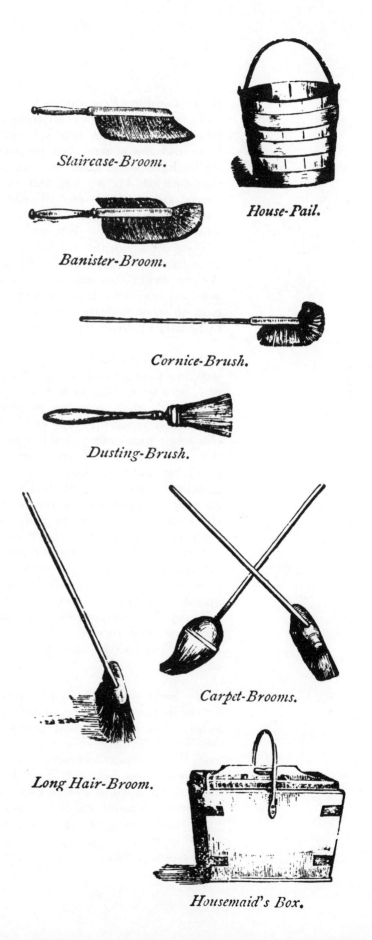

Staircase-Broom.

House-Pail.

Banister-Broom.

Cornice-Brush.

Dusting-Brush.

Carpet-Brooms.

Long Hair-Broom.

Housemaid's Box.

House Cleaning Perplexities Solved
"The confusion usually attending house-cleaning arises, nearly always from lack of system. No preparations have been made for when the dreaded day arrives. All the rooms are thrown into disorder, and when night comes the mistress and maid are in any but amiable temper, and no perceptible progress has been made in the work. Do not begin cleaning the rooms until the season for heating them is past, on account of the dust created by furnace or stoves."[10]

A very reasonable approach, logically thought out by Mr. Morrow, who wrote the book. But like a man, he then goes on to give minute instructions for seasonal cleaning which ends up taking two full weeks. Included are instructions on what to wear for this occasion: "Dress yourself in a neat calico or cambric dress, the skirt short enough to clear the floor, a linen collar fastened at the throat with a simple pin or bright ribbon; arrange your hair nicely under a sweeping cap, put on a long full apron, and you are prepared to work. And by simply removing the apron you may receive with perfect ease any person who may chance to call".[10]

Mr. Morrow thought it advisable for the hard-working woman to take a brief rest before eating dinner, and was thoughtful enough to suggest that oatmeal porridge made with water was especially good for mothers upon whose nervous forces too great a demand had been made.
A well thought-out seasonal cleaning schedule was a boon for most women. They all knew there were a thousand untold things to be done, particularly in the spring: "The nits or eggs of vermin have lain dormant through the cold months, and will now begin to hatch and unless preventives are promptly applied the increase of bedbugs and cockroaches will be without number. Prepare for soap-making by either sending all the soap-grease to the factory, or be mixed with strong lye preparatory to soap-making. All refuse vegetables ought to be thrown out; the potatoes selected; the small ones given to the cow, if there is one, and the best reserved for spring use. The meat barrels will now need looking after; if there is much corned beef on hand, unless very salt, it should be used as fast as possible. See that the pork is well covered with brine, and the sides of the barrel free from vermin. If the hams have not been protected before, bag and bury them in a barrel of strong, hard-wood ashes, and do the same with dried beef; examine the cheese, if inclined to mould or infested with vermin, make it into pot or brandy cheese. Examine the pickles and sweetmeats; if pickles are moulding, renew the vinegar; if preserves are fermenting, boil them up for tarts; if entirely spoiled, put the syrup in the vinegar-barrel. If butter on hand, is in danger of becoming rancid, melt it over water slowly, when melted let it boil up once with slices of raw potatoes cut very thin boiled in it, strain into very small jars, stirring salt through the butter. If crockery is tea stained boil it up in white lye. Place all barrels on a low staging, to prevent their moulding; scatter lime under each. . . .

"Cover all furniture, pictures, and books before taking up carpets; throw the carpets from the windows."[7]

Bedroom carpets were often made at home, and the following formula had great appeal to the economical:

Bed-Room Carpets for Twelve and a Half Cents Per Yard
"Sew together the cheapest cotton cloth the size of the room, and tack the edges to the floor. Now paper the cloth as you would the sides of a room, with cheap room paper; putting a border round the edge if desired. The paste will be better if a little gum arabic is mixed with it. When thoroughly dry give it two coats of furniture or carriage varnish, and when dry it is done."[3]

Mattresses were filled with either economical corn husks, hair, straw, moss or feathers. Feather beds were the most luxurious, but they often smelled, particularly when the feathers were not well-cured.

How to Manage Feather Beds
"As often as a bed is thought to need airing, lay it exposed to the outdoor air, high and dry from the ground, and in the shade. Do not lay it out until the sun has been up long enough to drive away the morning moisture, and take in before evening. It is an erroneous notion that beds should be exposed to the sun. The warmth extracts the oily matter in the quill end of feathers and makes them rancid. By being always in the shade, this oily substance in time becomes concrete and inodorous."[5]

It was one thing to air a feather bed, another to prepare the feathers, and for many years this had to be done at home. Feathers were well dried, it was suggested, when they were put in the oven after bread-baking was finished. When they were thoroughly dry the housewife spread them over the attic floor, and covering her head in a veil, proceeded to whip them with a small stick.

Beds were nearly always damp and the arrival of guests brought about a flurry of housekeeping. It was customary for the hostess or for a pernickety guest to test the bed by introducing a goblet between the sheets immediately after the warming pan had been withdrawn. "After a few minutes if drops of wet adhere to the inside of the glass, it is a certain sign of a damp bed. But if only a slight steam appears, all is safe; otherwise take off the sheets, and sleep in the blankets".[4] At the end of the century the glass was discarded and a hand mirror substituted. Guest rooms were to be made more inviting by leaving some albums, scrapbooks or portfolios of engravings beside the bed.

Sometimes regardless of the best house-keeping skills, a distinct smell pervaded the room. Some women resorted to the old-time pomander — an apple or an orange stuck with cloves. Sometimes they used perfume or sweet bags filled with aromatic herbs and spices. If the odour still persisted, a number of writers suggested the reason: "The bedroom odour, noticeable in three out of every five bedrooms in the land, is mostly derived from the urine that is allowed to stand uncovered, or in but partly closed receptacles 12 out of each 24 hours, in these rooms. The extent to which this source of mischief in bedrooms is overlooked by people otherwise highly particular in their house-keeping is indicated by the number of delicately shaped, finely decorated and coverless pieces of pottery sold to well-to-do-people for use in their bedroom".[13]

From smells, it was just a step away to that almost national pastime for more than a hundred years — the killing of bed bugs. In our world of screens, pesticides, public health and emphasis on personal hygiene it is hard for us to understand this preoccupation with bugs. Obviously nothing was successful, because over a period of some one hundred and twenty years, the methods kept changing. It was no doubt complicated by the perfunctory examination of steerage immigrants, and earlier still, by the fact that Canada was one of the last places where wigs were worn. With no great hope of success, an eighteenth century manuscript suggests: "To keep clear of Buggs for one night. Take the leaves of Kidney Beans and lay them under your Bolster, it will draw all the Buggs to them. To get entirely quit of them, rub all the Bedstead with Spirits of Turpentine".

In 1831: "Take the white of four eggs, ten cents worth of quicksilver, put them into a bowl, beat them until perfect froth, take a feather and dip in and apply it to every part of your bedstead where bugs ever conceal themselves, do this but once a year, and you will never see a bedbug in your house".[12]

In 1899: "Take varnish and thoroughly paint your bedstead, ten cents' worth will do for one bedstead, easily used and safe, the application must, however, be thorough, the slats, sides, and every crack and corner receiving attention".[13] Maybe the bugs slid off! Bugs in store closets were eliminated by painting the shelves with mercury dissolved in whisky.

To Keep Free from Vermin
"Crickets: Scotch snuff upon the holes where they come out of or powdered arsenic on a roasted apple."

"Beetles: use the parings of cucumber near their holes."

"Caterpillars: put a tallow candle in storage trunks."

"Rats and mice: use a trap, or a good cat is the best remedy or equal quantities of old cheese and hemlock will poison them but this renders the house liable to the inconvenience of a bad smell."

"Moths: use pepper, red cedar chips, tobacco or indeed any strong spicy smell but nothing is so good as camphor."

"Ants: put green sage in the closet or grease a plate with lard and set it where they are troublesome, then place a few sticks around the plate for the ants to climb upon."[14]

Flies were kept from the pictures by washing the frames with a solution made from soaking onions five or six days in a pail of water. Other ladies found an effectual barrier to dust and flies was to cover the frames with yellow cambric as near the colour of gilt as possible. Others placed saucers around the room filled with a mixture of cream, brown sugar and black pepper. Cedar boughs hung from the ceiling were a common fly trap. Travellers took with them small muslin bags filled with pennyroyal as a talisman against the fleas, although the beauty writers thought that strong perfumes would do the trick. If by chance a bee or wasp was swallowed, the cure was a drink of salty water,—"it kills the insect and cures the sting".[15] When bees swarmed around the head, the victim should smoke tobacco and hold an empty hive overhead. The bees would enter it.

Disinfecting, fumigating and purifying were all part of the job; the worse the smell of the fumigant the more successful it was bound to be.

To Destroy Putrid Effluvia
"Mix a spoonful of salt with a little powdered manganese in a glass cup, pour on the mixture at different times a spoonful of strong vitriolic acid, and the vapour arising from it will destroy the putrid effluvia "[4]

Quite often housewives put this mixture on a red-hot shovel and ran through the house spreading the vapours. Water stored in hogsheads and cisterns became smelly, black and oily; to clear the water a large spoonful of pulverized alum was stirred into the barrel, and in a few hours the dirt sank to the bottom, leaving it as fresh and clear as spring water, or so it was said. Most books suggested that four ounces each of alum and borax was

sufficient to clear fifty barrels of drinking water.

Everything had to be polished or scoured and all the cleaners were home-made. The black iron cooking pots were scoured with sand and the interiors freshened with rhubarb (pie plant) and water. Treen (woodenware) was washed in soap suds but dried away from the hearth to prevent warping. Pewter was cleaned with wood ashes, tin and Britannia (poor man's silver) were rubbed with lamp oil and polished with whiting and buckskin. Magnesia was used to clean silver and any black spots removed with sulphuric acid. Knives of course were not stainless and were cleaned and sharpened on a leather-covered board with a mixture of emery, crocus martis and oil. Less fastidious women used brick-dust, but this was thought to wear the knives excessively.

In a frugal, economical age, special care had to be taken of new household items. For instance, brooms were dipped in hot suds once a week to prolong their lives and a new broom always had a few straws removed for cake-testing. New earthenware was strengthened by placing in cold water, bringing to the boil and then cooling. "A handful of rye, or wheat bran thrown in while it is boiling will preserve the glazing so that it will not be destroyed by salt or acid".[5]

In an age when fine furniture was highly polished, white heat marks were vexatious. They were usually cured by holding a shovel of hot coals over the spot. Wax or lamp oil stains on the floors were also removed with hot coals, but black walnut was rubbed with butter-

milk to restore its glow. The mica windows of stoves were bathed in vinegar.

Open fires throughout the house played havoc with oil paintings. The annual cure for dingy pictures was to dissolve a little common salt in stale urine and rub the pictures with it until they were quite clean. They were rinsed with clear water, dried gradually and finally polished with a clean cloth. Towards the end of the century, pictures were being cleaned with a mixture of whisky and water.

Inks were home-made and the varieties included permanent, washable and even invisible. The reason for the latter was the rather casual approach to privacy of mail in some early post offices — usually the postmaster's living-room or the tavern counter.

Durable Ink
"The milk or gum that exudes from the sumach is a good substitute for durable ink. Break off the stalks that support the leaves. Squeeze them into a cup, expose the writing to the sun and it will become a fine black."[14]

Boot blacking was also home-made and the recipes were as varied as a witch's brew. In 1861 Mrs. Isabella Beeton offered the following suggestion, which would be perhaps a little heady for most present-day women:

"1 oz. each of pounded galls and logwood-chips, and 3 lbs of red French wine (ordinaire). Boil together till the liquid is reduced to half the quantity, and pour it off through a strainer. Now take ½ lb each of pounded gum-arabic and lump-sugar, 1 oz of green copperas, and 2 lbs of brandy. Dissolve the gum-arabic in the preceding decoction, and add the sugar and copperas: when all is dissolved and mixed together, stir in the brandy, mixing it smoothly. This mixture will yield 5 or 6 lbs of a very superior polishing paste for boots and shoes."[16]

The more usual recipe in Canada was to take elder-berries, mash them in water and leave to ferment. It was then boiled for at least half a day, water being replaced as it evaporated. "Then strain it through a coarse thin cloth, then boil it down to the thickness of molasses, and it is fit for use"[17] Boots were waterproofed with equal quantities of beeswax and mutton suet melted together and brushed over the boots, including the soles.

The Frugal Housewife
"When plain tortoise-shell combs are defaced, the polish may be renewed by rubbing them with pulverized rotten-stone and oil. The rotten-stone should be sifted through muslin. It looks better to be rubbed on by the hand. The jewellers afterwards polish them by rubbing them with dry rouge powder; *but sifted magnesia does just as well* — and if the ladies had rouge, perhaps they would, *by mistake* put it upon their cheeks, instead of their combs; and thereby spoil their complexions."[6]

A cautionary tale!

REFERENCES

[1] *Boston Cook Book*, D. A. Lincoln, Boston, 1883.

[2] *A Treatise on Domestic Economy*, Beecher, New York, 1849.

[3] *Dr. Chase's Recipes*, A. W. Chase, London, Ontario, 1868.

[4] *The Housekeeper's Receipt Book*, Anonymous, London, 1816.

[5] *The American Frugal Housewife*, L. Child, New York, 1838.

[6] *Home and Health*, Anonymous, London, Ontario, 1882.

[7] *The Housekeeper's Encyclopedia*, E. Haskell, New York, 1869.

[8] *The Home Cook Book*, Anonymous, Toronto, 1877.

[9] *The Art of Cookery Made Plain and Easy*, H. Glasse, London, 1765.

[10] *The New Household Manual*, R. Morrow, Saint John, N. B., 1901.

[11] *The Household Guide*, B. G. Jefferis, Toronto, 1894.

[12] *The Cook Not Mad*, Anonymous, Kingston, Ontario, 1831.

[13] *The White House Cook Book*, Zieman and Gillette, Toronto, 1899.

[14] *The Lady's Receipt Book*, Leslie, Philadelphia, 1847.

[15] *The New Household Receipt Book*, S. Hale, London, 1854.

[16] *Household Management*, I. Beeton, London, 1861.

[17] *The New England Economical Housekeeper*, E. A. Howland, Montpelier, 1845.

Domestic Duties

Making candles and tending the oil lamps were part of the housekeeping chores. There was a period in the nineteenth century when home lighting ran the gamut from primitive rush lights burning melted fat, to candles, to oil lamps and in some areas, to gas-lights.

Candle-making took time and patience. They were made by the dipping, moulding or forming methods. When dipping candles, the prepared wicks were slowly and steadily dipped in hot wax, cooled and hardened and the process laboriously repeated. It was important to maintain the correct temperature: if the wax was too hot it would not cling to the wick, if too cold it clung to the bottom of the wick. Poured candles were much easier and the candle moulds are still to be seen to-day. Beeswax, being soft and pliable, was often moulded around wicking.

The itinerant candle-maker was one of the earliest tradesmen, taking this chore away from the housewife. Candles were made in cool weather and were stored in closed boxes away from rats and mice. The ends of wax candles, never to be wasted, were used in making starch to give an extra gloss or else the home-made starch was stirred with a wax candle. Spicy-smelling bayberries were used for candles in maritime areas where the wax myrtle grows. These berries were also sewn into small muslin bags to grease slow-moving irons.

The cheapest and most common candle was made of tallow: melted clarified animal fat, usually mutton or beef. But in the early days of the eastern settlements and when the west was pioneered and cattle were scarce, deer, bear, coon or hog fat was used. In some backwoods settlements candles were so scarce they were used only on such occasions as Christmas Eve or a birthday. At other times, the light of the fire sufficed. An early status trick was to dip evil-smelling tallow candles into hot wax to give them a more expensive look.

Lamps brought problems: grease on the carpets, hearth and clothes. Also they had a tendency to explode when not well treated or when the fuel merchant cheated, and a dropped lamp could be a disaster. The care and the mixing of the fuel was complicated. Contemporary household advice from the middle of the end of the century speaks for itself:

"Lamps are better than candles, as they give a steadier light and do not scatter grease like tallow candles.

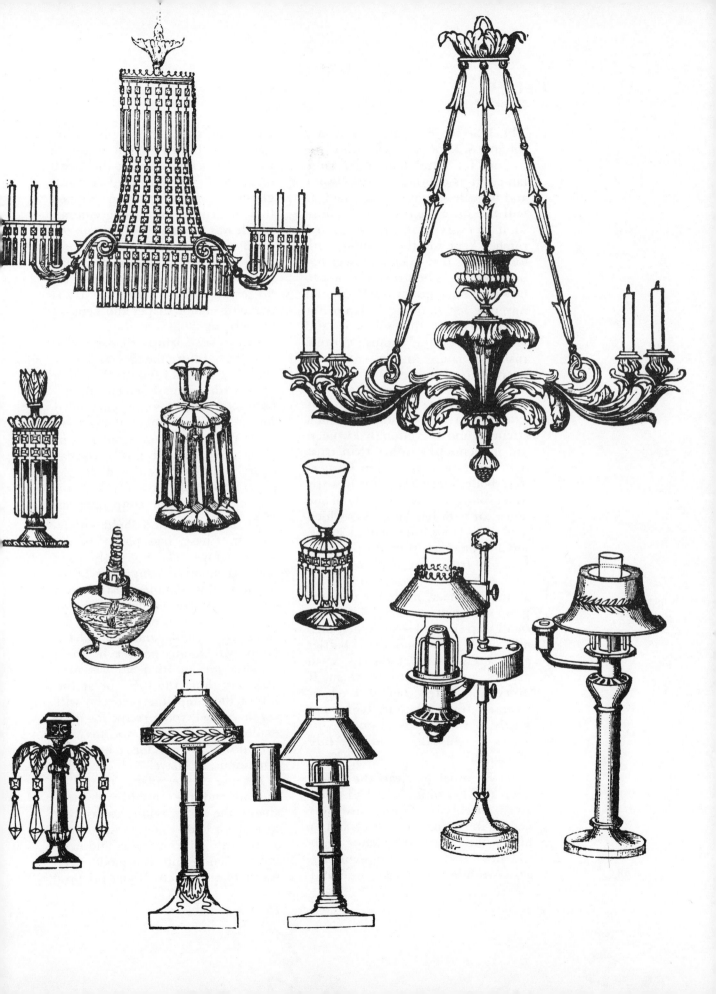

The best oil is clear, and nearly colourless. Lard is a good substitute for oil, for astral and other large lamps. It is cheaper, burns clearer and has a less disagreeable smell. It will not burn well in small lamps. Melt it every morning in an old pitcher kept for the purpose. Oil, long kept grows thick and does not burn well. It is best therefore not to buy it in large quantities. It should never be left standing in lamps for several days as this spoils it, and often injures the lamps. Cleanse inside of lamps and oil-cans with pearlash (soda) water."[1]

The preparing of the lamps was a daily ritual that required so much attention and discretion that women did it themselves rather than trust it to domestic help. Lamp burners were boiled once a month in soapy water, but every day the lady of the house sat with her lamp tray which held — "a lamp filler, with a spout, small at one end, turned up to prevent oil from dripping, a ball of wick yarn, and a basket to hold it, a lamp trimmer, made for the purpose, or a pair of sharp scissors, a small soap-cup and soap, some pearlash, in a broad-mouthed bottle; and several soft cloths to wash articles, and towels to dry them. If everything after being used is cleansed from oil, and then kept neatly, it will not be so unpleasant a task as it usually is, to take care of lamps."[1]

It was usual to clean the lamps after the morning fires had been given attention. Great care was needed in trimming the wick and in filling the reservoir. Lamps with too little fuel generated explosive gas; overfilled ones ran over and left grease stains. New lamp chimneys were boiled in salt water to prevent cracking. In fact this treatment was recommended for all glassware. Some women dipped their wick yarn into strong vinegar, which was thought to eliminate the smell of the burning oil. Others drew the wick through melted wax until stiff and smooth to make tapers for sealing letters. When dry it was twined in fancy shapes and kept on the writing-table.

Cut glass lamp shades were thought to injure the eyes, and weak eyes were shaded from the flickering light with a small screen. Broad-bottomed lamps were recommended for the kitchen. Night lights were made of floating tapers burning in a teacup of oil. It was a regular household task to fold and cut old paper into strips or spills, kept on the mantelpiece for lamp lighting.

That complete household authority, Dr. Chase, had plenty to say about lamps. He not only gave many economical recipes for burning fluid, but detailed instructions about safety. He recommended that lamps be filled in daylight, "or far from fire or lights; and also to have lamps which are perfect in their construction, so that no gas may leak out along the tube, or at the top of the lamp; then let who will say he can sell you a recipe for non-explosive gas or fluid, you may set him down at once for a humbug, ignoramus, or knave".[2]

Because of the volatile nature of the oil and the cupidity of merchants, the doctor said it was as well to make a handy home test: "pour a little into an iron spoon, and heat it over a lamp until it is moderately warm to the touch. If the oil produces vapour which can be set on fire by means of a flame held a short distance above the surface of the liquid, it is bad. Good oil poured into a teacup or on the floor does not easily take fire when a light is brought in contact with it".[2]

Soap was made at home, although many women passed this chore along to the soap works as soon as possible. Others continued to supervise this operation well into the twentieth century and are still making soap today. Before the soap came the ley (lye) and this was home-made from the collected hardwood ashes.

To Put Up a Leach:
Say a Large Tierce
"Lay sticks across the bottom, then a covering of straw, one peck of lime should come next, after which the ashes, these to be well beaten down several times in the course of filling up, pouring in a pail of water each time after pounding. If you are in no hurry for your lie, (lye) water your leach occasionally until it shows a disposition to run at the bottom, then stop up until you are ready to commence making soap. It will make two barrels."[3]

The straw prevented the coarser ashes from blocking the hole at the bottom of the barrel. Lye had to be tested to determine its strength. The usual way was to take a sampling and to float an egg.

"If the egg rise so as to show a circle as large as a ten cent piece, the strength is right; if it rise higher the ley must be weakened by water; if not so high, the ashes are not good, and the whole process must

be repeated, putting in fresh ashes, and running the weak ley through the new ashes, with some additional water."[1]

Once there was lye, fats had to be collected, generally during the fall killing and throughout the winter months.

To Preserve Soap Grease
"Make your cask clean, when you throw in fresh rinds or any thing of the kind, sprinkle salt enough to preserve it, the same when you put down hog's inwards, and be as careful to keep it tight as any other meat and you will have no disagreeable smell nor waste of grease by vermin."[3]

Soap-making was an art, and not always successful, and for this reason it was polite to wish soap-makers luck or to ask God's blessing for them. The superstitious felt that soap would set only if it was stirred one way. There were as many different recipes for making soap as there are for making cakes.

To Make Boiled Soap
"For a barrel take thirty-five pounds of scraps or other grease that is made daily in a family and put half the quantity into a five pail kettle, a pailful of strong lie (sic), boil it thoroughly with a moderate fire or it will run over, then keep adding strong lie until full, put it in a barrel and add weak lie. Then take the other half of the grease and proceed as before."[3]

In the Canadian edition of his book of household recipes, Dr. Chase appealed to the economical with a recipe for "One hundred pounds of Good Soap for $1.30". "Sal-soda and lard each 6 lbs; stone lime 2 lbs; soft water 4 gals; dissolve the lime and soda in the water, by boiling, stirring, settling and pouring off; then return to the kettle (brass or copper) and add the lard and boil until it becomes soap; then pour into a dish or moulds, and when cold cut it into bars and let dry. (This recipe was found in the pocket of an overcoat, along with a piece of the soap)."[2]

Substitutes for soap included pine or fir sawdust, and fine sand was often added to softened soap to help wash small boys.

The question that now arose was when to wash the clothes. Housewives and the authorities could not agree whether wash-day should be Monday or Tuesday. Everything hinged on whether the housewife believed in the soaking of dirty clothes. If so, then Tuesday was wash-day, because to soak clothes on a Sunday night was a profanation of the Lord's Day.

In the pioneer years of a settlement, wash-day depended on a spell of good warm weather, a supply of soap and water, and the time to launder. Some early illustrations show women standing in the wooden wash tubs pounding away with their feet, much as they fulled cloth in some areas.

By the time the first shanty was left behind, wash-day was a thoroughly organized and dreaded day. The laundry area had a wet floor, steam billowed from the special stoves, and the women were naturally exhausted and short-tempered.

The number of articles that were provided for a laundry in a mid-nineteenth century home gives some idea of the scale of operation.

"A plenty of soft water is a very important item. When this cannot be had, ley or soda can be put in hard water, to soften it; care being used not to put in so much, as to injure the hands and clothes. Two wash-forms are needed; one for the two tubs in which to put the suds, the other for blueing and starching-tubs. Four tubs of different sizes are necessary; also, a large wooden dipper, (as metal is apt to rust); two or three pails; a grooved wash-board; a clothes-line, (seagrass or horse-hair is best); a wash stick to move clothing when boiling, and a wooden fork to take them out, soap dishes made to hook on the tubs, saves soap and time. Provide, also a clothes-bag, an indigo-bag, of double flannel, a starch-strainer, of coarse linen; a bottle of ox-gall for calicoes; a supply of starch, neither sour nor musty; several dozens of clothes-pins, which are cleft sticks, used to fasten clothes on the line; a bottle of dissolved gum Arabic; two clothes-baskets; and a brass or copper kettle, for boiling clothes, as iron is apt to rust."[1]

Although many areas were primitive and undeveloped, it should not be forgotten that household appliances came on the scene early. It was partly the lack of servants or their indifference to service that spurred the demand for machines to replace them. Travelling pedlars, salesmen and wonderfully lurid free almanacs and advertisements all helped to make sales.

By 1874, the writer of the *Gentle-*

man Immigrant speaks thus of the Canadian housewife: "If it is washing day, she helps her help in the laundry. But in well organized households, washing-day has no terrors; it is a 'heavy wash' that cannot be got through in two hours. There is no messing and slopping and soaping, and rubbing as in an English farmhouse. With one of Doty's patent washing machines and wringers the linen is washed and wrung without the operator as much as wetting her fingers. It is only the ironing that is tedious, but in the woods a little ironing goes a very long way".[4]

Starch was made at home from various farinaceous vegetables and there was a tendency for it to become mouldy. Frequently starch was made from potatoes and salt was added to prevent sticking, but the most common way was to use grain.

To Manufacture Starch

"Cleanse a peck of unground wheat, and soak it, for several days, in soft water. When quite soft, remove the husks, with the hand, and the soft parts will settle. Pour off the water, and replace it, every day, with that which is fresh, stirring it well. When, after stirring and settling, the water is clear, it is done. Then strain off the water, and dry the starch, for several days, in the sun. If the water be permitted to remain too long, it sours and the starch is poor. If the starch is not well dried it grows musty."[1]

Laundering was more than washing. It meant the restoring of faded colours, the setting of non-fast dyes, the removal of spots and stains and general refurbishing. Clothes were expensive and precious and many hours were spent in caring for them. To this end, one item used was beefgall: "Send a junk-bottle to the butcher, and have several gall-bladders emptied into it. Keep it salted, and in a cool place. Some persons perfume it; but fresh air removes the unpleasant smell which it gives when used for clothes".[1] Ox-gall in water improved and set coloured calicoes. Undiluted it removed grease, especially from coat collars.

Hay water was used to wash and stiffen brown or buff linen; men's white gloves were washed and dried on the hands; beaver and white fur hats were cleaned with warm Indian meal (corn meal) and salt; woollens were washed in very hot suds — "it is the lukewarm water that shrinks them".[5] Stains were sometimes removed by holding them over steaming brimstone and calico was often set with a spoonful of sugar of lead to a pail of water.

The Best Way to Clean a Veil

"Mix 1 Tea cup Strong Black Tea, 1 tea spoon Gin, 1 tea spoon Ammonia, dry just enough to make smooth."[6]

To Clean Silks and Ribbons

"Mix half a pint of Gin, half a pound of honey, half a pound of soft soap, one eighth pint of water. Mix then lay each breadth of silk on a table and scrub well with the mixture."[5]

White flannel was stored with lumps of wax to keep it white, and charcoal prevented stored clothes from smelling. Dry cleaning was done with grease balls made of soap, fuller's earth and ox-gall. Finally, two cleaning hints concerning frequent mishaps:

To Remove Carriage Wheel's Grease from Clothes

"Rub with butter, then with blotting paper and a hot iron or use a bit of charcoal on a silver spoon, you may then take it off as you would a drop of wax or tallow."[7]

Against Piss Spots

"Boil some chamberlye (sic) and wash the place with it. Then rinse it with clear water."[7]

Smell of House Drains Prevented

"Any collection of filth whatever may be completely neutralized by pouring upon it a mixture of lime water and the ley of wood ashes or suds that have been used in washing. If you have a strip of land, do not throw away suds. Both ashes and suds are good manure for bushes and young plants."[6]

Ironing day followed washing day, and for this a further long list of necessities had to be stocked. There were different irons to cope with all the complicated frills, scallops and draped dresses. Some irons had their own built-in heat, charcoal. Others were heated on the fire or range and covered with protectors to keep the clothes clean. Equipment included frames on which to air clothes, bosom boards on which to iron and even polish the starched shirt fronts to a deep shine. Women used odd little irons like curling tongs to cope with the frills of the caps, dresses and aprons. There were special sleeve boards, and shirt boards, and in the days of the sweeping skirt they were at least five feet in length.

In the early days, the yarns and homespun were dyed at home with natural dyes. These gave soft muted colours, but often had little strength or lasting power. Once again, as soon as it was possible to have professional dyeing, the family sent the yarns out. But the women continued to restore the faded calicoes and cottons. With the growth of foreign trade, longer-lasting and more concentrated dyes were imported for the finer fabrics. By 1856, chemical dyes had become available and these resulted in brighter fabrics. New shades were possible and colour lasted longer. Popular shades of the period were Solferino pink and magenta.

Yarns dyed at home were usually wool, since cotton and linen were difficult to master with home equipment. Among the natural dyes were onion skins for a soft yellow; the purple paper from loaf or cone sugar was saved for the fine slate colour; and tea leaves were saved and boiled in a rusty iron kettle for drab, a dull brown suitable for small boys' breeches. Walnut shells gave a pleasant brown, and balm blossoms gave a pretty, easily faded pink for little girls' bonnets and pelisses. White maple bark gave a light slate; lye and copperas gave nankin, a yellow brown that was popular. This was one of the long-lasting dyes, and so was recommended for the linings of bed quilts, comforters and petticoats. The ever-economical housekeeper cut down old gowns to dress little girls and the adults' stockings were mended, cut down and re-dyed for the children.

Dyes were set with mordants and the one most used, because of its cheapness and availability, was alum.

One of the most interesting household tasks was the making of food colouring at home; the pioneers enjoyed highly coloured jellies and icings. Spinach juice was strained and bottled for green colourings; indigo was often used for blue; and red was usually beet juice. For many years it was not possible to buy flavourings, but this did not mean that their syllabubs and custards were bland. Small, well-stoppered bottles were filled with brandy; in one, rose leaves would be added, in another, orange or lemon peel, and yet another would have peach leaves. The kernels of peaches were saved, dried and boiled in milk to flavour custard. Some women even beat their batter with fresh peach twigs to give flavour.

The staples we have come to take for granted were prepared at home. Sugar cone was not only expensive, it was hard. Certain days would be set aside to cut cubes with special scissors or nippers. Salt was bought in large damp lumps and first had to be dried in front of the fire, then crushed with a rolling-pin or pounded in a mortar, and finally stored in a wooden salt box. Coffee not only was ground at home, it also had to be roasted.

Because coffee was very expensive, various substitutes were used; dandelion roots, dry brown bread crusts, roasted rye grain that had been soaked in rum, or roasted and ground peas. "Where there is a large family of apprentices and workmen, and coffee is very dear, it may be worth while to use the substitutes, or to mix them half and half with coffee; but, after all, the best economy is to go without".[5] Fish skin was considered the secret of good coffee; it was easier and cheaper than clarifying with egg shells. "A bit of fish skin thrown into coffee while it is boiling tends to make it clear. If you use it just as it comes from the salt-fish, it will be apt to give an unpleasant taste to the coffee; it should be washed clean as a bit of cloth and hung up till perfectly dry. The white of eggs or even egg shells are good to settle coffee. Rind of pork is excellent".[5]

Buying, making and restoring vinegar took considerable time, and was a very necessary part of the preserving of food for winter use. So much was used that it was thought poor economy to buy by the gallon. "Buy a barrel, or half a barrel, of really strong vinegar, when you begin housekeeping. As you use it fill the barrel with old cider, sour beer, or wine-settlings, &c. left in pitchers, decanters or tumblers; weak tea is likewise said to be good: nothing is hurtful, which has a tolerable portion of spirit or acidity. Care must be taken not to add these things in too large quantities, or too often: if the vinegar once gets weak, it is difficult to restore it. If possible, it is well to keep such slops as I have mentioned in a different keg, and draw them off once in three or four weeks, in such quantity as you think the vinegar will bear. If by any carelessness you do weaken it, a few white beans dropped in, or white pepper dipped in molasses, is said to be useful".[5]

A recipe handwritten in an 1880 notebook says: "To 8 galls Rain Water add 3 Qts Molasses put into a good Cask, shake well then add 2 or 3 Spoonsfull of Yeast in summer put into the sun, in winter in a Warm place. In ten or 15 days add to the other ingredients a sheet of Brown paper torn in strips dip(p)ed in Molasses. The Paper form the Mother".* Some women thought that old pickle brine was better than new and to this end the brine from cucumber pickles was drained, boiled and cooled, then stored from year to year.

To keep cheese the housewife took a clean barrel and put fresh clean hay on the bottom, put in a cheese and added more hay over and around it, and so on until the barrel was filled. It was covered and kept in a cellar or in a frost-free attic, and examined periodically for vermin. Suet was packed in stone

*This is almost identical to the recipe in *The New Household Receipt Book* written by Mrs. S. Hale, London, 1854.

This Cut is a fac-simile of package.

The greatest tribute to its extraordinary merits is, that it was awarded FIRST PRIZE AND DIPLOMA at

TORONTO EXHIBITION,

HAMILTON EXHIBITION,

LONDON EXHIBITION,

MONTREAL EXHIBITION,

1880.

Over all other Yeasts.

Try it and be convinced

MANUFACTURED BY

PEARL YEAST CO.

39 Front Street East, TORONTO.

jars and covered with molasses, and parsley—"to garnish viands all winter"[3]—was kept green in a strong salt pickle.

Poultry was not kept on a commercial scale until the middle to later years of the century, but most women kept a few chickens. To keep the money received from selling eggs was always the housewife's prerogative. In times when barter was common, eggs were often traded for tea, bonnets or other luxuries. There were a number of ways to store eggs and each woman had her favourite method. First the eggs were selected for freshness: "If they shake like water they are not. If both ends of the egg when put in the mouth are of the same temperature, they are bad; but if a perceptible difference in the heat is perceived, they may be depended upon as good eggs".[8] It was said that eggs packed in a pail of salt and unslaked lime would keep almost for ever. Another way was to put eggs in strong cabbage nets and every day hook on a fresh mesh so that the eggs were gradually turned.

Yeast was made at home for many years. At first it was made as needed, but later Indian meal (corn) was added to make a paste and the mixture spread on boards to dry. Then it was cut into portions and stored until needed.

Many early settlers stored their precious root vegetables in pits or cellars without adequate air ventilation, thinking that the cold would penetrate and suffice. To their horror everything rotted. Fruit was preserved in many ways, pumpkin and apples were dried on racks, or dried with sugar to make "leather". Here is an early ready-mix pie-fill:

An Excellent Way to Preserve Pompions

"Boil and strain them through a sieve fit for pies, put them in dishes and dry them in the oven or sun till hard and dry — lay them up for use and they will keep for years. When to be used, dissolve it in milk and it is as good as when first boiled."[3]

Grapes and other delicate fruits were paper-wrapped and stored in jars filled with bran or dry sand. Apples were packed in barrels for winter eating; some people favoured pricking each one with a goose quill before tightly packing them into casks. Sometimes prize cabbages were brought indoors complete with root, and buried in dry sand. Fruits were of course preserved in syrups and in brandy, as had been done for a long time.

At first the bottle tops were either parchment soaked in brandy, or fine leather or bladders. It was not until mid-century that bottles had stoppers cemented on, and shortly after came the preserve bottle with its lid and ring, very like the one we know today. One of the curious things about home canning is that it is one of the few food processes that was started outside the home, enjoyed a commercial success, and was then adapted for the small kitchen. On the other hand, the making of jams, sausage, hams and candles all began in the kitchen, and then went commercial.

Curious and Simple Manner of Keeping Apricots, Peaches, Plums, &c. Fresh All Year

"Beat up well together equal quantities of honey and spring water;

pour into an earthen vessel, put in the fruits freshly gathered and cover them quite close. When any of the fruit is taken out, wash it in cold water, and it is fit for immediate use."[3]

Other household duties included the making of "sticking paste" as well as various glues for paper, leather and china. Razor strops were made and quills sharpened for pens. Spices were purchased, pounded, sieved and stored. The nutmeg was a tricky item to buy and brides were warned about the Yankee pedlars who would not hesitate to sell wooden ones to the unsuspecting. The test of quality for a nutmeg was to prick it with a pin. If it was good, fresh oil would spread around the puncture.

There were no laws to ensure the purity of packaged foods and prepared staples. The first pure food law was not passed until the 1870's. So light was competition that manufacturers and tradesmen did not police each other. It was up to the buyer to beware and keep alert for signs of adulteration. The sharper the tradesman the more knowledge the women needed. Books of this period were helpful and describe the many tricks used. Of course, these books were equally helpful to the tradesmen. It was common practice to put copper in pickles to give a fine green colour. To detect this you had to use ammonia and water, and any copper then showed up as a fine blue colour.

Good flour was a creamy yellow white, never pure white. "If it feel damp, clammy or sticky and gradually forms into lumps or cakes it is not the best". Baker's bread was adulterated particularly when the price of flour rose. The foreign mixtures added were usually alum, chalk, bone dust and plaster of Paris. The use of alum was frequent because it has a high water absorption and added to the weight. Brandy was watered and restored with burnt sugar and cayenne pepper. Cayenne itself was cut with brick dust, red lead or vermilion. Cocoa had flour, starch and animal fat; custard powder had turmeric and sand; sugar was mixed with sand or sawdust. Loaf sugar was expensive because it was harder to tamper with. Plum, chestnut, poplar and willow leaves were dried and added to tea.

It is interesting to see these adulterations from the trade point of view:

To Give Body to Diluted Milk
"Use the following nutritive and healthy compound at the rate of 8 oz to every 5 gals., stirring it up in the milk until all is dissolved: arrowroot, 6 oz., magnesia, 6 oz., starch, 1 lb., flour, 6½ lbs., white sugar in powder 1 lb., mix all intimately together and keep in a dry place for use."[9]

Frequently food had to be restored because of an unwise purchase, or because of a change in temperature. Although ice boxes were known by 1840, they were rare. Many farmers had their own ice houses, but sometimes the supply ran low. Meat was such a problem in the summer that some food editors suggested a meatless diet. Others advocated meat being covered with bran and hung in a wire cage in an airy room. This was thought to keep mutton, veal or beef perfectly sweet and good for nine or ten days.

Occasionally the brine in the pork barrels soured and tainted the meat. Then it had to be poured off, reboiled and the meat would be restored "even when much injured". Mrs. Dalgairns, a Scottish writer popular on both sides of the Atlantic, recommended in 1845 that tainted meat be washed in camomile tea. Some sixty years later charcoal was still being used.

To Restore Tainted Meat
"Fly blown meat can be completely restored by immersing it for a few hours in a vessel containing a small quantity of beer; but it will taint and impart a putrid smell to the liquor."[5]

To Sweeten Meat
"A little charcoal thrown into the pot will sweeten meat that is a little old. Not if it is anyway tainted — it is then not fit to eat — but if kept longer than makes it quite fresh."[6]

French Method of Purifying Rancid or Tainted Butter
"Let the butter be salted and scummed as for clarifying, then put into it a piece of bread well toasted all over. In a minute or two the butter will lose its offensive taste and smell, but the bread will· become perfectly fetid."[5]

Odd Scraps for the Economical
"The true economy of housekeeping is simply the art of gathering up all fragments, so that nothing be lost. I mean fragments of time, as well as materials. Nothing should be thrown away so long as it is possible to make any use of it, however trifling the use may be; and whatever be the size of the family, every member should be employed either in earning or saving money."[5]

Finally here is a miscellany of household hints for the pioneer woman. They first appeared in *The American Frugal Housewife*.[5]

"Cheap as stockings are it is a good economy to knit them. Cotton and woollen yarn are both cheap; hose that are knit wear twice as long as woven ones; and can be done at odd moments of time not to be otherwise employed. Where there are children, or aged people, it is sufficient to recommend knitting as an employment. It is a foolish waste of time to tear cloth into bits for the sake of arranging it anew in fantastic figures; but a large family may be kept out of idleness, and a few shillings saved, by thus using scraps of gowns, curtains etc."
"It is wise to keep an exact account of all you spend — even a paper of pins. This answers two purposes; it makes you more careful in spending money, and it enables your husband to judge precisely whether his family live within his income."

"If you would avoid waste in your family, attend to the following rules, and do not despise them because they appear so unimportant: 'many a little makes a mickle'. Look frequently to the pails, to see that nothing is thrown to the pigs which should have been in the grease-pot. Look to the grease-pot, and see nothing is there which might have served to nourish your own family, or a poorer one."

"Count sheets, towels, spoons &c. occasionally; that those who use them may not become careless."

"Attend to all the mending in the house, once a week, if possible. Never put out sewing."

"Make your own bread and cake. Some people think it is just as cheap to buy of the baker and confectioner; but it is not half as cheap. True, it is more convenient; therefore the rich are justifiable in employing them, but those who are under the necessity of being economical, should make convenience a secondary object. In the first place confectioners make their cake richer than people of moderate income can afford to make it; in the next place your domestic or your-

self may just as well employ your own time, as to pay them for their time."

"Buy your woollen yarn in quantities from someone you can trust."

"There's no need of asking the character of a domestic, if you have ever seen her wash dishes in a little greasy water."

"Tortoise shell and horn combs last much longer for having oil rubbed into them once in a while."

"The first young leaves of the common currant-bush gathered as soon as they put out, and dried on tin, can hardly be distinguished from green tea."

REFERENCES
[1] *A Treatise on Domestic Economy*, Beecher, New York, 1849.
[2] *Dr. Chase's Recipes*, A. W. Chase, London, Ontario, 1868.
[3] *Cook Not Mad*, Anonymous, Kingston, Ontario, 1831.
[4] *The Gentleman Immigrant*, W. Stamer, London, 1874.
[5] *The American Frugal Housewife*, L. Child, New York, 1838.
[6] *Manuscript Book*, Anonymous, Cobourg, Ontario, 1870.
[7] *Valuable Secrets*, Anonymous, Boston, 1798.
[8] *The Housekeeper's Encyclopedia*, Haskell, New York, 1869.
[9] *The Artizans' Guide*, Moore, Montreal, 1873.

The Canadian
Haberdashery

CHAPTER NINE

Fabric had to be turned into garments by the housewife or by the itinerant tailor who was sometimes engaged to make clothing for all the family. Everyone was clothed at home including the adult sons, but in some areas adulthood was marked with a "freedom suit." This was the last set of clothes made at home, and the receipt of it brought the privilege of keeping earned money and of buying future clothing. Women designed and sewed their own dresses and up to mid-century the only way to do this was to rip up an old garment for a pattern. However, by Confederation this was revolutionized when paper patterns became available.

Some of the drudgery was removed also by the first sewing machines. These, together with washing machines, were among the first appliances to be sold on the instalment plan, aided by colourful advertising, throughout the second half of the century. Paper dress patterns were first available in mid-century in England, where they were pioneered in *The English Woman's Domestic Magazine* published by Samuel and Isabella Beeton. Full-size patterns were available through mail order and this labour-saving innovation was such a success that publications in both Britain and the United States were quick to copy.

The purchase of fabric was not without the adulterations and trials of the period. Most books had hints for detecting doctored cloth.

"Seek for that [linen] which has a round close thread, and is perfectly white, for, if it be not white, at first, it will never afterwards become so. Much that is called linen, at the shops is half cotton, and does not wear so well as

J. David del

Lavieureux Imp. r. Lacepede, 38, Paris

AD. GOUBAUD, Edit. à Paris

cotton alone. Cheap linens are usually of this kind. It is difficult to discover which are all linen; but the best way is, to find a lot, presumed to be good, take a sample, wash it, and ravel it. If it be good, the rest of the lot will probably be so. If you cannot do this, draw a thread, each way, and if both appear equally strong, it is probably all linen."[6]

Many facets of life in the nineteenth century provoked public argument and clothes were no different. It is obvious that the low-necked dress would draw controversy.

The Evil of Low-Necked Dresses

"No lady should wear her dress so low as to make it quite noticeable or a special subject of remark.[7] . . . The fashion of wearing low-necked dresses on certain occasions thus leaving the neck and the upper part of the chest bare, is fraught with evil consequences. It would be less objectionable in countries uniformly warm; but that our daughters here in frigid and changeable climate, should expose to the chilling winds a vital part of the body, is one of the evils of fashion which should be discountenanced by every mother, and father, and brother. Of the unseemliness and reckless immodesty often connected with this exposure, it is not necessary to speak in this discussion."[8]

Whether wool should be worn next to the skin, and the exact number of undergarments needed, occupied the time and thoughts of many writers throughout the century. At the turn of the nineteenth century those who could afford woollen night clothes were pleased to wear them, but by mid-century there were second thoughts:

"Wearing flannel next the skin, through the night, is especially injurious, and therefore the woollen night-gowns of young children and invalids should never be worn next the skin. It has often been found that persons who have suffered from rheumatism, and on this account have worn flannel next the skin, have been relieved from this disease by simply leaving off the flannel."[8]

By 1882 the tide had turned, and wool next to the skin was favoured and thought to prevent early death, coughs, colds, diarrhea, dysenteries and fevers of all kinds. In fact, anything that prevented cold and kept the body warm was definitely in.

Newspapers as Protectors From Cold

"A newspaper, folded several times and laid across the chest during a cold walk or ride, is a most excellent protector. If the bed-clothing is not sufficiently warm, especially at hotels, two or three large newspapers spread on the bed between the blanket will secure a comfortable night, as far as cold is concerned."[8]

The corset was of great public concern, and although both medical and churchmen thundered against them, women went on wearing the garment. They were not new in the nineteenth century but during this time they reached their peak of restraint and became the subject of much moralizing. Corsets in the early years of the century were not confined to grown women. They were used also on little girls, who were laced into cotton and bone "stays", and were not unknown to gentlemen wishing to preserve a more youthful and military appearance. Women in the bush naturally discarded any form of stay, but as life prospered and fashion came to the forefront, the corset returned. It gave great impetus to the whaling industry. When both whale-bone and whale-oil were discarded, the depression was felt at sea. Towards the end of the century a new method of stiffening corsets was discovered, — Coraline, manufactured from the natural fibres of the Mexican Ixtle plant. Its use revolutionized the industry. These new-style garments were advertised extensively and quite often sold on the basis of money returned if not satisfied, after three weeks' wear. Women used elastic cord to lace the corset so that even tight-lacing would give somewhat with breathing.

Search Lights on Health

"About one-half the children born in this country die before they are five years of age, and no doubt this terrible mortality is largely due to this instrument of torture known as the *modern corset*. Tight lacing is the cause of infantile mortality. It slowly but surely takes the lives of tens of thousands, and so effectually weakens and diseases, so as to cause the untimely death of millions more."[9]

That there should be profound moralizing discussions on the clothes of the working classes was inevitable. Their clothes were bright and colourful and all followed fashion. This was something unheard of in the mother countries, and those with status resisted strenuously.

"But a love of dress has its perils for weak minds. Uncontrolled by good sense, and stimulated by personal vanity it becomes a temptation at first, and then a curse. The sewing girl, the chambermaid, and even the cook, must have their elegantly trimmed silk dresses and velvet cloaks for Sunday and holiday wear, and the injury done by this state of things to morals and manners of the poorer classes is incalculable."[8]

Fashion Hints

"A vulgar girl wears bright and glaring colours, fantastically made; a large flaring, red, yellow, or sky-blue hat, covered with a rainbow of ribbons, and all the rings and trinkets she can load upon her."[7]

"Single ladies dress less in fashionable society than married ones, and all more plainly and substantially for walking or travelling, than on other occasions."[7]
"Colours that harmonize forming the most agreeable combinations, in which are included all the latest and most fashionable shades and colours: black, yellow, bronze and light blue; black and scarlet; blue and chestnut; blue, brown, crimson and gold; orange, black and white; green, gold and mulberry; lilac, scarlet and white or black."[10]

"A fur hat for four or five dollars lasts longer and looks better than a silk hat."[7]

"Be as particular as you like about the cut of your pantaloons. Buy strong cloth that will not be tearing at every turn, and if you consult economy and

taste at the same time, let them be either black or very dark grey, when they will answer upon all occasions."[7]

"The vest allows of some fancy, but beware of being too fanciful. A black satin is proper for any person or any occasion. Nothing is more elegant than pure white."[7]

"The best dressed men wear the least jewelry. Of all things avoid showy chains, large rings, and geegaw pins and broaches (sic). All these things should be left to Negroes, Indians, and South Sea Islanders."[7]

"Keep a small whisk broom, wherever gentlemen hang their clothes, both upstairs and down, and get them to use it if you can."[6]

The first shoes were made at home or by travelling shoemakers who stayed long enough to outfit the family for a year. As villages grew, shoemakers established shops and took on apprentices. There are many early records of small boys damaging their shoes and going barefoot until it was too cold to step outdoors. Shoes were made at first from home-tanned leather and were fashioned on crude wooden lasts. In some areas they were pegged rather than sewn, because of the excessive dampness of some of the clearings, which rotted thread. Flax thread for shoes was often waterproofed and strengthened with beeswax. In women's shoes the height of the heels and the narrowness of the soles increased as the century progressed.

For Burnt Shoes
"Spread soft soap on them while still hot and when cold wash them, this softens the leather prevents it drawing up and will make them nearly as good as new."[11]

The knitting of stockings was a household industry with everyone taking part, often boys as well as girls. Old stockings were unravelled and remade for younger children. Silk stockings, owned of course only by the rich, brought about another household gadget — the wooden leg on which to dry them smooth and shapely.

Muddy roads dirtied clothes and, as a result, fastidious ladies wore travelling or overskirts. In some areas it was a common sight to see a row of muddy overskirts hanging in the drive shed or porch while the ladies were quilting or in church. Loyalist settlers were very familiar with the long over-petticoat called a foot-mantle or a weather skirt. As time went by, weather skirts became less cumbersome and were made of lighter and more waterproof materials.

To Render Great Coats Water-proof
"It is only necessary to melt an ounce of white wax in a quart of spirits of turpentine; and, when thoroughly mixed and cold, dip the coat in and hang up to dry. By this cheap and simple process any kind of cloth may be rendered impenetrable to the hardest rains, without sustaining injury."[12]

As money and industry flourished, more jewelry became fashionable. Some of the best examples are now collectors' pieces. There were a wide variety of pocket watches, many with ingenious alarm or striking devices. Women favoured the fob watch pinned to the dress bosom. Watches were also carried in a leather-lined pocket concealed in the waist seam of dresses. In a sentimental age, and in a period when families were often parting to take up new land, sentimental jewelry was in favour. Scenes of childhood, locks of hair and early photographs were often framed or enclosed in lockets.

At the beginning of the century, silver, gold and horn buttons were prized possessions, as were seal rings or fob seals for correspondence. Ear-rings and cameos were in fashion. Coral necklaces were given to lucky babies to ward off evil spirits and to ensure an easy teething. Diamonds sparkled with the growing wealth towards the end of the eighties, but good taste dictated that diamonds be worn only when the lamps were lighted. Because of the extraordinary preoccupation with death, there was a tremendous amount of mourning jewelry: pins, lockets and rings. Indeed, it was customary to give such souvenirs to close friends attending a funeral.

Towards the end of the century a different type of fashion note was printed for the "new" women:

Women in Employment

"For women who are engaged in some daily employment such as teachers, saleswomen and those who are occupied in literature, art or business of some sort, the dress should be somewhat different from the ordinary walking costume. Its material should be more serviceable, better fitted to endure the vicissitudes of the weather, and of quiet colours such as brown or gray and not easily soiled. Linen cuffs and collars are best suited to this kind of dress, gloves which can be easily removed, street walking boots, and for jewelry, plain cuff buttons, brooch and watch chain. The hat or bonnet should be neat and tasty with but few flowers or feathers."[10]

By the last quarter of the century there were clothes for every possible occasion for the well-dressed and the monied woman. She was now allowed to participate in a number of sports, for which suitable clothes were designed. It was recommended that she have a row of shot stitched to the bottom of skirts used when horseback riding, and she now acquired clothes to swim, play tennis, for croquet and archery.

Swimming

"There is no doubt that the less cumbersome the clothing the more beneficial the bath, and ladies who are fortunate in having private bathing places will find a flannel dress, made with a loose blouse waist and short closed drawers, very nearly perfection; but for the ordinary bather, who has to take her chance with many others, there is no better design than the one which also serves as a gymnastic suit, and consists of a sailor blouse, skirt and trousers. The skirt is plain in front, and there is no more fullness in either blouse or skirt than is necessary to its good appearance. The amount

of material required for this entire suit is a little less than nine yards. Twilled flannel, dark blue or Russian gray, is the most serviceable material for a bathing dress, as it does not chill or hold the water. White, black or red braids are the usual trimmings, put on broad and in clusters, or simply as bindings, according to taste."[8]

"The best form is the loose sacque, or the yoke waist, both of them to be belted in, and falling about midway between the knee and the ankle; an oilskin cap to protect the hair from the water, and marine socks to match the dress complete the outfit."[10]

In the main, fashion followed London and New York, but there were some truly Canadian ways of dressing. Some fashions were very colourful but have, unfortunately, been all but lost to us. The most authentic Canadian dress, of course, was that of the many Indian nations who in the early years did not wear white men's clothes. Their beadwork was remarkable. Among some groups social position was shown by the type of dress, particularly the headdress, ornaments and leggings. The voyageurs developed their own colourful costume of open shirt, blanket coat and brightly woven sashes. The dress of French Canada was similar, and in 1832 Joseph Bouchette, the Surveyor-General, had time to pen the following fashion notes:

"Till lately, the chief clothing of the population was wholly of their own manufacture, but the cheapness of English goods has in some degree induced a partial use thereof. Canadian cloth is, however, still almost universally used; and the grey *capot* of the *habitant* is the characteristic costume of the country. This *capot* is a large coat reaching to the knee, and is bound round the waist by a sash, which sash is usually every possible bright colour within the power of the dyer. This, with a straw-hat in summer, a *bonnet rouge* or a fur cap in winter, and a pair of moccasins made out of sole leather, complete the dress of the peasant. The women are clothed nearly after the fashion of a French peasant: a cap in place of a bonnet, with a dark cloth or stuff petticoat, a jacket (*mantelet*) sometimes of a different colour, and moccasins, the same as those of the men, form their every-day dress. On Sunday, they are gaily attired, chiefly after the English fashion, with only this difference — where the English wears one the Canadian girl wears half a dozen colours. Here, as in the case of the food, no penury is manifest: an exceeding neatness in their persons, and cleanliness, that first requisite to comfort, mark the people to be above the influence of want, and to be in that state of ease which permits them to pay due attention to decency of external appearance."[1]

Two short-lived fashions in Canada were the wearing of knee breeches and silk stockings, and the use of the wig. For a brief time after the Revolutionary War, knee breeches were much in vogue among government people and other officials. It is recorded that at the opening of the first parliament of Upper Canada at Newark,

"The people were in their best holiday attire. The men in long stockings, garters and shoes, with their hair in queues, surmounted by tri-corn hats; the women in high-waisted dresses, with tight sleeves and bunched-over elaborate petticoats."[2]

The knee breech fashion continued longest among the English establishment and the New England Loyalists. Other Canadians favoured trousers or pantaloons. It was not very long before women of all classes discarded their hoops and many-bunched petticoats which were both uncomfortable and clumsy, particularly in the clearings.

Canada was probably the last place where men wore powdered wigs over shaved heads. Towards the end of the eighteenth century, wigs were going out of style in Europe, but the slowness of communication and the tendency of the officials to cling to European formal finery no doubt made York, Montreal, Quebec and Halifax among the last places where the wig was seen. Confined to the wealthy, it was worn on dress occasions or for any public appearance outside the home. In the privacy of his home, a gentleman wore a cap, one type for reading another for sleeping. Wigs were extremely expensive and styles varied from year to year. They varied also with different professions. Some swelled out at the sides, others rose in puffs, some were turned under in heavy rolls, others hung in braids, or curls known as queues. Wigs were hard to keep clean, but a wealthy man would own several in different styles. The most expensive were made of human hair, but others were made of horse, goat and mohair and even cows' tails. Each type of wig was named: grave-full-bottom; giddy-feather-top; fox-tail, etc. The back was bound and braided with ribbon, usually black, but colours were permissible if the wearer were young.

As wigs went out of fashion they were replaced in the same society, for a very short time, with powdered hair, — an untidy, dirty and troublesome fashion that ruined clothes. Hair was soaked in oil or rubbed with bear grease or pomatum to make the white powder adhere. Frequently the hair ends were tied with ribbon and put in a "wig-bag" to protect the coat collar. Regardless of the rising costs of wheat and its periodic scarcity, the British Army during the reign of George III used over six thousand pounds of flour annually for hair powder. Men made their own from flour mixed with a favourite perfume and stored it in glass bottles or cedar boxes.

Many visitors as late as the eighteen-seventies seemed to detect a difference in the Canadian way of dress even though most settlements were very close to the United States border.

"It may be imagination, but we fancy that we can already detect a difference in general appearance of our fellow passengers — that the men are shorter and broader built, the women plumper and rosier. Their style of dress is certainly different. Across the frontier chimney-pot hats, Melton or beaver overcoats, bonnets and mantles are most in vogue; here fur caps, frieze and homespun dreadnoughts, hats with 'clouds' drawn over them, and stout Scotch plaids. That in our eyes they should seem more prepossessing is only natural — are they not our own people?"[3]

How did they dress? Status, climate and local conditions had a great deal to do with the choice of clothing. Among the most colourful Canadians were the prisoners at Kingston described by Mrs. Moodie as being warm and comfortable . . . though certainly not very elegant, consisting (for it was late in the fall)

"of a thick woollen jacket, one side of it being brown, the other yellow, with trowsers to correspond, a shirt of coarse factory cotton, but very clean, and stout shoes, and warm knitted woollen socks. The letters P.P. for 'Provincial Penitentiary', are sewed in coloured cloth upon the dark side of the jacket."[4]

The extremely severe climate, before large areas of forest were cleared, dictated as much clothing as possible. Mrs. Trail[1] mentions a work garment known as "logging shirt". It seems to have been an over-shirt of coarse hempen cloth. In the days before the bush was filled with sportsmen, the hunters tried to distinguish themselves from the game by wearing white overgarments. While the winters were cold the summers were unbearably hot with swarms of nipping insects. The following from *Adventures in Canada* describes a summer of the eighteen-forties in western Ontario.

"My sisters never went with so little clothing before; and, indeed, it was astonishing how their circumferences collapsed under the influence of the sun. As to us, we thought only of coolness. Coarse straw hats, with broad brims, costing about eight-pence a piece, with a handkerchief in the crown to keep the heat off the head; a shirt of blue cotton, wide trowsers of dark printed calico or, indeed of anything thin, boots, composed our dress. But this was elaborate, compared with that adopted by a gentleman who was leading a bachelor life back in the bush some distance from us. A friend went to see him one day, and found him frying some bacon on a fire below a tree before his door; — a potato pot hanging by a chain over part of it, from a bough — his only dress being a shirt, boots, a hat, and a belt round his waist, with a knife in it."[5]

The heavy leather belts, known in the vernacular as "leathern", were much commented upon by English visitors, because of their heaviness and their numerous attachments, including an axe and a large Bowie-knife.

It is not correct to believe that all settlers were clothed in sombre home-spun. Nothing could be further from the truth, for as soon as there was a little money available there was a great tendency to buy bright and gaudy materials. In Quebec, the discarding of commercial fabrics and the resuming of sombre grey homespun by both men and women, particularly towns-people, was one of the overt signs of the 1837 rebellion. This was a form of boycott of imported British goods, a protest against the Establishment.

Homespun was woven in many soft colours as well as in intricate patterns. The many quilts and comforters still to be found are evidence of the exciting colours and patterns that were known. The early fashions were diverse and

so they continued throughout the century. As time, money and leisure increased the people adopted clothes for every occasion.

Many religious denominations had a style of dress peculiar to themselves. To "dress gaudy" was considered by some to be a sign of pride and worldliness. Subtle differences among such groups included the tall stand-up collars worn by Mennonites and Tunkers, and the scoop bonnets for Quaker women.

All women wore caps, both day and night. They chose elaborate starched and frilled ones for day wear, with the strings and ribbons falling down either side of the face or tied under the chin as fashion demanded. Night caps were plainer and were usually made of linen, with linen ruffles "as cotton borders will not last as long as the cap."[6] Nightwear in general was voluminous. Men's nightwear was made like their shirts, except longer. Women's night gowns had some goring, but the fabric requirements at mid-century were five yards for a long gown, two and one half for a short one.

In the early years, expensive broadcloth was known and owned, but such professionally made fabric was kept for formal wear: weddings, funerals and dances. It was expected to last for many years. Ordinary clothing was homespun and "linsey-woolsey" (a mixture of linen and wool) was a favourite for women's dresses, often woven into stripes of different widths and colours. Early clothing was completely home-made, from the wool carding and dyeing to the spinning and weaving. Gradually, as mills were established, one less chore was done at home. Sometimes homespun continued to be made, but the dyeworks might first colour the raw wool, or the finished cloth would go to the mill for a final gloss finish, or to be fulled to prevent shrinkage.

DR. WARNER'S
❖ CORALINE ❖ CORSET. ❖

Patented Nov. 27, 1878, April 20 and Nov. 23, 1880.

Its Advantages are:

1st. It CANNOT be broken. **A Reward of $10** will be paid for every strip of Coraline which breaks with four months' ordinary wear in a corset.

2d. It is more pliable than whalebone, and so adapts itself more readily to the movements of the body. This makes it much more comfortable and healthful.

3d. It is not affected by cold, heat or moisture. A corset boned with Coraline will last one half longer than one boned with whalebone.

The Coraline Corset is made throughout of superior materials, and is warranted in every respect. If not found entirely satisfactory the purchase money will be refunded.

In many areas cloth fulling was the occasion for a bee. All the neighbours came to help twist and pull the dampened cloth. This was the occasion for singing songs with a strong rhymthmic beat as teams of men and women twisted and pounded the wet cloth. Other customs connected with spinning included the courting etiquette of a young man riding across country to help a young woman spool the quills of her loom, when his intentions were serious.

Finally came the horseless carriage and with it a new way of life, and a new approach to dressing. Since there had never been anything quite like it before, the designers and fashion writers were somewhat puzzled at first, but not for long.

"Of late certain ladies' tailors have pointed out that there should be a great similarity between a motoring costume and any forms of sensible yachting dress; also it has been proved by experience that every form of short fur is preferable to the long-haired kinds, and that in some ways the two ideal furs for horseless carriage wear are Persian lamb and sable. A veil must also be regarded as a necessity.

"A word may be said concerning the motor garments worn by men. The King, who has now for some years past led the fashion, not only with regard to the Anglo-Saxon race, but also as regards the dandies of every nation, when motoring wears in preference a neat dark blue suit and a yachting cap."[13]

No wonder the more unsophisticated and curious ran alongside to have a second look.

In the early days, a bride wore a new dress of style and fabric which would make it serviceable for many years to come. This custom was long retained in many parts of the country. Silk and printed muslins were popular fabrics and the shades were usually neutral, but she was allowed to have it a little more elaborately trimmed than was usual. "But if the bride wishes to attract as little attention as possible, she will not make herself conspicuous by a too showy dress".[10]

By the 1880's, the bridal dress as we know it was popular with all classes of society and in all the more settled areas. The full dress was white from head to toe, with a high neckline and covered arms. It was customary for the bride to wear on her head a wreath of maiden-blush roses and orange blossoms. The blossoms were sometimes removed after the ceremony, but the roses remained until she left for her wedding journey, or to go to her new home. Widows too were married in white, the only difference being the lack of veil and orange blossoms.

From mid-century the preoccupation with death demanded a rigid mourning etiquette. Whether this stemmed from the Queen's widowhood, or the decimation of families from epidemics, or the loss of loved ones who went to settle new lands, or whether it was the superficial sentimentality that then permeated life, it is hard to say. Nevertheless, the rules were so rigid that some families must have been in mourning almost constantly. A widow wore deep lustreless black for one year, the second year she wore silk trimmed with crape, and during the final six months she could with propriety wear grey, violet and white. Parents were mourned for a year, so was a child. Grandparents were mourned for six months, as were friends who left legacies.

Mourning

"Deep mourning requires the heaviest of black serges, bombazine, lustreless alpaca, delaine, merino, or similar heavily clinging material with collars and cuffs of crape. Mourning garments should have little or no trimming; no flounces, ruffles or bows are allowable. If the dress is not made en suite, then a long or square shawl of barege or cashmere with crape border is worn. The bonnet of black crape; a hat is inadmissable. The veil is of crape or barege with a heavy border; black gloves and black bordered handkerchief. In winter dark furs may be worn with the deepest mourning. Jewelry is strictly

forbidden, and all pins, buckles etc. must be of jet. Lustreless alpaca and black silk trimmed with crape may be worn in second mourning, with white collars and cuffs. The crape veil is laid aside for net or tulle, but the jet jewelry is still retained. A still less degree of mourning is indicated by black and white, purple and grey, or a combination of these colours. Crape is still retained in bonnet trimming and crape flowers may be added. Light gray, white and black, and light shades of lilac, indicate a slight mourning. Black lace bonnet, with white or violet flowers, supersedes crape, and jet and gold jewelry is worn. The deepest mourning excludes kid gloves, they should be of cloth, silk or thread; mourning handkerchiefs should be of very sheer linen with a border of black, very wide for close mourning, narrower as the black is lightened. Mourning silks should be perfectly lustreless and the ribbons worn without any gloss. The mourning for children under twelve years of age is white in summer and gray in winter, with black trimmings, belt, sleeve ruffles and bonnet ribbons."[10]

Some Questions on Dress

1. Are the mothers of men who rule the world found among the loose-robed women, or among the women who dress in closer-fitting apparel?

2. Is there not the greatest improvement of the human race where fashions of dress are most subject to change?

3. Can a people who go naked, or only half-clothed, be Christian, or ever become Christian unless they clothe themselves?

4. Are not those nations most morally refined in civilization and Christianity where the costume of men and women differ most essentially?[14]

REFERENCES

[1] *The British Dominions in North America*, J. Bouchette, London, 1831.
[2] *Pen Pictures of Early Pioneer Life in Upper Canada*, M. Sherck, Toronto, 1905.
[3] *The Gentleman Immigrant*, W. Stamer, London, 1874.
[4] *Life in the Clearings*, Moodie, London, 1853.
[5] *Adventures in Canada*, Geikie, Philadelphia, n.d.
[6] *A Treatise on Domestic Economy*, Beecher, New York, 1849.
[7] *Ladies' Indispensable Assistant*, Anonymous, New York, 1851.
[8] *Home and Health*, Anonymous, London, Ontario, 1882.
[9] *Search Lights on Health*, B. G. Jefferis, Toronto, 1894.
[10] *Our Deportment*, Young, Paris, Ontario, 1883.
[11] *The Improved Housewife*, Webster, Boston, 1856.
[12] *The Housekeeper's Receipt Book*, Anonymous, London, 1816.
[13] *The Woman at Home*, A. Swan, London, 1903.
[14] *Manners*, Hale, Boston, 1868.

Ladies' Indispensable Assistant

CHAPTER TEN

Everything we know today in the way of cosmetics, from rouge to eyelash dye, was made and used, although a glance at the paintings and photographs of the period makes it hard to believe. The women look so well scrubbed and innocent of all artifice; and who would know that the man hiding behind a flowing beard had dyed it with walnut shells for the picture-taking occasion.

Cosmetics were used by both sexes and instruction was available in almanacs from drug houses and in books on etiquette, fashion and cooking. To say that everyone was using them is generalizing. Much depended on the social and economic status of the user, the progress of a particular settlement and the local religious beliefs.

Loyalist women certainly knew all about scent and cosmetic making and how to take advantage of the many natural dyes and sweet-smelling plants. There does not seem to be any evidence that Canadian women distilled their own essential oils. However, this was not really necessary because manufacturing commenced quite early and drug houses both wholesale and retail were able to take care of the demands. As early as 1836, Anna Jameson[1] wrote of the high quality of the apothecary shop in Toronto, which had a large selection of imported products as well as the home produced mixtures.

How well scrubbed our subjects were is disputable. All agreed that beauty and social acceptance began with the bath, although the general public was reluctant. Reminiscing of his boyhood in the settlements of western Ontario, George Stanley talks of toilet facilities in the 1840's.

"Most of them were content to put up with the very rudest accommodation and conveniences; one room, containing several beds, often holding not only the whole household, but any passing stranger. How to get in and out, unseen, was the greatest difficulty. I have often been in trouble about it myself, but it must surely have been worse for the young women of the family. As to any basin or ewer in the room, they were Capuan luxuries in the wild bush. 'I'll thank you for a basin, Mrs. Smith', said I, one morning, anxious to make myself comfortable for the day, after having enjoyed her husband's hospitality overnight. It was gloriously bright outside, though the sun had not yet shown himself over the trees. 'Come, this way, Mr. Stanley; I'll give it to you here', said Mrs. Smith. Out she went, and lifted a small round tin pie-dish, that would hardly hold a quart, poured some water into it from the pail at the door, which held the breakfast water as well, and set it on the top of a stump close at hand, with the injunction to 'make haste, for there was a hole in the bottom, and if I didn't be quick the water would all be gone'. Luckily I was all ready; but there was no offer of soap, and so I had to make my hands fly hither and thither at a great rate, and finish as best I could by a hard rubbing with a canvas towel".[2]

It is not surprising that North Americans were thought to be the least washed of all civilized nations. The majority felt that water applied occasionally to face, feet, hands and neck, was sufficient. There were, of course, portable bathtubs made of metal, wood and papier maché, but it was not until the latter years of the century that installed tubs were common, and then only for the wealthy. Early baths were often made of lead, surrounded with luxurious cabinet work. Miss Beecher, in 1849, had designed a system of running hot water, but this idea was considered merely curious. Judging by the admonitions in the press, most folk thought that pulling silk stockings over unwashed feet was acceptable. However, by the end of the century the bath was accepted and women were making their own water-softeners — usually bags containing almond meal, oatmeal or orris root and sweet smelling herbs.

Hair was worn long, and all were advised to brush and comb it every

day until the tresses were like those of a well-groomed horse. In the early days, women wore caps indoors and these gave some protection from the dust and soot. When caps went out of style, morning or dusting caps came in for housework.

A beauty writer at the turn of the century came up with this startling observation and opinion:

"Among the lower classes, who give little or no attention to their hair, one often sees girls endowed with tresses of enviable thickness and lovely colour. I have noticed many a domestic servant whose opulent though dusty mass of twists and plaits beneath her cap many a mondaine might envy. There have been speculations as to the reason for the scanty heads of hair which women to-day lament. My own opinion is that our foremothers owed their

127

luxuriant locks to the pomades which were sedulously rubbed into the scalp. We have transferred the pomade to our faces, and the hair has followed it."[3]

Macassar oil and pomades of all kinds were used to give additional sheen to the hair. Their universal use led to the hobby of making small protective furniture covers, known as anti-macassars. Similarly, hats and bonnets were lined with yellow oiled silk to prevent injury to the hat itself and to preserve its appearance.

Pomatum was first introduced not only as a hair restorative and an aid to shining hair, but also to keep hair powder sticking to the hair when powdered hair was still fashionable. It long remained a hair dressing when powdering was barely a memory. One of Canada's first exports was bear pomatum, which went both to the United States and Europe. The following advertisement comes from a Buffalo drug house catalogue for the year 1856.
"*Bear's Pomatum*: This is manufactured by ourselves from the bear's fat as it is supplied to us in the fresh state by the hunters of Canada and the West. Our arrangements with the backwoods enable us to supply the pure and genuine article. Bear's oil has an unfailing reputation as an article of the toilet. It is as popular now as fifty years ago."[4]

People worried about losing hair particularly as it was cut off at the first sign of serious illness. Recurring migraine headaches were thought responsible for thinning locks. A salve of bay rum and glycerine was used to counteract thinning hair, although some favoured the cut half of an onion rubbed over the scalp. The most common hair rinse was milk.

An Excellent Way of Improving the Hair
"Once in three days take some rich unskimmed milk that has been made sour by standing it in the sun. Stir it up, so as to mix all through it the cream that has collected on the surface. Wash the hair with this, rubbing it well into the roots. Let it remain on the hair about a quarter of an hour or more. Then wash it off. This is an Asiatic process, and if continued every third day, seldom fails to render the hair of young people thick, soft, and glossy."[5]

Men encouraged the growth of hair with the use of brandy rubbed over the skin. When the growing temperance movement put an end to that method, they turned to salt and water. All felt the real enemy was the "stove pipe hat".

As time passed, men cut their hair shorter, but the beard was more flourishing than ever and a great deal of attention was lavished on it.

"It should be thoroughly washed and brushed at least twice a day, as dust is sure to accummulate in it, and it is very easy to suffer it to become objectionable to one's self as well as to others."[6]

Many lotions were used to encourage the more luxuriant growth of hair, mostly based on ammonia and colognes. Shaving was done with a straight razor, and the village barber shop became the local men's club. Most men left their own shaving mug with the proprietor, with the result that in the days before public hygiene was enforced, "Barber's Itch" was a common complaint. Mixtures of suet and olive oil were the salves, used with lavender and thyme to hide the smell. Razor strops were made at home and the best came from the belts of old threshing machines. Alternatively, well-greased kip-leather was used.

"Oil it well with wagon grease. Be sure not to take the grease from the outside of the wheel, as it is filled with too much dust and dirt."[7]

There were after-shave lotions of sweet oil, lime water and oil of roses — always applied in small quantities with the forefinger.

Because of the prevailing fashions, women needed large numbers of hair pins. This required careful shopping because most were heavy, large, crudely made and sharply pointed.

Something New for the Ladies!
"These hair pins are made of the best steel wire, the only metal that will retain magnetism. The fact of the pins being magnetized can be tested by the power one has for attracting another. By being constantly in contact with the hair they impart to it vigor and strength. *Preventing the hair turning grey.* Preventing the *headache.* Preventing *soreness in the head.* We do not claim that these *hair pins* will cure all diseases that females are liable to but what we allege above we can prove by thousands of ladies in New York and elsewhere who have used Them." (An advertisement of 1882)

Dandruff was eased with mixtures of egg yolk and bay rum, but babies' scalps were anointed with chicken fat, unsalted butter, or sweet cream.

Cure for Dandruff
"A cooling diet, free use of seltzer water and the free use of the ointment made according to the recipe given, will cure most obstinate cases: Take of lard one tablespoonful and rub in a quarter of a teaspoonful of tar (not coal tar, but pine tar). Rub this salve well into the scalp every night, and by morning the disagreeable odor will be gone."[7]

With the passing of years, fashion changed from straight hair for women, looped and braided in the Grecian manner, to curls and frizzes augmented with false pieces. Hair was curled with soft paper or kid rollers, and waves were pinched-in with hot irons. One of the favourite setting lotions was gum tragacanth and rose water, nothing more than gummy water. No wonder it was claimed to keep hair in any position regardless of the weather! A tea made of boiled quince seed was recommended to keep the forehead hair in place when out in the wind.

Most commercial hair dyes were harmful, being based on lead and its derivatives. Many people therefore made their own, using such wild plants as vines, willow bark, raspberry canes, myrtle leaves, butternut hulls, green walnut shells, as well as beet seeds and alum. The colouring was cooked in rainwater, wine or vinegar with the addition of sage and marjoram. These herbs were in the cephalic group and were thought to contribute to the well-being of the head and brain.

To Restore False Hair

"The switches and curls and frizzes which fashion demands should be worn, will fade in course of time; and though they matched the natural hair perfectly at first, they will finally present a lighter tint. If the hair is brown this can be remedied. Obtain a yard of dark brown calico. Boil it until the colour has well come out into the water. Then into this water dip the hair and take it out and dry it."[6]

Eyebrows and eyelashes were darkened with India ink and walnut juice, and the sought-after arched brow was obtained by "pinching them between the fingers several times a day".[6] Lashes and brows were rubbed with olive oil to promote growth, and the split lash ends were trimmed with scissors. When eyebrows were burnt off by fire, (a common accident), growth was encouraged with a mixture of quinine and alcohol. Until they grew back, burnt cork or cloves disguised the bare spot. Although there was much preoccupation with beautifying the eyes, there was little real care for the health of the eye. Regardless of advice, the thrifty liked to keep the lights dim and the use of glasses was not encouraged.

"Short-sightedness is not always a natural defect. It may be acquired by bad habits in youth. A short-sighted person should supply himself with glasses exactly adapted to his wants; but it is well not to use these glasses too constantly, as, even when they perfectly fit the eye, they really tend to shorten the sight. Unless one is very short-sighted, it is best to keep the glasses for occasional use, and trust ordinarily to the unaided eye."[7]

The extreme range of temperature between indoors and out during the winter months, plus the hot sun of summer led to the making of salves, lotions and various skin creams, mostly based on oil or lard. There were astringent washes, ranging from horse-radish grated into milk to brandy mixed with rose water.

The medical men, of course, disapproved of cosmetics and recommended greater use of a fruit and vegetable diet. Cucumber was at last to reach the table raw, and it served a double purpose. Faces were also to be rubbed with it. Indeed, all fruit and vegetable waters were to be saved and used as lotions. Women were warned that they could not use cosmetics undetected; their gentlemen friends would soon find them out. Pesky pimples were washed with either carbolic acid or corrosive sublimate diluted with oil of almonds. This was said to remove all pimples within a few days.

Fair skin was a mark of beauty, and certainly a status symbol indicating that the woman did no work outdoors in the strong sunlight. To this end women usually veiled themselves before venturing forth. If the worst happened and the skin became tanned it had to be bleached, usually with a concoction of milk, lemon juice and the best brandy. Freckles were removed with corrosive sublimate or the older remedy of chickweed juice or elderflower juice diluted in water. Age spots were eliminated with sulphur water and lemon juice.

Hands reddened by the weather and the use of strong home-made soaps were whitened with a variety of lotions, including Laureline which is still being made and sold at church bazaars seventy years later.

Laureline —
The Perfect Hand Whitener
"Take two ounces of glycerine, one ounce of alcohol, one-fourth ounce of gum tragacanth, one half ounce of rosewater or violet perfume, one pint of water; soak the tragacanth in the water two days, then strain and add the other ingredients. Cut the glycerine with the alcohol. If it should be too thick add a little more water and alcohol. Bottle, and it is ready to use."[7]

Other hand-softening and whitening remedies included the application of a coat of mutton tallow just before going to bed. "Beauty gloves" were prepared by filling large soft gloves with a mixture of tallow and glycerine, to be worn while doing housework as well as when sleeping. A surprise for husbands was the wearing of cloth mittens to bed. These were filled with wet bran or oatmeal. Alternatively, Jamaica rum

and lemon juice was rubbed into the reddened skin.

To Cure Reddened Hands
"Soak the hands nightly in hot water for two weeks; this will also be of benefit to those who have flushed faces."[7]

Hot water and massage was used also to whiten arms in time for the winter balls. "Many women are much annoyed when the season for wearing ball dresses comes around, by the red and rough appearance of their arms and necks. Powder is useless to remedy the evil, since the white coating speedily rubs off upon the broadcloth of the wearer's luckless partner".[8]

A Soothing Cream
"This prescription is used by hunters to keep away the black flies and mosquitoes, it is said to leave the skin very clear and fair, it is as follows: Mix one spoonful of the best tar in a pint of pure olive oil or almond oil, by heating the two together in a tin cup set in boiling water. Stir till completely mixed and smooth, putting in more oil if the compound is too thick to run easily. Rub this on the face before going to bed, and lay patches of soft cloth

How to Take Care of the Hands.

A PERFECT ARM AND HAND.

on the cheeks and forehead to keep the tar from rubbing off."[6]

Wrinkles were helped with lotions, (always keep the skin damp), and moralizing, (never scowl even if the sun be in your eyes). Scrawny necks were considered the result of feather boas and constricting clothes, and lines around the mouth were the result of bad passions and cunning curiosity.

To Remove Wrinkles and Facial Lines

"Put some powder of best myrrh upon an iron plate, sufficiently heated to melt the gum gently, and when it liquifies cover your head with a napkin and hold your face over the myrrh at a proper distance to receive the fumes without inconvenience."[7]

Oral care was rudimentary. One of the suggestions to keep the front teeth white was to wrap a handkerchief around the finger and massage them twice a day. Slightly more hair-raising was this advice:

To Whiten Teeth

"This preparation is used by dentists. Pure muriatic acid one ounce, water one ounce, honey two ounces, mix thoroughly. Take a toothbrush, and wet it thoroughly with this preparation and briskly rub the black teeth, and in a moment's time they will be perfectly white. Then immediately wash out the mouth well with water that the acid may not act on the enamel of the teeth."[9]

Gums were strengthened with washes of red wine and oil of almonds. Women firmly believed they were the weaker sex when it came to teeth. It was thought that a tooth was lost with every childbirth.

To Sweeten the Breath

"Take three hours before breakfast a dose of chlorate of potassa in sweetened water and the breath will be as sweet as an infant's of two months."[10]

Lipsalve was used both as a cure and protection for sore lips, and to colour them a becoming red. Many women bit their lips to make them glow, others coloured mixtures of beeswax and lard. Rouge was made by boiling scarlet cuttings left after dressmaking with lemon juice and thickening slightly. Other women, particularly in Quebec, favoured the juice of the beet. By mid-century, commercial preparations were being sold. The following is taken from a drug house catalogue of 1856:

"The force of the objection to the use of rouges depends very much on the motives of the fair one who employs them. An 'old campaigner', flushing her withered cheeks with colour long since denied by nature, in the vain hope of inveigling some imaginary admirer into a sacrifice of his bachelor independence, is, in very truth, a 'painted Jezebel'. But where its use originates in an innocent desire to please; where the red tinge of the cheek is not falsified by wrinkled, yellow forehead above, and a scrawny neck below them; or when the gay season has been lengthy, and Lent comes on but slowly; when gas light, and dancing, and late hours, have paled the cheek which on Christmas day glowed like the rose, it is a fair stratagem to call on art to come to the assistance of nature. There is a degree of humbug about all this, certainly, but rouge is not the only humbug known to ladies fair; as witness cotton and whalebone! We have liquid rouge (safe, innocent, and stands perspiration); also Theater Rouge and Vegetable Rouge. Lip salve at once a rouge and an emollient."[4]

Face powder was obtainable commercially, although many women preferred to make their own from flour and starch sifted through silk. In the eighteenth century, pearl face powder was known, and as late as 1829 druggists were told to stock it for the use of the curious and the rich. Generally, commercial face powder had injurious ingredients like lead and other metallic substances and this sometimes played the lady quaint tricks:

"If they [powders] contain mineral ingredients, any exposure to sulphuretted hydrogen gas, or to the sulphurous gas of a soft-coal fire, will decompose them, and the lady who left her toilet with a brilliant pearly complexion, may look in the glass an hour afterward and find herself turned to a dingy brown, or a very dirty black."[4]

Colognes and perfumes were used by all. Many of the familiar names sold today were known and used. In remote areas women followed the old custom of steeping sweet smelling plants in alcohol. So important was scent to a well-bred woman that in 1836 Mrs. Anna Jameson[1] travelled Lake Huron in an open bateau, equipped with her notebooks and a

supply of cologne. Colognes were advertised with give-away cards impregnated with scent. Some of these are still faintly fragrant almost a hundred years later. Perfumes were advertised then, almost as much as they are today, and gave as many promises. Some were for both men and women. Hence this advertising of 1856, when there were "German" colognes, "Hungary Waters" as well as the following:

"*West End*: a perfume that is aristocratic, gentlemanly, dignified. Just the thing for statesmen and statuesque women."

"*Lavender*: it is chaste and lady-like, yet spicy. Just now it is very fashionable, and it can never be long otherwise."

"*Geranium*: a neat spicy fragrance, the emblem of the flower is 'Gentility'."

"*Jasmine*: very neat perfume. It is always in good taste."

"*Patchouly*: much admired a few years ago, and still popular. Brought into use as a preventive of moths in clothing, it now holds a permanent rank among perfumes."

"*Orange Flowers*: sprinkled on the head and bridal wreath or artificial orange flowers used at weddings."

"*Mignonette*: a little too pungent for common use, but appropriate to a little spicy woman, with jet black eyes, and given to repartee."

"*Sweet Pink*: fresh and grateful. Rather juvenile, and does not harmonize with old ladies."[4]

A summertime occupation was making pot-pourri for the parlour, and pomander for the linen closets. Pot-pourri was basically dried highly perfumed plants mixed with common salt and orris root, plus the addition of spices. The mixture was kept in stoppered pottery jars and uncorked before the parlour was used. Pomanders were clove-studded apples developed from the Elizabethan moth preventive. The fruit was again rolled in spice and orris root. Orange pomanders were made only when oranges became cheaper and less of a luxury.

Towards the end of the century, the increase in money and leisure brought a greater interest not only in cosmetics, but in deportment and the figure itself. White arms and a languid figure were esteemed, and girls spent hours with arms stretched overhead to attain this goal.

"As the arm is always in proportion with the other portions of the body, consequently a well-shaped arm, small hands and small wrists, with full muscular development, is a charm and beauty not inferior to the face itself and those who have well-shaped arms may be proud of them, because they generally keep company with a fine bust and a fine figure."[7]

The fine figure is somewhat ample to our eyes, but even in those days, those of too fine a figure sought to reduce it with strong sassafras tea. There was a great emphasis on the bust measurement, which hardly tallies with our preconceived ideas of nineteenth century propriety.

"Full busts — In the female beauty of physical development there is nothing than can equal full breasts. It is an indication of good health and good maternal qualities. Cotton and all other false forms simply show the value of natural ones. All false forms are easily detected because large natural ones will generally quiver and move at every step, while the artificial ones will manifest no expression of life. As women look so much better with artificial paddings and puffings than she does without, modern society should waive all objections to their use."[7]

To obtain this desirable form without puffings, women took enormous doses of cod liver oil and massaged themselves with linseed oil and rosewater. Other peculiar beauty problems that set women writing to their favourite magazine were round shoulders (stretch several times a day) and knock knees. For these the advice was more detailed:

"I commenced the practice of placing a small book between my knees, and tying a handkerchief tight round my ankles. This I did two or three times a day, increasing the substance at every fresh trial, until I would hold a brick with ease breadthways."[11]

As late as the 1860's men put small sweet-smelling sachets in their jacket pockets. They were called "casselettes" and were thought to be "a very neat and tasty piece of foppery".[4] Mothers warned their headstrong daughters against making the acquaintance of men who had the smell of scented lozenges or aromatic cachous on their breath.

". . . the use of them is a confession, out of one's own mouth, that he has either a naturally bad breath, bad teeth, uses tobacco, or has been drinking. Such a story does the little cachou tell to the nostrils of the fair damsel who inhales its fragrance; but with the usual charitable forgiveness of her sex, she attributes it only to the mildest of the sins enumerated—that abominable cigar — and unhesitatingly waltzes down the room with a young reprobate who is so 'chuck' that he dances out of time, treads on her toes, bangs her against the piano, and finally, his eyes growing glassy, and his lips indicating a rebellious condition of the inner man, he professes himself 'vewy tiawd', and makes off for the fresh air and a little brandy to kill that 'dooced champagne'."[4]

REFERENCES

1 *Winter Studies and Summer Rambles in Canada*, Jameson, London, 1838.
2 *Adventures in Canada*, Geikie, Philadelphia, n.d.
3 *Woman at Home*, Swan, London, 1903.
4 *Hints on Various Subjects*, Anonymous, Buffalo, 1856.
5 *The Lady's Receipt Book*, Leslie, Philadelphia, 1847.
6 *Our Deportment*, Young, Paris, Ontario, 1883.
7 *Household Guide*, B. G. Jefferis, Toronto, 1894.
8 *Home and Health*, Anonymous, London, Ontario, 1882.
9 *The White House Cook Book*, Zieman and Gillette, Toronto, 1899.
10 *The Peerless Cook Book*, Anonymous, Montreal, n.d.
11 *The Economical Cook Book*, Warren, New York, n.d.

Treasures of
Use and Beauty

Fortunately for us our forebears were collectors who never threw anything away, because it might be useful. Indeed it is useful to us to help complete a picture of everyday living. They filled their attics and barns and conscientiously collected and saved vast amounts of ephemera in albums which otherwise might have been lost or used to light a fire. Albums were the rage throughout the period, and their numbers and complexity grew as time went by. They were set on parlour tables together with folio books of drawings, steel engravings, water colours of the Holy Land, and volumes of pressed flowers and ferns. In many homes looking at albums was the only distraction offered to children on a Sunday, when all else was forbidden.

The covers of albums showed the excessive ornamentation beloved by book-binders of that time. Some were home crafted with poker work, tastefully decorated with sea-shells or covered with woven raffia. Autograph albums made the scene around the 1880's and the vogue continued well into this century. Friends and acquaintances had to record suitable poems, uplifting thoughts or witticisms for posterity. Books on etiquette, home encyclopedias and housekeeping books had chapters to help people through this fad. How they scan can be seen from these 1881 examples:

> *Though oceans now between us roll,*
> *And distant be our lot;*
> *Though we should meet nor more, sweet maid,*
> *Forget me not.*[1]

> *I kissed her little tiny hand,*
> * I pressed her fairy form,*
> *I vowed I'd shield her from the blast,*
> * And from the world's cold storm,*
> *She raised her gentle eyes to mine,*
> * They were filled with drops of woe*
> *With trembling lips she faintly said,*
> * "Confound you — let me go!"*[1]

> *Woman's love*
> *Like ivy, it is often seen*
> *To wear an everlasting green —* (no sarcasm)
> *Like ivy too, it's apt to cling*
> *Too often 'round a worthless thing.*[1]

If nothing else, it was a time of the poetaster.

Depending on circumstances and social position, time and money could be spent by increasing numbers of women on hobbies, collections and general trivia. The advent of the more leisurely life varies with the area of the country, but generally from mid-century onwards there were many well-established families and an increasing number of people, women particularly, who had time to spare.

Women sewed and embroidered but no longer was it a necessity to keep the family clothed with their own efforts. Indeed, the fashionable now favoured seamstresses. A great deal of time was spent on embellishment and, eventually, everything was ornamented. There was not a corner of a home that was not crammed with decorated items. The activities of the Queen were followed closely; many favourite embroidery stitches were called "Kensington", or pieces were worked "in the manner of Windsor". Shawls too, both for the person and to drape over furniture, gained their impetus from Victoria, as did the popularity of tartan, paisley and lace, and no doubt the excessive indulgence in mourning and all its appurtenance.

The ladies knitted, crocheted, tatted, beaded and embroidered all manner of household items. Innumerable patterns were available in magazines and needlework books to help them. They favoured bird cage covers, hyacinth bowl mats, gold fish bowl cosies, music stool couvrettes, cheese serviettes, cruet mats, caps for morning wear, candlestick doilies, antimacassars and tasselled watch-holders. There were pillows for sofas, needlecases, slipper holders, wall protectors (for greasy heads that leaned against a wall) wall protectors (behind wash stands) firescreens, paper and letter holders, screens, handkerchief cases, pin cushions (filled with iron filings and bran), foot-stools, work baskets, lace work and net work. They made a form of many-coloured patchwork known as Kaleidoscopic, or Kensington, used for pillows, bedspreads and table covers — and much much more.

There was beadwork for purses, reticules and slippers, borders for rugs, Gothic chairs embroidered to look similar "to those in the private apartments of Windsor Castle", flower work and braiding, cording and tasselling. There were slippers of satin to bead, silver-wire baskets to work with silks, fireside caps with gems, flowers to be embroidered and raised on velvet. There was gold-braid work and the re-embroidering of lace. The possibilities were endless.

Fine needlework had been for centuries an inherited tradition among educated women and the task was started early with young daughters. Certainly a sampler of the more common stitches was under way by the sixth year. Many examples still exist of completed samplers dated in the eighth year, usually worked on unbleached linen or canvas. Many are as bright today as when they were finished.

In the 1860's stamped needlework was invented in Germany and although this brought the art to the masses, the working of the sampler was eventually lost, as were many of the finer and more intricate stitches. However, embroidery became easier and much more popular. Eventually it was even worked on perforated paper. These mottos embroidered on paper, with their shaded wools and Gothic lettering, have a nostalgic charm, although they do not show the craftsmanship of the earlier sampler. Of the perforated work the most common was a single proverb or phrase: "God Bless Our Home"; "Faith, Hope and Charity"; "Honour Thy Parents"; "Jesus Saves".

The preoccupation with death and mourning brought about the pastime of preparing souvenirs of those "who have passed over". Locks of hair of the deceased were now twisted into swags and loops for bracelets or lockets.

Often in Quebec the silver coffin labels and the handles were incorporated together with some preserved funeral flowers in a picture frame. When photography became more common, a hand-coloured picture might be added. This mourning montage was displayed prominently under a glass dome or framed.

The arts benefited from this death preoccupation. People, particularly children, were often subjected to an expensive portrait by an itinerant primitive painter when death seemed imminent. This accounts for the strange glassy and sickly look on most children's portraits of that period. Later, the hobby of hair sculpture was extended to both the living and the dead. It was not uncommon for a family to have a glass-cased wreath of many coloured hair-flowers, formed of the different colours of hair from the heads of children, parents and close relatives, living and dead.

This concern for the dead led to the attempt to make flowers everlasting. Some flowers are naturally dry and with little effort will keep, although brittle, for many years. In the 1880's, many of the fleshy flowers such as roses and carnations were laboriously preserved and then kept under glass. It was a job that took hours of painstaking care. A household book of the time says: "Preserved or embalmed flowers are chiefly to consecrate the chamber of death as there are very few but love to keep some of the floral offerings to their cherished dead".[2]

139

First, the flowers were bleached to remove all colour, in a solution of chloride of lime, carbonate of soda and soft cold water. The flowers were dipped, individual petals were then pressed and dried. Very thin sheets of wax were used to sandwich each separate petal. Special colours were used to tint the petals, some before waxing, others after. Colours, shadows, and tints were added and the sandwiched petals were then carefully cut out and reassembled using warm wax. Stamens and calyx were all modelled from coloured wax. Once the flowers were embalmed they were glued on a wire form covered with moss. Funeral wreaths or crosses were put in a box frame with a black velvet background. Or the background might be white satin, particularly if the deceased were young and unmarried. Other flower arrangements were put under glass bell domes. The very talented were able to give a downy effect to some flowers by brushing with thin gum and flocking powder.

Fresh flowers were popular but the arrangements were not the deceptively simple designs favoured by lady gardeners today. Nor were they the marvellous mixed bouquets beloved of the eighteenth century: they were more like a gangster's funeral tribute.

In 1885, ladies read articles such as this: "In the days gone by, the floral bell was considered as being a decoration only appropriate for marriage ceremonies. It was then made of pure white flowers with a very little green for bordering. But in these days, when the confluent time of aesthetic taste has washed away conventionalisms, it take its place for any occasion among the many designs for floral decorations. The most effective situation for this design is between portieres, and it should be suspended by a bright-coloured ribbon".[2]

Other floral pieces included a butterfly, or a boat, often a three-master, of smilax, roses, carnations, pinks, pansies, azalias, fuchsias and forget-me-nots among the suggested flora. Suitable for a christening was a cradle filled with primroses, polyanthus, pink daisies, sweet alyssum and candytuft. Floral fans were in good taste for the guests to carry at weddings, full evening dress parties, balls and the opera. There was always the private Easter Cross to be erected on the parlour table, made of wood about twenty-one inches high and covered with granite-coloured paint. It was put on a base and surrounded by stones and small boulders. Wax was then used to imitate ice and snow around the foot of this rugged miniature and icicles could drip from the arms. Wax flowers such as violets, snowdrops and arbutus were trailed around the base, over the rocks and up and around the arms.

The wealthy had conservatories. As early as 1837, Anna Jameson[3] mentions that two wealthy ladies of Toronto had such showplaces and sent her hot-house flowers in mid-winter. Later Victorians particularly loved the ivy and the geranium in all their many forms and varieties, using the designs in embroidery, metal work, and wall papers.

The love of flower arranging, the plentiful supply and the sentiment of the age led to "a novel and pretty entertainment for a summer evening that can be given by setting apart an hour for 'floral conversation'. Large bunches

of various plants and flowers named must be arranged on tables, from which
the guests selected blossoms neeeded".[4]

Every flower, every shrub, every tree had a known but secret message to
give to those who understood the code. It was further complicated by
different colours of the same flower having different meanings. Many books
were published with the listing of flower meanings as their sole subject and
the list could run into thousands. Here is a very small list:

The Language of the Flowers

alyssum, sweet — worth beyond beauty
apple blossom — preference
arbutus — welcome
ash — grandeur
ash, mountain — prudence
bachelor's button — hope in love
basil — hatred
borage — bluntness
briar — envy
bugloss — falsehood
coreopsis — love at first sight
currants — you please me
dandelion — coquetry
evergreen — poverty
flax — I feel your kindness
geranium, ivy — your hand for the next dance
honeysuckle — the colour of my fate
marigold — cruelty
myrtle — love
pansy — think of me
rose, bridal — happy love
rose, dog — pleasure and pain[5]

Leaves and foliage were carefully collected as the summer ended. Some were used in tall vases together with bullrushes and ornamental grasses, others were carefully arranged and glued in albums. In any event, the first move was to press the leaves in newspaper under heavy books, then dip them quickly into warm melted wax. Glossy surfaces were coated with varnish. In the same way, ferns were dried and "a butterfly on a cluster of ferns is pretty on picture-cards and you can make pretty lambrequins by pinning Autumn leaves and ferns in graceful forms on your lace curtains".[2]

Some leaves were reduced to phantoms or skeletons by rotting the fleshy parts under water for at least six weeks. The mess was washed off and the veiny part pressed and dried in blotting paper. These were glued into albums or leaf prints were made. This was done by spreading printers' ink on a marble slab, using a roller and inking the leaves; the branch was then placed inkside down on paper and pressed.

Other ornaments included bouquets "made of natural leaves and sprays artificially frosted. This is done by means of powdered glass, which can easily be obtained by pounding some bits of glass with a heavy hammer, care being taken to protect the eyes against flying splinters. Dip the objects in thin gum water, and shake the powdered glass over them. When dry handsome bouquets can be arranged".[6]

Small baskets were made of pliable copper wire, covered with gauze, and flowers were attached to the basket. Everything could be used "except full blown roses".[2] The whole was then immersed in a solution of alum and water and left until crystallized. "These baskets make a beautiful parlour ornament, and for a long time preserve the freshness of flowers".[2]

Other hobbies included china painting. Some ladies cast and moulded in wax and then bronzed and buffed the result. A favourite was an urn covered with draperies and swagged with waxed oak, holly and small maple leaves. Mottoes could be done in this way using a heavier wax and gluing the

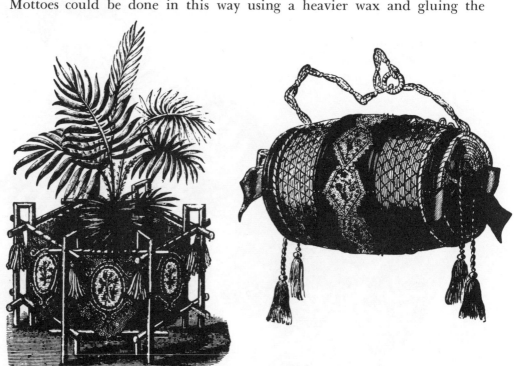

142

letters to black velvet: "A pretty style of motto is clasped hands in the centre of pure white wax, surrounded with sprays of fine flowers and buds, finished in Fire Bronze".[2]

There was Decalcomanie — the use of transfers on crockery, china, glass, bookcases and even on ribbons and dresses. Japanese-style lacquer ware was done painstakingly because the outsides of boxes were decorated and were "pretty when arranged with fine fish-scales to form leaves, butterflies, etc. These may be gummed on".[2] The whole arrangement was then sealed with size. Flowers were made of silk and satin; a "Banner made of velvet or satin or plush and a spray of flowers embroidered in ribbons on it, looks very handsome".[2]

Those who could not afford the elaborate flower vases and the carved picture frames could ingeniously make their own. "Pretty imitation vases may be made of cards, painted, and left without a bottom, so that they may be set over a glass of flowers. Picture-frames are also easily cut from paste-board, covered with pine cones, glued on and varnished".[7]

Families now began to consider household pets. If fish were kept, the bowl was often displayed on specially embroidered lace mats tatted and crocheted to form a wreath of flowers around the tank. Or else, in rustic style, the bowl was displayed on a table made from the rough trunk of a tree. Ivy wound around was considered "nice". Small lap dogs appeared again, but the pet that cut across all social strata was the canary in every parlour. For a treat this little bird was regaled with crackers, sweet apples, and worms. "A little sponge cake may be given occasionally".

By 1850 they were worried about the canary's health: "Here is a good remedy for a canary's cold: Boil an egg very hard. Make a paste of the yolk with a little olive oil, sprinkle well with cayenne pepper. Give this to him. You also might put a few drops of brandy in his drinking water, like a good fellow". Brandy for the birds too! no wonder the temperance movement grew apace.

REFERENCES
[1] *Mother Hubbard's Cupboard*, Anonymous, Hamilton, Ontario, 1881.
[2] *Treasures of Use and Beauty*, Anonymous, Windsor, Ontario, 1885.
[3] *Winter Studies and Summer Rambles in Canada*, Jameson, London, 1838.
[4] *The Home Manual*, Logan, Columbus, 1889.
[5] *Our Deportment*, Young, Paris, Ontario, 1883.
[6] *Manuscript Album*, Anonymous, Toronto, 1889.
[7] *Manners; or, Happy Homes and Good Society All the Year Round*, Hale, Boston, 1868.
[8] *Ladies' Indispensable Assistant*, Anonymous, New York, 1851.

Our Deportment

CHAPTER TWELVE

For many years life was rough and ready and many of the sensitive, sheltered wives of men of rank shuddered at the Canadian lack of etiquette and manners. There was, however, a code of manners. It simply took in new situations and differed from the standard practised in Europe, because occasions for old-time etiquette rarely existed. Of course, a social revolution was under way, with wealth coming into the hands of those unaccustomed to its responsibilities. A rigid code managed to maintain a façade over the scandals of the time, effectively keeping them from public knowledge for many years. In all codes of etiquette what is polite to one generation becomes outmoded, laughable and even vulgar to the next, and so it was in Canada in the nineteenth century.

In the early years, the fashionable world was restricted to a small number. But as the century advanced, fashionables could be found in ever-increasing numbers, always in suprisingly close contact with London, New York and Paris. In rural areas the people were cut off and had little time or inclination to bother with changes of style and manners. It is in the remoter villages that something of the old-time way is still preserved. Joseph Bouchette had this to say of society in Canada in 1831, and it is still true: "However remote from the vortex of the *haut ton* on this side of the Atlantic, the high circles are by no means strangers to the delicacies, etiquette, and refinements of European society; and by the agreeable union of French and English manners, that forms so peculiar a feature of the society in Canada, a degree of vivacity prevails, which holds a medium course between the austerity of English reserve and the ebullitions of French rhapsody".[1]

Bouchette, who was Surveyor-General of Lower Canada, goes on to discuss the various settlers at that time. Like other writers of the period, he came in contact with the Yankee-Canadian, a special breed and a law unto himself, with an uninhibited way of life, dislike of the British immigrant, and lack of manners. The explanation was, "The Americans, from a desire to mark their independence, their freedom from all the pernicious restraints of European despotisms, too often forget the common courtesies of life. The Canadian, on the contrary, while acting with independence, is polite; while guarding himself from becoming a dupe, is honest".[1]

Some ten years later, N. Willis thought that those newly arrived from Ireland, Scotland and England still retained their original ideas and habits, with the exception, however, of those in western Ontario: "The tone especially in the western districts appears to have been in a great measure given by such Americans as came, not from the civilized portions of the Union, but from the back-wood tracks, breathing rather the spirit of Kentucky than of New England".[2]

Eighteenth century people of culture were well-versed, from an early age, in the social niceties. They knew how and when to bow and curtsy, and the exact required depth of this salutation. The tricorn hat, a marvellous all-weather covering because the sides let down in wet weather, was worn with a point directly over the left eye, and most important, it was part of a man's dress worn indoors; the times it was removed were carefully prescribed. In contrast, eighty years later, men were told never to wear a hat in the house, or in the theatre, or when in the presence of ladies.

The ladies at the beginning of the nineteenth century kissed each other on meeting, but by the end of the 'eighties this was considered ill-bred. Early in the nineteenth century, people were emotional and often cried, although laughing had to be controlled. Their affectation was to talk as if all were deaf, and to orate rather than converse. An etiquette book of 1850, however, said "Avoid a loud tone of voice in conversation, or a 'horse laugh': both are exceedingly vulgar, and if practised, strangers may think you are a retired politician, who has acquired the practice in bar-room harangues".[3] And of course, according to *Our Deportment*: "Suppression of undue emotion, whether of laughter, of anger, or of mortification, of disappointment, or of selfishness in any form, is a mark of good breeding".[4]

Snuff-taking and smoking were popular. It is estimated that men took a pinch every twenty minutes. This called for elegant gestures and the proper handling of the snuff-box, which for ease was kept inside the vest or waistcoat, rather than in the deep hard-to-get-at coat pockets.

Smoking was enjoyed until society decreed that no man could smoke in front of a woman, even if permission were granted. (There was a strong anti-tobacco movement parallel with the temperance and food reform leagues. They had mutual members as well as some members in "rights for women" groups. These are among the most interesting social phenomena of this period.)

A definite code of smoking manners was established. On a train, smoking was permissible if all the other passengers were agreeable. However, permission could not be asked if there were a woman present. It was courteous to offer tobacco to a fellow traveller, but vulgar to offer any to a churchman above a curate.

Publications had much to say about the evils of the tobacco habit. Etiquette books have gory engravings of inner organs attacked by smoke. However, this has been a subject of admonition ever since King James I broke into print against the weed. "In those homes where the husband is permitted to smoke in any room of the house, the sons will follow the father's example, and the air of the rooms becomes like that of a public house",[5] said many Victorian writers.

A distinct backwoods ceremony was observed when borrowing coals to re-start a fire. Notwithstanding the stock of finely split pine sticks tipped with brimstone, pieces of decayed wood called "punk", or even the firing of the family gun into the coals, sometimes nothing would revive the fire. This was the time to take a special pan and go to the nearest neighbours to "borrow some fire". It required a speedy return and gave rise to an expression still occasionally heard when speaking of a rushed visit: "You must have come to borrow the coals". If the borrower arrived while butter was being churned, there was nothing for it but to wait until the housewife was ready to leave her churn and offer the coals. It was unneighbourly and ill-mannered to help oneself to the fire while the woman was churning.

An exaggerated formality characterized town life. To understand the nineteenth century one must understand the etiquette of the call, the visit, the card and above all, the "cut". Introductions merely required a bow, a complete change from the deep curtsy of the 1800's. However, it was still the lady's privilege to determine whether she would recognize a gentleman with a bow. If she did, he had to bow in return. Calls were made for all occasions, — for condolence, congratulation, friendship, for invitations received, for marriage, and the birth of a child. Purely social calls, called "Morning Calls", were never made earlier than noon nor later than five o'clock. Evening calls had to terminate by nine o'clock.

Rules were observed in formal calls. The hostess rose on the entrance of guests, but not on departure, except when the visitors were ladies. Strangers were introduced to other guests, "but it is not customary to introduce residents of the same city, unless the hostess knows this will be agreeable to both parties".[4] Return courtesy calls were made within three days of a dinner, if it was the first entertainment offered. If not, the call was returned within a week. Return calls were made for any kindness shown and for any entertainment from a tea-party to a ball. A lady, of course, never called on a gentleman.

Visitors left their personal calling cards, engraved with their names. No other embellishment was correct, although gentlemen could add their military rank or any title. "A lady's card should not bear her place of residence, such cards having, of late been appropriated by the members of the demi-mondaine".[4] By a code attached to calling cards, different corners were turned down if the card was left while the lady of the house was absent. A left-hand corner meant "felicitation"; left-hand lower corner, "condolence"; the right-hand lower corner, "to take leave", and right hand end turned down, "delivered in person".

It was not customary in cities to offer refreshment. A hostess receiving callers was allowed to sit and embroider or do light needlework because "a lady looks much better employed than in absolute idleness".[4]

A woman kept her bonnet on while calling and did not remove it even if urged to do so. A gentleman was even more formal: "He should retain his hat and gloves in his hand on entering the room. The hat should not be laid upon a table or stand, but kept in the hand, unless it is found necessary from some cause to set it down. In that case, place it upon the floor. An umbrella should be left in the hall".[3] Naturally, children and pets were not to be taken visiting.

The "cut" was a way of discouraging others who wished to be friendly. Etiquette demanded that a bow must be returned if seen. However, if one turned the head so that one just could not quite see the bow, it was not returned — a marvellous example of late-century hypocrisy. Another type of "cut" was the "cut direct" given by a prolonged stare at a person. If justified at all, it could be given only in case of extraordinary and notoriously bad conduct on the part of the individual being "cut", and was very seldom called for. If any one wished to avoid a bowing acquaintance with another, it could be done by looking aside or dropping the eyes. It was an invariable rule of good society, that a gentleman could not "cut" a lady under any circumstance, but circumstances might arise when he might be excused for persisting in not meeting her eyes, "for if their eyes meet, he must bow".[4]

Other tips on general social etiquette include: "Pulling out your watch in company unasked is a mark of ill-breeding. It looks as though you were tired of the company, and that time dragged heavily. If you desire to know the time, retire to some corner, or into another room and look at your watch unnoticed".[3]

One should avoid excessive modesty: "Do not use the word 'limb' for 'leg'. If legs are really improper, then let us on no account mention them. But having found it necessary to mention them, let us by all means give them their appropriate name".[4]

"Indelicate words or expressions should leave no shadow of a smile because a lady will always fail to hear that which she should not hear, or having mistakenly heard, she must not understand". And finally, "No lady should make use of any feminine substitutes for profanity. The woman who exclaims, 'The Dickens', or 'Mercy' or 'Goodness' when she is annoyed or astonished, is vulgar in spirit".[4]

In an age when a great many girls, talented or otherwise, were taught to sing and play a musical instrument, it was necessary to note: "A lady in company should never exhibit any anxiety to sing or play; but being requested to do so, if she intends to comply, she should do so at once, without waiting to be urged. If she refuses, she should do so in a manner that shall make her decision final. Having complied, she should not monopolize the evening with her performances, but make room for others".[4]

In all the etiquette books throughout the period there seems to be much

147

concern about how to refer to a spouse. In 1860 it was thought abominable for a woman to speak of her husband as Mr. B., but even more so for him to register them at a hotel as "Mr. B. and lady". Neither was he to refer to her in conversation as "my lady". By 1865 it was considered unbecoming for a married woman to refer to her husband by his surname without prefix of any kind. Some years later, in 1881, *Practical Life* mentioned that in some places "it is the custom, when there is an old lady of the same name as one or more younger ladies, to give the senior lady the style madame, instead of Mrs.".[6]

In this game-playing period, when evenings were devoted to theatricals and summer afternoons to outdoor games such as croquet, rules were necessary to guide behaviour. When playing games it was the height of ill-manners to show anger if the opponents were found to be cheating. On the other hand, a good guest played any part in charades assigned by the hostess "even if they are obscure or distasteful".[6]

But perhaps the rules prescribed for a man attending a picnic sum up a forgotten way of life in Canada: "It is the duty of gentlemen to do all they can to make the occasion enjoyable and even mirthful. They should also look to providing the means of conveyance to and from the spot selected for the festivities, make such arrangements as are necessary in the way of providing music, games, boats and whatever else is needed to enhance the pleasure of the day. The ladies provide the luncheon or dinner, which is spread upon the grass or eaten out of their baskets and at which the restraints of the table are withdrawn. At picnics, gentlemen become the servants as well as the escorts and guides of the ladies, and perform such services for the ladies in the way of procuring flowers, carrying baskets, climbing trees, baiting their fish-hooks, and many other things that are requested of them".[4]

Letter writing was of course an art, and the fashionable Spencerian script needed much practice. Both books of exercises to upgrade the penmanship and books on how to write letters were very popular among the less educated and were available in French and English. Men always used white paper but ladies might use delicately tinted papers. Scented notes were in and out of fashion from time to time. Letter-writing books contain examples to cover every contingency from asking for a loan to writing a love letter. One of the most charming is "Chesterfield's art of letter-writing simplified. Being a guide to friendly, affectionate, polite and business correspondence, containing a large collection of the most valuable information relative to the art of letter-writing, with clear and complete instructions how to begin and end correspondence, rules for punctuation and spelling, etc." It was published at thirty-five cents in 1857, sent anywhere in the United States and the Canadas. One copy owned by a man, inscribed "Lytton, British Columbia, 1871" has been found. The concern for proper form reached far into the wilderness.

Fans were carried by women on formal occasions. The material they were made of changed with fashion's whims, but always there was the secret language of the fan. Like the flower code, if you understood the lady's action you might be rewarded, or discouraged. When the open fan was held against the face, touching the lips, it meant, "be quiet, we are overhead"; to touch the right cheek, "yes"; the left, "no". If it touched the nose, the observer was not trustworthy. The closed fan held towards the heart meant, of course, "love". To hide the eyes behind the open fan, the same message; and to slowly lower the open fan held in the right hand until pointed to the ground was the final, "I hate and despise you".

There was a great deal of home entertainment, but it had gradually changed from the spontaneous visiting and the work bees of the earlier days. Even home entertaining had its rules. For example, a man about to be married always gave the bachelor dinner to his friends. This was understood to end their friendship unless the bridegroom chose to renew their

Notes of Invitation.

Mr. Walter Hood presents his regards to Miss Jennie Mason, and requests the pleasure of escorting her to the Grand Opera, to-morrow evening.

246 Monroe Ave., April 10.

Miss Jennie Mason presents her compliments to Mr. Hood, and accepts with pleasure his kind invitation to accompany him to the Opera.

April 11th

Invitation to Spend the Evening.

Mrs. M. Bell requests the pleasure of Mr. and Mrs. Howard Wilson's company, on Thursday evening, March 30th, at seven o'clock

Acceptance.

Mr. and Mrs. Howard Wilson have much pleasure in accepting Mrs. Bell's kind invitation for Thursday evening, March 30th.

Mill Avenue,
Thursday, March 19th.

Regret.

Mr. and Mrs. Wilson regret that, owing to previous engagements, they are unable to accept Mrs. Bell's kind invitation for Thursday evening, the 30th instant.

Mill Avenue,
Tuesday, March 19th.

acquaintance. In the same way, a newly married couple was not expected to give parties at their home during the first year of marriage, but, says an 1860 guide, "after that time they must no longer play the part of exceptional beings, but blend with the herd, and give and take as others".[3]

What kind of parties were popular? Around 1870 the oyster evening was in vogue. Barrels of them were shipped hundreds of miles inland across this country. It is true that this was done only in winter, but the amount of oysters consumed was prodigous. Every cook book of the period has at least two dozen recipes. The oysters, like the lobsters at that time, were very large. "There is no pleasanter frolic for an Autumn evening, in the regions where oysters are plentiful, than in an impromptu roast in the kitchen. There the oysters are hastily thrown into the fire by the peck. You may consider that your fastidious taste is marvellously respected if they are washed first. A bushel basket is set to receive the empty shells, and the click of the oyster-knives forms a constant accompaniment to the music of laughing voices".[7]

A similar evening party, most fashionable from the 1890's onwards, was the chafing-dish supper. As today, this little table cooker was popular. A number of books cautioned the hostess that only the finest butter should be used when cooking for guests and wearing evening dress!

At afternoon teas the ladies wore carriage dress, and light refreshments were served. The cups were either "a harlequin tea service, each cup different, or a set of choice East Indian China".[8] Tea was brought in and placed on a table by the hostess. Often there were urns of black or green tea. Food included, "a basket of wafers, delicate sandwiches of chicken or thin sliced meats, and a basket of fancy cake. If the English style is followed, the cups of tea are carried to the guests on a tray, and a tiny table to rest the cups on placed in reach of each group".[8]

In fact, tea entertaining was so popular throughout the century, as soon as a woman had the feel of "gentility", that books discussed tea-making at length. In 1852, Mrs. Hale wrote, "Presuming all ladies to be intimately acquainted with the mode of making tea, yet, to some, a few hints on the subject may not perhaps be found objectionable".[9] Teapots had to be scoured and the tea served hot. Preferred was "one of those metal tea-kettles warmed by a spirit-lamp, as formerly used by our grandmothers, and now — thanks to good taste in tea-drinking — again coming into fashion".[9]

Invitations to tea parties were issued on the lady's visiting card with the time and place written in the left hand corner. The pouring of the tea and the passing of the refreshments was usually done by the family or close friends.

By 1880, Canada had the forerunner of the cocktail party, known as a "Kettle-Drum". Some say it was introduced from England, but it was also becoming fashionable in the United States. It is hard to say where the intriguing name came from. Some contemporary books suggested that wives of officers held informal receptions using regimental drums as tables. Another theory claimed that the noise of the voices was like the kettle-drum. "For a kettle-drum there is usually a crowd, and yet but few remain over half an hour — the conventional time allotted — unless they are detained by music or some entertaining conversation. A table set in the dining-room is supplied with tea, coffee, chocolate, sandwiches, buns and cakes, which constitute all that is offered to the guests. There is less formality at a kettle-drum than at a larger day reception. The time is spent in desultory conversation with friends, in listening to music, or such entertainment as has been provided. Gentlemen wear the usual morning dress. Ladies wear the demi-toilet, with or without bonnets".[4] There were also "Breakfast Parties" at which the dress of the ladies was simpler than at dinner or supper parties. (See Omnium-Gatherum.)

Friends enjoyed many evening pastimes, from showing pictures with the magic lantern to home theatricals. Card games were played when religious convictions did not forbid this activity. There was, of course, whist of which Governor Simcoe was particularly fond, in addition to euchre, bezique, cribbage, all-fours, Loo, poker, brag, piquet, écarté, cassino, Boston, and backgammon. They played checkers, chess, dominoes; billiards too became fashionable. They amused themselves with amateur conjuring, and many books taught the banjo and how to play solos, hornpipes, jigs, reels and "walks around". There were joke books and monologue books as well as collections of *bon mots*, puns and riddles. In 1860, one of the most popular books was *Mrs. Partington's Carpet Bag of Fun*, mailed anywhere for 35 cents.

Blind Man's Buff.

The Feather Game.

Shadow Buff.

Houses with a double parlour and folding doors lent themselves to evenings of charades and *tableaux vivants*. If one did not have a double parlour "a temporary curtain will suffice".[6] The stage was set with as much scenery as could be found, costumes were assembled and friends were invited. Some were tapped to become actors, the rest an audience. A tableaux evening meant that a complete book would be enacted with two-minute tableaux arrangements while an unseen commentator read the appropriate passage. Between scenes, while the curtain was drawn, there might be other monologues, or someone would sing. Suggested plays included Longfellow's *Evangeline*, Tennyson's *Maud*, or even *Pilgrim's Progress*. All this was accompanied by soft music, "the organ or piano to have a good light, the rest in darkness, one light on the stage for the reader."[6] The stage itself was lit by a reflector lamp hidden behind the curtains and there was much cautioning because of the danger of fire. By 1881, a writer suggested the best light to borrow or hire was a train headlight. There were also shadow parties. Taut sheets were hung from the ceiling and players were lit from behind to make silhouettes.

Evenings ended with refreshments, passed on trays while people were seated in the parlour, or else at the dining-room table. The usual foods were cake and lemonade or cake and fruit, strawberries, raspberries and poundcake. Another suggested menu: oranges sliced, sugared and some cocoanut grated on top, served in saucers, and a basket of macaroons and cream cake sent around with them. "This will be ample. After all I think your friends will most fancy, even in winter, sponge cake, jelly cake and ice cream".[6]

Some evenings were rather like our informal buffet suppers, if anything of the late nineteenth century could be considered informal. In 1871, advice to the bride considered the "standing supper of oysters, chicken-salad, sandwiches, coffee, ice-cream, jellies and cake, is not a formidable undertaking when you have had a little practice".[7]

Another event was the evening soirée, when the ladies sat and embroidered, while the gentlemen moved among them chatting, or else one of them would read from a current book. Later, tea and small cakes were served. But by the 1850's this elegant evening entertainment was going out of fashion, much to the regret of many women including Mrs. Sara Hale, who thought it not only in good taste but economical too.

Our predecessors gave formidable dinner parties, that probably set back several decades the convivial institution of eating with friends. Canada had dining clubs before they ever became a modern gimmick. Possibly the very first was Champlain's Order of Good Cheer, followed by the Beaver Club banquets of the Montreal fur entrepreneurs. The Agricultural Society of Newark (now Niagara-on-the-Lake) held monthly supper meetings before the end of the eighteenth century. But by no stretch of the imagination can these be classified as domestic happenings. They were convivial occasions.

The nineteenth century dinner party meant hand-written invitations, to be sent from two to ten days before the event. When the guests were assembled there was the ritual of the host escorting with his right arm the lady honoured either by rank or age. A bride on her first appearance took precedence over all. It was necessary for the hostess to mention to each gentleman, as unobtrusively as possible, which lady he was to take into the dining-room. "This saves half a dozen rushing 'for the honour of escorting, la plus belle' of the party, while some plain demoiselle is under the painful necessity of escorting herself".[10]

The setting of the dinner table, as well as the table etiquette, changed during the period. In the first years of the century the table was set with a full course. That is, soup, fish and several game or creamed dishes went on at once. It was important to have abundant food and to set the table in a good geometric pattern. From this we get the expression "a side dish". A side dish was of pickles or some small amount of food put on the table to help form the geometric pattern. This complete course would be removed and replaced with an equal number of dishes, including roasts, game pies and other meats. Depending on the circumstances, a third table setting would now appear with some meats and an increasing number of desserts, cakes, pies, jellies and pastries. This practice continued for some fifty years.

In 1852, these instructions were given to make the formal dinner table not only elegant but comfortable. "Two or three cloths make the table look much handsomer; and it is astonishing how meagre to an eye accustomed to that style, a table with only one appears; but this may be easily obviated, if the cloth is not removed during the service, by having a stout coarse one under it; or a scarlet cloth under a fine thin damask gives it an imperceptible glow; but, if such is used, the cloth must not be taken off, as nothing can look well in removing but linen. A scarlet cloth, fitted to the table, and slid between the table-cloths, preserves the polish, as well as adds to the appearance".[9] (The earlier method to prevent marring the mahogany was a thin cloth of soft leather.)

Table flatware and appointments changed over the years. The fork was the last instrument introduced to the table. At the end of the eighteenth century it was three-tined, picking up the fourth tine by mid-century. Spoons were much larger and the knives were blunt-ended, but no longer used to convey food to the mouth. Many etiquette books stress this non-use of the knife. It was used earlier as a food conveyor because the fork, until the tines increased and were subtly curved, was a difficult instrument to use, except as a spear for food. Out of habit the older generation still conveyed solids to their mouths with the knife.

How and when to use the finger bowl occupied a writer of 1860, and many others before and since. The following excerpt presents not only an interesting social picture but shows that the custom of rinsing the mouth with the bowl was still practised, regardless of social disapproval. This habit is mentioned in many English eighteenth century etiquette books and it is interesting that this rather unpleasant habit crossed the ocean. It accounts for the word "rinser" often being used to describe a finger bowl — some of them actually having a lip to facilitate the function. "Finger glasses when used, come on with the dessert, and are filled with warm water. Wet a corner of your napkin, and wipe your mouth, then rinse your fingers; but do not practice the filthy custom of gargling your mouth at table, albeit the usage prevails among a few, who think that because it is a foreign habit it cannot be disgusting".[3]

The word "napkin" was used rather than the genteel "serviette" that came in towards the end of the century. In 1868, "napkins may be folded according to fancy, varying much with the varying fashion. Sometimes they are placed on the plate, with a roll of bread inside, and sometimes arranged in a fan-shape in the champagne-glass".[11] By the 'nineties, napkin folding had become very elaborate. Pages are devoted to the "swan" and various complicated twists. By the sixties, two white cloths were placed upon the table, the one on which dinner was served was removed when the dessert appeared. Formal dinners among the educated affluent always ended with the old English custom of passing the port, with nuts and fruit on the polished table. (Doilies were invented by a man named D'Oyley at the end of the eighteenth century to prevent plates and coasters marking the fine polished tables.)

Table-ware was of pewter, bone, and silver, and later of silver plate. "Silver dishes, where the means permit, should also be used; and also the finest kind of glass, cut, never blown or moulded".[11] By 1877, "small can-shaped pitchers of engraved crystal, holding a quart, are placed with ice water between each pair of guests. A cruet stand and silver salt cellar is at each corner and a silver butter dish at each end".[8]

This was the beginning of the harlequin china period for the dinner table too. Later the fashion went out and has only begun to revive today. "Large dinner services of one pattern are no longer chosen. The meats and large dishes are in silver of electroplate ware, and the sweets come in heavy English cut crystal, and each course brings with it plates of a different ware".[8] By 1881, tables were furnished with little glass or silver rests for knife and fork while the plate was passed for a second helping.

In the early years, servants continued the custom of waiting on table wearing gloves. This was a hygienic precaution of the eighteenth century, when the toilet of the servants was rudimentary. However, by mid-century the white gloves were out, and instead, servants used a damask napkin with one corner wrapped around the thumb.

Table ornamentation became more elaborate as time went by. Towards the end of the century, the silver-plated epergne with its plated animals, crystal baskets for candies and its fluted flower and bud vases had to be seen to be believed. But like all fashions, during some periods the elaborate setting was in, other times it was banished. In 1877, it seems to have been out. "Decorations must be choice and used with discretion. Flowers should be fine but few. All artificial contrivances like epergnes and show-pieces, tin gutters lined with moss and filled with flowers for the edges of a table; or mirror plates to reflect baskets of blossoms, are banished by the latest and best taste. The finest fruit group in the centre of the table, set off with leaves, the garnished dishes, the lustre of glass and silver, and the colours of delicately painted china, need no improvement as a picture".[8]

In 1868 a pleasant practice appeared: "the French custom of a bouquet at each lady's plate is a pretty one, and frequently adopted here".[11] At that time readers were told "flowers must vary with the fashion; the present mode is to arrange them upon the table itself, perfectly flat, and it has the advantage of not interfering with the view of your opposite neighbours".[11]

Although the Temperance movement grew steadily with the years, its strength was usually in rural areas. Fewer gains were made among the prosperous townspeople. Wine, both home-made and imported as well as Canadian, were offered at most entertainments. Even a group of women meeting to embroider and gossip would stop for a glass of wine. Wines were decanted into cut-glass bottles. Claret and Burgundy were handed round at dinner in silver-mounted glass pitchers. Many of these still survive from the beginning of the century.

The rules for the service of dinner wines were set out by the Ladies of Toronto in their *Home Cook-Book*: "The order of wines is sometimes perplexing, and the novice should remember that Chablis or Sauterne comes with the small oysters before soup, and that Sherry is drank (*sic*) after soup. Claret may be taken by those who prefer it during a whole dinner with entire propriety. Champagne comes with the roast, and Burgundy with game. The French and Germans reserve champagne for a dessert wine, but we drink it with both roast and dessert".[8]

Ladies who really did not wish to drink a glass of wine at a dinner party were told to throw their gloves over the top of the glass. No lady would take a second glass of wine under any circumstances.

The Cook's Own Book describes an interesting wine ceremony begun in the eighteenth century and practised until late in the nineteenth century. "Soup being removed, the gentleman who supports the lady of the house on her right should request the honour of taking wine with her; this movement will be the signal for the rest. Should he neglect to do this, you must challenge some lady. Until the cloth be removed, you must not drink wine except with another. If you are asked to take wine, it is a breach of etiquette to refuse. In performing this ceremony (which is very agreeable if the wine be good) you catch the person's eye, and bow politely. It is not necessary to say anything".[10]

Until approximately the 1870's, carving was an important accomplishment of both men and women, the only difference being that women used a smaller carving knife and fork, but all sat down to carve. The terms of carving and the language employed to dismember almost any edible and some, to us, inedible birds go back to the fourteenth century.

All cook-books from the eighteenth century onwards have several pages of copper-plates showing exactly how to and where to cut. "Without a perfect knowledge of the art of carving, it is impossible to perform the honours of the table with propriety; and nothing can be more disagreeable to one of a sensitive disposition, than to behold a person, at the end of a well-furnished board, hacking the finest joints, and giving them the appearance of having been gnawed by dogs".[10]

The writer goes on to say: "Of course you will carve the meat yourself, or why did you buy this book? Surely not with the intention of teaching your servants to perform that important duty. You will not ask to be allowed to help your guests, but supply a plate in silence, and hand it to your

LOOK ON THIS PICTURE

AND ON THIS!

servants, who will offer it to such of the company as are unprovided. Do not attempt to eulogize your dishes, or apologize that you cannot recommend them — this is extreme bad taste. It is ill-bred, though common to press any one to eat; and, moreover, it is a great annoyance to be crammed like a turkey".[10]

For the would-be hostess with the problem of how many guests to invite and how many supplies to order, the Ladies of Toronto once again had the answer: "In inviting guests, it is safe to calculate that out of one hundred and fifty, but two-thirds of the number will be present. If five hundred are invited, not more than three hundred can be counted upon as accepting. Allow one quart of oysters to every three persons present. Five chickens (or, what is better, a ten-pound turkey, boiled and minced), and fifteen heads of celery, are enough for chicken salad for fifty guests; one gallon of ice cream to every twenty guests . . .".[8]

The Complete Book of Etiquette or Guide to Table Manners
"If you have children never introduce them after dinner, unless particularly asked for and then avoid it if possible."[10]

"When dinner is announced, never hasten into the dining-room."[11]

"If you desire a glass of water, or a knife from the servant, do not call him 'Waiter' as you would in a restaurant, but call him by his name, or better still, merely make a sign that you want him without calling."[11]

"Ladies should never dine with their gloves on, although it is not positively ungenteel."

"Every dinner must begin with soup."[11]

"Do not hold your knife and fork erect in your hands at each side of the plate nor cross them on your plate when you have finished, nor make a noise with them."[4]

"The knife should only be used for cutting meats and hard substances, while the fork, held in the left hand is used to carry food into the mouth."[4]

"When you send your plate to be refilled, do not send your knife and fork, but put them upon a piece of bread, or hold them in your hand."[4]

"Tea or coffee should never be poured into a saucer to cool, but sipped from the cup. If a person wishes to be served with more tea or coffee, he should place his spoon in his saucer. If he has had sufficient, let it remain in the cup."[4] (At the beginning of the century, a person replete turned his cup upside down in the saucer. Many visitors who did not understand this code suffered liquid torture.)

"The old-fashioned habit of abstaining from taking the last piece upon the plate is no longer observed. It is to be supposed that the vacancy can be supplied if necessary."[4]

"When sweet corn is served on the ear the grain should be pared from it upon the plate, instead of being eaten from the cob."[4]

"Bread should not be crumbed into soup or gravy. Cheese is crumbled with a fork. Cherries in pie, or natural, should have the stones passed to the napkin held at the lips and returned to the plate, and grape seeds and skins are disposed of in the same way."[8]

"It is beginning to be the custom to take soft bread as well as ice-cream with cake. Cocoanut pudding looks like pie, but is helped and eaten with a spoon."[8]

"A knife should never be put into the mouth. Many people, even well-bred in other respects, seem to regard this as an unnecessary regulation."[4]

"If a bone inadvertently gets in the mouth, the lips must be covered with the napkin in removing it."[4]

"Never use a napkin in place of a handkerchief for wiping the forehead, face or nose."[4]

"It is a mark of rudeness to pick your teeth at the table. To hold your napkin over your mouth does not avoid the rudeness of the act."[4]

"It is expected that the guests will remain from one to three hours after dinner. Eat cream cake with a knife and fork."[3]

REFERENCES

[1] *The British Dominions in North America*, Bouchette, London, 1831.
[2] *Canadian Scenery*, N. P. Willis, London, 1842.
[3] *Complete Rules of Etiquette and the Usages of Society*, New York, 1860.
[4] *Our Deportment*, Young, Paris, Ontario, 1883.
[5] *A Treatise on Domestic Economy*, Beecher, New York, 1849.
[6] *Practical Life*, Wright, Brantford, Ontario, 1881.
[7] *Commonsense in the Household*, Harland, New York, 1871.
[8] *The Home Cook-Book*, Anonymous, Toronto, 1877.
[9] *The Ladies' New Book of Cookery*, Hale, New York, 1852.
[10] *The Cook's Own Book*, Anonymous, Boston, 1845.
[11] *Manners*, Hale, Boston, 1868.

The Dinner Question

CHAPTER THIRTEEN

"The arts of cookery render many things unwholesome which are not so in their own nature. By jumbling together a number of different ingredients, in order to make a poignant sauce, or rich soup, the composition proves almost a poison. All high seasoning, pickles, &c. are only incentives to luxury, and never fail to hurt the stomach. It were well for mankind if cookery, as an art, were entirely prohibited. Plain roasting or broiling is all that the stomach requires. These alone are sufficient for people in health, and the sick have still less need of a cook."[1]

Tracing our culinary tradition is fascinating because the history of cooking in Canada is complex and, so far, almost unrecorded. Food ranged from basic porridges and stews to the sophisticated dinners of the gentry based on Hannah Glasse and Isabella Beeton's research. This variation existed throughout the century. While some families in eastern towns were enjoying imported luxuries, other families pioneering in the west were eating the staple salt-rising bread, bannock and slapjacks (griddle or pan cakes) which the east had known a hundred years earlier. There were, of course, people in the older settlements who continued to eat the pioneer diet, which was often heavy, usually greasy, but generally sustaining and frugal.

As the century advanced and affluence increased, so did the number of box stoves. The use of huge open hearths was less common: they were blocked off or otherwise altered. Progress was steady but slow. It is interesting to note that although the house itself was warmed by one or more cast-iron box stoves, food long continued to be cooked over the open fire.

The open hearth with the black iron pots was greatly encouraged by women's magazines and food writers who believed that flavour was lost when the new-fangled stoves were used. However, progress could not be halted, and the cook-books were forced to give both methods of cooking. Even so, Canadian women fared a great deal better than their counterparts in Britain and other European countries where the abundance of servants and inherent conservatism delayed progress in household equipment.

The nineteenth century continued to recognize distinct social classes, and food for each group was different, provided there was no famine. The "gentleman settler" lived a far different life from the survivors fleeing from the Irish disasters unless of course, he was completely unsuited to this country, feckless and unadaptable, as many of them were.

Settlers came from many different social and economic backgrounds. All brought their own food habits and prejudices which had to be adapted to local conditions and native ingredients. One of the great influences was that of the Indians. Without their teaching many early groups would have perished. They knew how to make the most of such indigenous foods as the plentiful game. They rendered down the pigeons and porcupine for lamp and cooking oil and they smoked and dried meat and fish. Indians grew patches of beans, pumpkin and corn, and they knew how to preserve the latter by drying and powdering it. Dehydrated corn was usually taken on long journeys and was eaten powdered for a quick meal or mixed with water or broth to make a porridge, if time and weather permitted. The early settlers also learned how to make corn porridge (samp), how to cook meat in maple sap, how to mix corn and beans (succotash) as well as how to make maple sugar. Whether one of the early traditional dishes of fish stew is Indian or French is hard to say. It comes down to us as chowder but the origin was possibly *chaudière* from its iron cooking pot. (Incidentally, it was quite common to add a dollop of beer or spirits to chowder.)

No matter what the social rank, all were levelled from time to time when the crops failed. When this occurred it was not uncommon for farms to change hands for a few sacks of flour or potatoes. Government grants to settlers included dry beans and this staple was distributed also from time to time to those who had lost their harvest. These navy beans were combined with molasses, and occasionally rum, to become another traditional food: baked beans.

There was a continual flow of people, ideas, books and goods from Europe as well as from across the United States border. Many domestic books are identical regardless of country of origin. After the Revolutionary War those of "German" background who wished to live under British rule, along with discharged Hessians, came north bringing their reputation for fine food, laden tables and immaculate housekeeping. Our heritage from them includes waffles, applecake, pies with crumb toppings, gingerbread, spiced meats, sauerkraut and doughnuts. They made prune cake and raisin pies — both were served at funerals, perhaps because of the dark colours. The French preserved and adapted the country cooking of the thrifty people from the coastal areas of northern France. The old dishes include *çi-pâte* or six layer pie, *tourtière* or meat pie, soups made from dried peas and beans, pork with apple and cinnamon, all of which can be traced back centuries.

After the Great Rebellion, many Scotsmen were exiled and some found their way into Canada. Others left the Highlands later for economic reasons and some took their army discharge here. Their food was similar to French food, and even today there is a connection between Scottish and French-Canadian food. Many names and culinary terms are similar. One of the oldest and perhaps the most interesting Franco-Scottish food is *çi-pâte* or sea pie (for recipe see Chapter XV). In many parts of Quebec women are still making their famous *çi-pâte*. The title is a corruption of six-pate or six-layer pie, traditionally layers of game and pastry sealed into a heavy iron pot, and very similar to game pies in early French cooking. Scotland long had historic and culinary ties with France. This pie is included in Scottish books as Sea Pie, but it has no connection with the sea and fish is never used. Generally, early Scottish cooks call for a mixture of beef and poultry between paste layers. Many cookbooks give variations of this pie, including the very Scottish Mrs. Dailgairn whose books were well-known to Canadian settlers, and the formidable Mrs. Beeton. By mid-century there are variations of Sea Pie in many Canadian cookbooks, and so a very old dish took on a new title and was adapted to new ingredients.

Some Culinary Terms From France and Scotland

assiette	ashet	a dish
armoire	aumrie	a cupboard for dishes
batterie	battry	kitchen equipment
cannelle	cannel	cinnamon
carâfe	caraff	water pitcher
groseille	grosset	gooseberry
hochepot	hotch potch	a thick vegetable soup

The United Empire Loyalists came with a tradition of hospitality, a knowledge of fine cooking and a taste for the elegant. They had been in the new world long enough to know how to handle corn bread, and to make bread from a mixture of rye and corn known as rye and Injun. They developed pumpkin and lemon pies, preserved the cranberry, and were familiar with cookbooks coming from the American states as well as from England and France.

The British too were familiar with a wide variety of cooking and house-keeping books, and because many of the men had been with the army in India they knew a great deal about curry. They knew about food for travelling, including home-made bouillon cubes called Soup-in-the-Pocket. The British brought with them the national preference for hearty portions of roast meat and meat pies, when such foods were available. They enjoyed fruitcakes, custards, steamed pudding and fruit dumplings. (It is said that the favourite dessert of George III was apple dumplings, and all his life he wondered how the apple got into the pastry.)

Mayonaise of Salmon.

Raised Pie.

Lobster Salad.

Cherry Tartlets.

Game Pie.

Fancy Pastry.

Open Tart.

Tomato and Cucumber Salad.

Ratafia Pudding.

Pigeon Pie.

Meat Pie.

Perhaps it is from the Negroes who were familiar with cooking in the southern states that the butter tart developed. This confection is now found only in Canada, but it is obviously related to the pecan tarts and pies. Many Negroes returned to the United States after the Civil War. Their departure was regretted by contemporary writers who mention that the free Negro was the most devoted of household help in a period of saucy servant girls. No doubt these visitors left behind the instructions for Brunswick Stew and Country Captain, — recipes no longer used or even remembered in Canada, but still part of the southern United States' tradition.

Among those to bring no dowry of food lore were the impoverished settlers escaping from England's industrial revolution. They had long forgotten their ancestors' foods and had resorted to bake shops. The Irish peasants too had merely subsisted for many generations.

As settlement moved westward, people with other European traditions added their cuisine so that the best cooking of this country still remains regional. Unfortunately, in Canada the written record of cuisine which might enrich the country as a whole is inadequate.

The most usual question about the food of the early days is, "Can this be made today?" In many cases, it is not possible. Recipes have to be adapted to suit current ingredients and the changed taste buds of today. It is hard to say exactly what results were achieved in pioneer homes. There is always the mist of nostalgia, although many early travellers were far from flattering about our food.

Bread was somewhat gritty because of the milling process. Our custom of sifting flour before use stems from those days when it was wet, lumpy and often included foreign matter. Bread soured quickly, yeast was not always reliable, and food scorched easily or contained ashes or cinders. Flour was coarse; sugar was wet and with a distinct molasses flavour; butter was often stale or very salty, even though it was washed before use. The scrawny hens laid small eggs with a gamey flavour, and milk was neither homogenized nor pasteurized, often with an unpleasant flavour when the cattle ate turnips or wild herbs.

One example of the change in food is Johnny Cake, or more properly Journey Cake, which was a staple corn bread made for travellers at the beginning of the century. It kept indefinitely, was cheap, easy to prepare, and, above all, filling. The recipe was refined about mid-century when milling was more standardized. Affluence added sugar and more eggs, and it was served with iced butter and pitchers of maple syrup. To duplicate even the later version is difficult, because the corn was stone ground and the type used has long since been hybridized out of existence.

There was slow but constant progress towards easing the lot of those catering to the large households. At the beginning of the nineteenth century almost everything had to be made at home, whether it was yeast or sausage. Only the wealthy could afford the spices, dried fruits and wines imported into the country, but towards the later part of the 1880's many packaged goods were commonly available in towns. It was no longer necessary to roast coffee at home, make yeast, cook tapioca for hours or steep lemon rind in brandy for flavouring. Almost from the beginning of the century stores in towns had carried stocks of imported goods and food. They were always ready to introduce something new, whether it was condensed milk, a patented baby food or a fruit, such as Shaddock, the sour ancestor of the grapefruit.

But right up to 1900 many women still purchased the minimum of packaged goods and made almost everything at home. They were not only conservative and frugal, they were also afraid of the many adulterations. As a single instance, the scandals of the poorly canned food used during the Crimean War set that industry back internationally several years.

The particular problems of a pioneer farming country brought about the early Canadian way of cooking. There was need for everyone to help in the clearings, where the men usually ate out. Meat was generally tough and had to be extended with beans and barley. These factors combined to make slowly cooked stews popular because they bubbled away unattended and could be left for hours. The double-crust pie (with crust top and bottom) was more convenient to transport. This took precedence over the top-crust pie more popular in the British Isles.

The long hot summers soon brought the demand for refrigeration. The invention of the mechanical ice cutter made it possible to cut and store ice in year-round ice houses. There was even some export of ice, although the Americans held the lion's share of that trade. Refrigeration brought about the perfecting of ice-cream, which gradually became available as a Sunday dessert in even the most modest homes. The plentiful ice, plus the invention of carbonated waters in the 1830's, brought into existence a new drink quickly latched onto by the Temperance movement. The adding of syrups to ice-cream and the opening of ice-cream parlours in the 1880's brought a change into the social life of young women, who could now meet there unescorted.

Before the century was half over, the continent became involved in a never-ending series of food and diet fads. Out of the hubbub came new recipes, a new approach to food, a new flour, and what are today our ready-to-eat breakfast cereals but were then diet foods designed for those with chronic indigestion. What started all this concern? Although not all food was poor, a great deal was. A reform was due in diet because menus consisted largely of salt pork, pickled or smoked meats, hot breads, fried and baked pies, boiled suet puddings and dumplings. The growing wealth of the middle class brought "made dishes" to the tables. These were mixtures of several ingredients in a heavy sauce and can be considered the forerunners of today's casseroles. It was common to find a dinner table set with two kinds of soup, a "made dish", a roast, possibly some fish, and hot bread; for dessert, pie, a fruit pudding and several kinds of rich cake. It is not unusual to equate success with a bountiful table. This has been true in all periods of food history, but at this time also in the United States and Canada the cooks turned to the grease-filled frying-pan with a vengeance. No doubt this was a speedy way of cooking, but the food became heavy and indigestible.

Sam Slick on "Made Dishes"

"Sam Slick, in his truthful, but satirical vein, enumerates the disguises of fashionable cookery. 'Veal (he says) to be good, must look like anything else but veal. You mustn't know it when you see it, or it's vulgar; mutton must be incog., too; beef must have a mask on; anythin' that looks solid, take a spoon to; anythin' that looks light, cut with a knife; if a thing looks like fish you can take your oath on it, it is flesh; and if it seems rael *(sic)* flesh, it's only disguised, for it's sure to be fish; nothin' must be nateral — natur is out of fashion here. This is a manufacturin' country; everything is done by machinery, and *that* that aint, must be made to look like it, and I must say, the dinner machinery is perfect'."[2] *(sic)*

A number of men tried to exert influence for a plainer diet, comprising fewer rich "made dishes", and more fruits and vegetables. Among them were Dr. Graham and Father Kneipp. The former was an evangelical minister involved with societies for the suppression of spirits. His popular lectures also included observations on tobacco, vivisection, women's rights, bathing, sex and food. Judging by the many quotations and recipes in Canadian books, he had a large following here. Although he had no knowledge of nutrition he believed that putting the bran back into flour would make bread lighter and more digestible. Dr. Graham had some sound advice on toothbrushing, room ventilation and moderation in diet. He also advocated cold water both inside and outside the body, stale bread, rice, oatmeal porridge, no salt, no condiments, and cold puddings if they had to be eaten. Dr. Graham was an extremist who believed that every mouthful should be chewed thirty-two times. Nevertheless, he guessed correctly at the need for an enriched flour long before food chemists were able to demonstrate the deficiency of the early flour, and "Graham flour" we know even today.

Father Kneipp was a world famous Bavarian priest who wrote diet books, designed healthful undergarments, and built an empire based on cold water cures for those suffering from such diverse illnesses as ulcers and migraine. It is interesting to find that this man, living in an obscure mountain village, generated so much influence that a French-Canadian cook-book developed for teaching in the schools generations later has a recipe named after him.

Pain Kneipp

"Ce pain est composé de toutes les farines et du son des céréales et seigle dans la proportion de deux du premier contre un du second. Le seigle a la très remarquable qualité de tenir le pain plus longtemps frais, et lui donne une saveur légèrement sucrée qui n'est pas sans charme."[3]

The amount of cake eaten daily in every household also gave concern to the food reformers. Not only were there cakes for special occasions from weddings to funerals, but no self-respecting dinner ended without at least a seed and a plum or currant cake. Most mornings began with fried cakes, crullers and doughnuts.

No story of food in the nineteenth century is complete without a reference to the change in the art of cake-making which took place then and which can be considered one of North America's contributions to culinary art. Up to the middle of the century cakes had been the same for hundreds of years, — solid, heavy and flat because they were leavened with homemade yeast or eggs. Lavish cakes required many dozen of eggs and continuous beating for several hours. By the 1830's a purified potash made from the plentiful wood ashes or from burnt corn cobs was used fairly generally. It was called pearlash. The abundance of that natural resource, fresh snow, led to experimental use when freshly fallen. Cooks were known to add sal volatile or smelling salts to the batter just before baking. The forerunner of baking soda, saleratus, also made its appearance, but basically cakes were still the same as ever.

Leavening

"Snow is an excellent substitute for eggs, either in puddings or pancakes. Two large spoonfuls will supply the place of one egg, and the article it is used in will be equally good. It should be fresh-fallen snow. The under layers of snow may be used. The surface which is exposed to the air loses its ammonia by evaporation very soon after it has fallen. It is the ammonia contained so largely in snow which imparts to it its 'rising power'."[4]

It took the advances of mass production and technology, the new super-fine factory-ground sugars, the changes in flour milling, plus the invention of baking powder to bring about the new type of cake in the second half of the century. Baking powder was invented almost simultaneously in the United States and Great Britain. Shortly afterwards it was for sale in Canada, although well into this century many women still preferred to buy ingredients from the druggist and mix their own. Baking powder brought about the well-risen, light and fluffy cake with which we are still familiar. It was known in England as "American cake".

These light cakes called for pans different from the old-style flat tins, hoops and baking kettles. The stores were soon selling tin layer-cake pans, many of them with scalloped edges. The cakes were now sandwiched together with jam or fruit preserves and known as jelly cakes. Angel cakes were now possible, so were rolled sponge cakes. Baking powder also brought into favour tea biscuits which soon overtook in popularity old time crumpets, fried cakes and "gems" — a kind of muffin.

It seems likely that the deterioration to heavier and greasier cooking took place gradually. There is little mention of really exceptionally poor and greasy food during the early years of the century, but rather a picture of rough comfort and plenty enjoyed by those who had cleared their land and were making headway.

Food in Upper Canada

"No people in the world live better than the inhabitants of Upper Canada. The abundance of produce, and the low price at which it can be sold, naturally inclines them to take the full use of it. Three copious meals, often of twelve or fourteen dishes each, are daily served up, called breakfast, dinner and supper, but consisting generally of the same component parts; among which are specially enumerated green tea, fried pork, honeycomb, salted salmon, pound-cake, pickled cucumbers, stewed chicken, apple tarts, maple-molasses, pease-pudding, gingerbread, and sour crout."[5]

Food in Lower Canada

"The comforts of the people, if compared with any other nation, are wonderfully great; their food, from their French habits, consists not of animal food to the same extent as that of the richer English, but is, nevertheless, nourishing and abundant. The food, indeed is oftentimes coarse, but always wholesome. From the length of winter it is found necessary to kill in the autumn such stock as is intended for that winter's food: a great proportion is immediately salted; some part is frozen; and thus though during the early part of the winter and the latter part of the summer the population live on fresh food, still for a great portion of the year their chief animal food is salted."[6]

Farmers slaughtered their own meat and drove herds of cattle into the nearest town, where the butcher shop and the slaughterhouse were usually one and the same establishment. There was, of course, no inspection of animals, meat or premises. Buying was always heavier as the colder weather set in and farmers brought loaded sleighs to the town. Some parked at the market square or the edge of town and did business from the sleigh. Others stationed themselves in the closest tavern, making it their headquarters.

Perishable foods were purchased and stored solidly frozen. To make a more enticing display some butchers displayed lambs and pigs standing on all four feet. Sometimes the animals were decorated with gilded faces, particularly around Christmas time, while at Easter garlands of paper roses were common.

The town stores had no set hours, owner and helpers worked from morn to night as long as there was a chance to sell. Saturday night was the big shopping night in many towns across Canada when all the family would go to make purchases, or simply to look. All who could afford it bought in bulk and cold weather found the storerooms bulging with barrels of flour, butter, sugar, lard and molasses.

The frequency of Canadian cook-books printing recipes for national delicacies such as "Mock Mince Pie", "Mock Apple Pie" and "Mock Goose" (see Chapter XV), all having in common nothing much more than a handful of soaked crackers, must testify to the frugality of the women or their poor calculations for winter supplies. The many variations of "Vinegar Pie" — a mock lemon pie — were developed because of the high cost and the periodic scarcity of lemons.

Foods were eaten in season; oranges were imported at Christmas, strawberries came in early summer, grapes in the fall, dried dates, raisins and currants for the winter. Each new season brought with it the natural excitement of a change in diet, — something that we have almost forgotten.

Because it was a period of "buyer beware" the first chapter of every household book was devoted to marketing: how to tell fresh meat and produce, the test for young and tender poultry, how to buy a cheese. It seems obvious to us that a chicken with a green tint is undesirable, yet most writers found it necessary to spell out such primary information.

Rules for Marketing

"*Beef*: The fat should look white rather than yellow; for when that is of a deep colour, the meat is seldom good."

"*Mutton*: Observe the neck of a fore quarter; if the vein is bluish, it is fresh; if it has a green or yellow cast, it is stale."

"*Pork*: Pinch the lean, and if young it will break. When fresh, the flesh will be smooth and cool, if clammy it is tainted."

"*Hams*: Stick a sharp knife under the bone: if it comes out with a pleasant smell, the ham is good: but if the knife is daubed and has a bad scent, do not buy it."[7]

Choice of Meat

"If people wish to be economical, they should take some pains to ascertain what are the cheapest pieces of meat to buy; not merely those which are cheapest in price, but those which go farthest when cooked."[8]

Choice of Butter

"For cooking on the chafing-dish I advise always using print butter. It may seem a little extravagant. But surely when one in evening attire prepares a dish which proves to be above reproach, one may say with the March hare, 'It is the best butter', without losing the reputation of being an economical as well as good housekeeper."[9]

To Make Chickens White and Tender

"The moment before they are to be killed, make them swallow 1 table-spoonful of best vinegar, then finish as usual."[10]

(This idea was also put forward by Vincent La Chapelle, Cook to the Prince of Orange in 1744.)

To Tenderize Mutton

"The day before you wish to use the piece of mutton, be it leg or saddle, have a hole dug in the garden, wrap your mutton in a clean, white cloth, lay it deep down in the hole, cover the earth tightly over it and leave it until next morning. Then dig it out, set it in a cool place where it can not spoil, and cook it for dinner."[10]

(Canadian mutton was greatly esteemed by housewives living in the north-eastern United States)

To Keep Pork

"There should always be a heavy stone on the top of your pork barrel to keep it down. This stone is an excellent place to keep a bit of fresh meat in the summer, when you are afraid of its spoiling."[8]

REFERENCES

[1] *Domestic Medicine*, Buchan, Dublin, 1784.
[2] *The Curiosities of Food*, Simmonds, London, 1856.
[3] *Manuel de Cuisine Raisonée*, Anonymous, Quebec, 1919.
[4] *The Practical American Cook Book*, Anonymous, New York, 1866.
[5] *Canadian Scenery*, N. P. Willis, London, 1842.
[6] *The British Dominions in North America*, Bouchette, London, 1831.
[7] *The Experienced American Housekeeper*, Anonymous, New York, 1823.
[8] *The American Frugal Housewife*, Child, New York, 1838.
[9] *On the Chafing-Dish*, Bailey, New York, 1890.
[10] *Liberal Living Upon Narrow Means*, Herrick, Boston, 1890.

Curiosities
of Food

CHAPTER FOURTEEN

*"Fair Canada is our Theme,
Land of rich cheese, milk and
cream."*[1]

There were some peculiar foods in nineteenth-century Canada as well as a number of curious cooking processes, so many in fact that Canadian food was the subject of discussion by scientists of the day as well as by travellers and visiting journalists, and a source of amazement to the newly arrived settlers. Some of these foods, of course, have vanished, others have gradually changed with greater knowledge of farming, food technology and mass production. Our native foods were bountiful and in the nineteenth century seemingly inexhaustible; enormous lobsters were for the taking and tree branches crashed under the weight of roosting passenger pigeons. In the field of food processing, both fish-canning and cheese-making were well advanced, highly profitable sources of foreign exchange.

It was the Indians who showed the settlers how to spear fish at night by the light of flares and how to chop holes in the ice to catch fresh fish in the middle of winter. All the rivers teemed with fish. Sturgeon were so plentiful that they were often sent brined to England and the continent. Sea salmon were large and, until the early years of this century, fresh-water salmon were to be found in rivers and lakes all over the country. The land-locked salmon of the east, the Ouananiche, was greatly esteemed as it still is today in New Brunswick and Quebec.

The building of much needed mills and the damming of streams spelled destruction to most of the eastern salmon, particularly since there was no understanding of the need for returning the fish to their spawning grounds. By mid-century the coming of the railway, with the availability of ice in commercial quantities made it possible for homes far from the lakes and ocean to be supplied with fresh fish. Ontario fish from Collingwood was sent to Toronto and exported as far as Oswego, Utica, Albany and even New York. Goderich sent fish to the markets of Cleveland and Cincinnati. As soon as the weather was cold enough, oysters were shipped across country in large barrels as far west as there were settlements. Lobsters were the wealth of New Brunswick, and the canning industry was highly successful and well established.

". . . at Shippagan and Caraquette, carts are sometimes driven down to the beaches at low water, and readily filled with lobsters left in the shallow pools by the recession of the tide. Every potato field near the places mentioned is strewn with lobster shells, each potato hill being furnished with two or three lobsters. Within a few years one establishment has been set up on Portage Island, at the mouth of the River Miramachi, and another at the mouth of the Kouchibougac River, for putting up lobsters, in tin cases, hermetically sealed for exportation. In 1845, no less than 13,000 cases of lobsters and salmon were thus put up on Portage Island. In 1857, nearly 10,000 cases of lobsters, each case containing the choicest parts of two or three lobsters, and one-and-a-half tons of fresh salmon in 2-lb and 4-lb cases, were put up at Kouchibougac. The preservation of lobsters in this manner need only be restricted by the demand, for the supply is unlimited. The price paid for lobsters, at the establishment on Portage Island, is 2s. per 100. They are all taken in small hoop nets, by the Acadian French of Neguac villages, who, at the price stated, could with reasonable diligence, make £1 each in 24 hours; but as they are somewhat idle and easily contented, they rarely exert themselves to earn more than 10s. per day, which they can generally obtain by eight or ten hours' attention to their hoop nets."[2]

Meats were many and varied. They ranged from the black squirrel, which made "capital eating" and tasted somewhat like rabbit, to the passenger pigeon, buffalo, turtle and moose. The pigeons have long been extinct and many other animals would have suffered a similar fate if legislation had not been applied just in time.

The cook-books of the period, in-cluding Mrs. Beeton's, said that no lady should ever be offered the leg of a bird. This was both vulgar and indelicate; only the breast and wings were permissible. And so it was with the pigeons, though probably plenty rather than politeness was the reason for discarding all but the breast when pies were made.

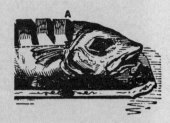

This killing of animals for the taking of one choice part, such as either the tongue or the hump of the buffalo, was prevalent throughout the period. But in 1851 buffalo hides were also used in tremendous numbers for a most curious reason, according to Peter Lund Simmonds:

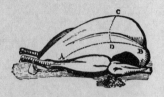

"During the time of the Great Exhibition in 1851, buffalo hides, and sheep and calf skins, advanced cent. per cent. in price. This was caused by the great demand for jellies in the refreshment rooms. Visitors then consumed jellies who never tasted jellies before; hides were purchased in tons in Liverpool, for the purpose of making these delicacies. Size and glue were used at first, but the hides were found to be cheapest."[2]

Jellied desserts had been known for a long time but had never been made in mass quantities. The usual jelling agent was isinglass, a fish glue derivative, and so it was in Canada. But as time passed animal gelatine in sheet form was used, no doubt spurred on by the 1851 success in London. Early gelatine was like sheet glue and had to be soaked for several hours to soften it.

Canadians were both intrigued and repelled by Indian feasts. These included on the menu specially fattened dogs; in some instances

white or light-coloured puppies were preferred. A native delicacy that did meet with popular approval was *mouffle*, the loose covering around the nose and lips of the moose or elk. Those who lived in eastern Canada, particularly in New Brunswick, thought highly of this meat when stewed or roasted. So did Mrs. Simcoe, who gamely tried the many delicacies of her new country and enjoyed mouffle at formal dinners in Quebec as well as at home in Upper Canada.

The beaver was considered delicate eating by both settlers and Indians, the greatest delicacy being the tail. Before cooking, the animals were singed to remove the hair but were cooked in the skin, which was peeled off before serving.

". . . and in some districts it requires all the influence of the fur-traders to restrain hunters from sacrificing a considerable quantity of beaver fur every year to secure the enjoyment of this luxury. The Indians of note have generally one or two feasts in a season, wherein a roasted beaver is the prime dish. It resembles pork in its full flavour, but it requires a strong stomach to sustain a full meal of it. The flesh is always in high estimation, except

176

VENISON.

when they have fed upon the fleshy root of a large water lily, which imparts a rank taste to it."[2]

Although the land teemed with game and fish most families considered pork to be the only possible kind of meat. Venison, either fresh or dried, was eaten of necessity. Generally men were too busy clearing and fencing land to spend time hunting, and, when possible, preferred to buy venison from local Indians. Dried and powdered venison was the main ingredient of pemmican, a long-lasting nourishing food known to the Indians and later used by anyone going on a long journey. Some settlers made their own in order to have control over the product, because the Indians pounded the dried meat on a buffalo hide, which added impurities to the mixture. The powdered meat was mixed with suet and dried service or June berries, which have an almond flavour, and packed in hide bags. These dried berries were often pounded into a paste and dried in cakes and eaten in lieu of bread and biscuit by both Indians and isolated settlers.

Another travelling food was "bean porridge", a thick stew made from corned beef (brined) or a mixture of fresh beef and salt pork cooked until thick, with white beans, hulled corn and corn meal to thicken the gravy. When the stew was tender and as thick as porridge it was poured into bowls ranging in size from a pint to two quarts. A clean tow rope was laid in a loop over the edge, and the porridge was put in the summer kitchen or outbuilding to freeze. Later the frozen stew was unmoulded and hung by the rope loop from a hook in the storeroom.

It was considered at its best when nine days old or more. According to a number of early accounts, the men who worked in the clearings took with them each day a skillet or a three-legged iron kettle, along with the frozen porridge which was wrapped in a clean cloth and hung on the sled stake. For the noon "bait" the stew was heated and eaten with thick slices of rye and Indian bread which had been kept warm all morning in jacket pockets.

The first settlers found the Indians growing patches of corn. They bartered for seed and did likewise. It became a custom to grow some corn even before the land was completely cleared and stumped. It was only after clearings were made and seed imported that other grains were grown. It is hard to realize that this country once had to have legislation passed in the British Houses of Parliament to "allow the Exportation of a limited Quantity of Wheat-meal or Flour, Oats, Oatmeal, Grotts, Barley, Pease, Beans, Malt and Biscuit, to Hudson's Bay, in North America, for the benefit of the Hudson's Bay Company, and their Servants residing there".[3] For many years there was a steady importing of seed by all the settlers who could afford to do so.

During the early days many homes were several days' journey from the closest mill, and families had to try and grind grain for themselves. The most laborious and primitive way was to use a coffee grinder or mill to make the children's porridge. Many Scotsmen, however, brought with them or made their native mortar-mill, the *quern*. This is a handmill made of two circular stones with a hole in the centre of the upper one through which corn or oats are fed. A wooden handle turns the mill, and the meal falls from the sides of the stones onto a tray. In some models the coarseness of the meal can be controlled by means of a wooden spindle. Corn was difficult to grind at home because of its tough outer skin. To overcome this a method of softening kernels in lye water was developed and used well into the twentieth century.

To Hull Corn

"Take 3 quarts corn, 2 quarts un-leached wood ashes (or ¼ pound potash); to ashes or potash add 6 quarts water, which boil and skim; strain lye into kettle; put in the corn; boil until skins break from kernels easily, stirring frequently; skim out the corn, rinse it several times, rubbing thoroughly last time; leave it to soak in clear water 10 minutes, then rub off black chits; rinse again; put back into kettle, cover with water, boil slowly till soft; keep hot water to add until boiled tender; salt. Eat with cream and sugar.
Take a ½ pint of yellow corn; roast it like coffee over a slow fire; clean out the coffee mill; grind 1 coarse, 1 fine; wet with milk and a little salt, after it has stood 5 or 10 minutes to swell."[4]

Wherever the Scots settled they ate oatmeal in various ways. One of the oldest traditional dishes was *sowans*, a mixture of slightly fermented oatmeal popular for many decades. When liquor was added, as it was from time to time, sowans was somewhat similar to the English flummery. "Sowans-Nicht" was another name for Christmas Eve when friends gathered around a big bowl. It was served also with plenty of butter on All-hallows Eve, when sometimes a ring was put in the communal dish to discover who would be the first to be married.

Old Time Sowans

"The old-time honoured dish of sowans is one of the most palatable, healthful and economical dishes that can be prepared for the evening meal of any family. If properly made and eaten with sweet milk it is extra nice. The following is the proper way to prepare it: Put into an earthen vessel three pints of rich oatmeal seeds, and two pints of good oatmeal (more or less can be used if desired), and stir enough lukewarm water in to make about the thickness of buttermilk. Set in a warm place for three or four days, or until the liquid becomes sour, keep the vessel covered and stirring occasionally; then rub and press the mixture well with the hands and strain through a fine sieve into a pot or saucepan; add salt to taste; place over a slow fire and boil constantly stirring until cooked, when it will be quite thick, if sufficient material has been used."[5]

With true Scottish thoroughness the residue was saved and used as a starter for another batch. It was guaranteed that this could go on every day for three weeks, with the result that the later batches were far superior in flavour to the early ones.
Quite new to all homesteaders regardless of origin was wild rice, a truly native plant. Technically it is

not a rice at all, but a tall water-loving grass growing along the edges and marshlands of lakes and rivers of Canada. The Jesuits in their writings misnamed it wild oats, and the English compounded the error by calling it wild rice. It was such an important food to the Indians that they battled each other over the more productive areas and from the time of the first treaties the harvesting of this food has been their perquisite.

The turning of maple sap into sugar, molasses, butter and taffy was a picturesque sight and an occupation quite new to all the settlers. It was also one of the most important household tasks at a time when sugar had to be imported. This was another food the Indians had known for generations. They used to boil the sap and evaporated it by dropping hot rocks into the syrup to speed up the process. This cooking method, as primitive as the first attempts to cook food, naturally adds much foreign matter to the syrup. It was the settlers who refined the process and made it economical and profitable. Sugaring went on day and night and was an excuse for parties, dancing and courtship. Children threw hot syrup onto freshly smoothed snow to make taffy, and young women tried to throw the syrup into initials to tell the name of a young man. Although it was a social occasion, sugaring was hard work, but it was often left to the women and young boys because, important as it was for household supplies, the men were needed for working in the clearings.

The first run of the sap in early spring was called the "robin run", and the final sap collecting was the "frog run". There were many weird and wonderful formulae to keep the boiling sap from running over. The most usual was to rub the edge of the kettles with lard, a custom still followed in some areas today when making jam. Another was to drop a lump of pork fat into the boiling mass at the critical moment. To clear the syrup, beaten eggs as well as milk were added. These curdled and rose to the surface bringing impurities with them, which were later skimmed off.

It did not take the settlers long to learn that it was possible to make a kind of beer from both maple and birch sap, and either of these would turn to vinegar. Mrs. Simcoe mentions in her diary eating another delicious sugar made from sap of the black walnut.

The taste of maple syrup was new to the recent arrivals in Canada, and because of the shortage of sweetening it was much relished. It was so popular among Lower Canadians that on fast days they would sometimes eat bread and maple sugar or butter, rather than fish. So rare was sugar, and so expensive, that many plentiful foods were not used because they took too much sweetening. For instance, pie plant (rhubarb) was considered a luxury by many, as were cranberries and other tart fruits.

Cheese-making was one of the earliest commercial enterprises, but it was first made in the home. Not only did the milk have to be collected and separated but rennet had to be made at home. Rennet separates the curds from the whey in cheese-making, and it was also used to prepare one of the favourite desserts of the period, a kind of junket. Rennet can be made from the stomach of many young animals, but most commonly it was the maw or first stomach of a sucking calf. The stomach was thoroughly washed and salted and then stored either dry or in salt, or sometimes in a mixture of aromatic herbs and water. If washed and dried between uses, rennet has the power of lasting through several curdlings. A maw would last a long time.

Many farms had bulky wood presses but a great many homes merely pressed the curds between two pieces of wood with heavy rocks to increase the weight. Some women simply hung the curds in fine cloth bags and allowed the whey to drip out slowly, but this type of cottage cheese had to be eaten quickly and could not be stored.

Cheese-making was hard work. Not only were the curds pressed, but the cheese had to be rubbed, turned, dried and examined. It was not much regretted when this chore left the home. Cottage and pot cheese was often flavoured with herbs such as sage, or even caraway seeds. German settlers made *schmier kase*, a sour curd cheese to which cream was sometimes added before serving. Many of these cheeses are still available in farmers' markets today. The monasteries of Quebec developed blue and a soft-ripening cheese similar to those made by the parent house in Europe. (The venturesome sprinkled flour between layers to encourage blue veining.) But the most important cheese was cheddar.

By the 1860's the first cheese factories began to purchase supplies from surrounding farms. So successful was this venture that very soon cheese became an important export. There was much competition to produce the finest cheese. Huge wheels were sent to agricultural fairs throughout the continent and overseas.

REFERENCES
[1] *Poems*, McIntyre, Ingersoll, Ontario, 1889.
[2] *The Curiosities of Food*, Simmonds, London, 1859.
[3] *Act. 13 Anno Regni Georgii III*, London, 1774.
[4] *Manuscript Book*, Anonymous, Toronto, 1877.
[5] *The New Household Manual*, Morrow, Saint John, N.B., 1901.

"THE COCK DOTH CROW, TO LET YOU KNOW,
IF YOU BE WISE, WHAT TIME TO RISE."

Mother Hubbard's Cupboard

CHAPTER FIFTEEN

*"Double, double, toil and trouble;
Fire burn, and cauldron bubble".*[1]

No attempt has been made to list completely the most used recipes, nor to give detail of everyday foods. Rather this is a personal selection of the most interesting and readable recipes in use during the greater part of the nineteenth century. Because this is not a full-scale cook-book, mention has not been made of the Ukrainian, Icelandic, Scandinavian, Slav and other European foods brought to this country, particularly to the west, by later settlers.

The complete history of changes in our daily food is a story in itself, but even a brief glance shows interesting sidelights. It took many years for cook-books, whether Canadian or American, to reflect the spirit of these new countries and to include recipes for the native foods, omitting the unattainable. Eventually the changes did take place.

"Griddle" or "girdle" cakes became "flapjacks", "slapjacks", and later "flatcars". The latter name was popular in early railroad days. They were always known as "flannel" cakes in lumber and mining camps. In our books "treacle" became molasses, and recipes appeared for corn meal, spruce beer and maple syrup. Gingerbread was made here as a soft spicy cake, instead of the hard cookie type of Europe.

Johnny, journey and hoe cakes were invented, and so were "rye 'n' Injun" breads, pumpion (pumpkin) puddings, pies, cakes and breads. Melon rinds were substituted for the rarer citron, and cranberries were plentiful. The lemon pie became acclimatized, and a national dish, changing gradually from an eighteenth century English pastry of treacle and sliced lemons to the creamy mixture we know, made possible with the general use of white sugar and the milling of cornstarch. For many years the *tourtière* had the same meaning to both English and French women. In fact, in seventeenth century England, tourtière meant a dish to hold a meat pie. By the mid-nineteenth century the word had died out among the English. All the early books have recipes for tea and coffee creams and jellies, invented by frugal women to use every drop of left-over of these expensive beverages.

Cook-books still current in the first thirty years of the nineteenth century were in the main written for "professed cooks". This eighteenth century terminology meant books for women already understanding the art of cooking. Beginners can search in vain to find recipes for simple daily foods such as toast, tea or boiled eggs. Cook-books were for the unusual and not for daily needs. Generally only the wealthy could read, and because ingredients were expensive, upper-class women learned to make their own confections. They were then able to direct the servants. Later, particularly in this country, when servants were few and untutored and when girls married extremely young, books were written to instruct the beginner.

For the greater part of the century, the time, method and ingredients for recipes are vague. It was not until the 1880's that standardized measuring equipment was advocated, and even then it was not common practice for women to use it. Of course, in the better kitchens, scales had been used for a long time, but there was a gradual shift from the European method of cooking by weight to the newer cooking by volume.

In selecting these recipes, where it was a case of the earliest or the most interesting presentation, I have taken the latter. As was mentioned in another chapter* these foods can be recreated, but the cook should remember the changes in eggs, sugar, butter, seasoning and flour. In most cases, today's milling means that at least a third more flour is required. Needless to say, these recipes are now for reading pleasure. None have been tested for present use, but this should not daunt the historically-minded experimenter.

"All these recipes are *reliable*. If they fail, it must be for want of that ingredient so necessary in every recipe, 'a spoonful of common sense.' They have been contributed by our best cooks, — have all been thoroughly tested — and will speak for themselves, if you will let them."[2]

Soups

Portable Soup

"Boil one or two knuckles of veal, one or two shins of beef, and three pounds of beef, in as much water only as will cover them. Take the marrow out of the bones: put any sort of spice you like, and three large onions. When the meat is done to rags, strain it off, and put it into a *very* cold place. When cold, take off the cake of fat (which will make crusts for servants' pies), put the soup into a double-bottomed tin saucepan, and set it on a pretty quick fire, but don't let it burn. It must boil fast and uncovered, and be stirred constantly, for eight hours. Put it into a pan, and let it stand in a cold place a day; then pour it into a round soup china-dish, and set the dish into a stew-pan of boiling water on a stove, and let it boil, and be now and then stirred, till the soup is thick and ropy; then it is enough. Pour it into the little round part at the bottom of cups or basons (*sic*) turned upside down, to form cakes; and when cold, turn them out on flannel to dry. Keep them in tin canisters. When they are to be used, melt them in boiling water."[3]

Cheat Soup

"Take of tomatoes 1 pint, canned or fresh; take a large teacup of nice white codfish, picked up fine; add to this 3 pints water; a small table-spoonful good sweet butter; when these have boiled 20 minutes; add 1 pint fresh milk — having ready ½

*See Chapter 13.

183

teaspoonful baking soda. Use immediately. The taste is similar to oysters or lobsters, all taste of tomatoes and fish are gone."[4]

Oysters

Oysters to begin a meal, oysters in soup, in pies, in rolls and even at times as invalid food were all part of the food picture in the nineteenth century. As soon as the weather became cold, barrels were shipped inland to be kept in summer kitchens and cold rooms for most of the winter. Oysters were kept in water and fed with occasional handfuls of meal, usually oatmeal. At this time these delicacies were not only cheap but still tremendously large in size, those six to eight inches in diameter were not uncommon. (The writer, William Thackeray, thought they were like swallowing a small baby.)

Oyster Pie

"50 oysters; 3 eggs boiled hard and cut up very fine; a few crumbs of bread; a large slice of butter; nutmeg, pepper and salt. Bake it in a paste."[5]

Tripe and Oysters

"Clean, scrape, and wash through many waters, three pounds of tripe, which boil in salted water until very tender, when done, cut it into small pieces, and put it into a stewpan with half a pint of boiling water, then take one quarter of a pound of butter, and mix well with one dessert-spoonful of flour, which add half at a time; then season with salt and pepper to taste, and for the purpose of browning the gravy, stir in one dessert-spoonful of sugar, browned until a very dark color.

After letting it simmer five or ten minutes, have ready about fifty broiled or pan'd oysters, stir all together, and send to the table hot."[6]

Breads

"Bread has, according to the computation of physicians, one fifth more nutriment in it when ripe, than it has when just out of the oven. It not only has more nutriment, but imparts a much greater degree of cheerfulness. He that eats old ripe bread will have a much greater flow of animal spirits than he would were he to eat unripe bread."[7]

"For a Child's Luncheon — Good sweet butter, with stale bread, is one of the most nutritious, at the same time the most wholesome articles of food, that can be given children after they are weaned."[8]

Sponge Bread

"Make a batter of flour and water, thickness of flatjacks; put it in a tin pail, and set this pail in a kettle of warm water, five or six hours, till it has risen; then mould it hard by adding more flour, and make it into loaves in basins, and let it stand till it begins to crack open. It is now ready to be put into the oven, and will bake in from thirty to forty-five minutes."[7]

(Breads made without yeast included forerunners of our present-day "quick breads" — salt-rising breads, often called "lightning bread", as well as sponge breads; these were popular because home-made yeasts were not only unreliable but time-consuming to prepare and difficult to store.)

It is **eminently needful** to any **lady**, who aspires to **excellence** in the cooking department of her household, that she should have a knowledge of what is good and reliable material, by the aid of which may be produced, in the best manner, the various substantials and delicacies of the table.

There exists no greater drawback to enjoyment of meals and health than to be compelled to consume heavy pastry, sad rolls, or pie crust comparable to horn in appearance and hardness.

These faults may all be avoided by the use of the

COOK'S FRIEND

BAKING POWDER

which is prepared with an especial view to

HEALTHFULNESS AND ECONOMY.

The **COOK'S FRIEND** may be used with the greatest advantage and satisfaction in the preparation of Sponge Cakes of every kind, Pie Crust, Boiled Puddings, Pancakes, Johnny Cakes, etc., etc., all which are thereby rendered **light** and **digestible**.

In the preparation of Biscuits or Rolls for the tea table the **COOK'S FRIEND** is invaluable as these may be eaten warm from the oven, even by dyspeptics, without injury.

Shortening, whether Butter or Lard, is economised when the **COOK'S FRIEND** is used, as in such case one fourth the usual quantity will produce better and more healthful results.

The Cook's Friend Baking Powder may be purchased at any respectable Grocery Store in the Dominion.

Purchasers should see that the correct name "Cook's Friend," is on every package as imitations bearing nearly similar names are being foisted on the public.

Name & Trade Mark the property of the Sole Manufacturer,

W. D. McLAREN,

55 & 57 COLLEGE STREET,

MONTREAL.

To Make Yeast Cakes for Yeast

"Take a quart of distiller's yeast if you can get it, if not the best you can get, add a quart of strong hop water, warm, but not scald your yeast; put as much Indian meal into it as you can conveniently mix, let it stand half an hour, make it into little flat cakes and lay them on a clean board, set them in the sun and dry until perfectly dry, put them in a dry place. When you wish to use yeast, take one cake and put it into a quart of warm water and dissolve it, stir in flour and make it as thick as thick cream, let it stand by a warm fire over night, it is then ready to make your bread in the morning."[9]

Communion Bread

1 pint flour
1 teaspoon baking powder
1 teaspoon sugar
  butter size of walnut

"Water or milk to make a proper consistency. Roll half an inch thick, put in pan, and score. Bake in a slow oven. Quantity is quite sufficient."[9]

Journey Cakes or Hoe Cake

"To one quart of coarse Indian meal, add as much warm water as will make the meal into a thick dough. Throw in sufficient salt to taste. Stir it well; spread the dough smoothly on a board; place it before the fire in an upright position. When done, cut it, and send it to table hot and eat with butter."[6]

Rye and Indian Bread

"Scald three quarts of finely sifted Indian meal till quite wet, add salt, and, when, cooked a little, work in three quarts of rye flour, two spoon-fuls of molasses, and two gills yeast. Bake three or four hours. It is better kept over night."[11]

Meats

"A steak without juice is like a woman without a soul — no account."[4]

To Boil Fowls or Chickens

"Time, one hour for a large fowl; three-quarters of an hour for a medium size; half an hour for a chicken."[12]

To Roast a Goose

"Time, a large goose two hours, a smaller, one hour and a half."[12]

Pork.

"Pig is in prime order for the spit when about three weeks old. It loses part of its goodness every hour after it is killed; if not quite fresh, no art can make the crackling crisp.

To be in perfection, it should be killed in the morning to be eaten at dinner: it requires very careful roasting. A sucking-pig, like a young child, must not be left for an instant.

The ends must have much more fire than the middle: for this purpose is contrived an iron to hang before the middle part, called a pig-iron. If you have not this, use a common flat iron, or keep the fire fiercest at the two ends."[13]

To Make Bacon

"Take fifty pounds of pork; hang it in the air four or five days; then put it in water for three hours; take three pints of molasses, five pounds of salt, six ounces of saltpetre, both very fine; rub it well with these, mixed; let it lie four or five days to make brine, then turn and baste it once a day for three or four weeks.

Instead of smoking this meat, boil three pints of soot in two gallons of water till it is reduced to three quarts; strain it, and pour it into the other liquor, with which baste it three weeks and dry it."[14]

Fried Pork

"Fried salt pork and apples is a favorite dish in the country, but it is seldom seen in the city. After the pork is fried, some of the fat should be taken out, lest the apples be oily. Acid apples should be chosen, because they cook more easily; they should be cut in slices, across the whole apple, about twice or three times as thick as a new dollar. Fried till tender, and brown on both sides — laid around the pork. If you have cold potatoes slice them and brown them in the same way."[15]

Mutton

"Select a large leg of Canada mutton. Let it hang, according to weather, as long as it will keep sweet. In winter, with care and favourable weather, it can sometimes hang 6 weeks and be all the better for it; of course the same is not the case in summer."[16]

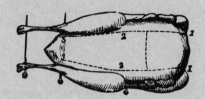

Partridge

"Let me note a Canadian receipt for cooking a partridge, which may be useful to sportsmen and travellers. Expedition is the maxim of all sylvan cookery, and as plucking the feathers of a partridge would be too great a tax on the time and patience of the voyageur, the method most in vogue is to run your hunting knife round his throat and ancles (*sic*) and down his breast, when, taking a leg in each hand, and pressing your thumb into his back, you pop him out of his skin, as you would a pea from its pod. Then make a spread-eagle of him on a forked twig, the other extremity of which is thrust in the ground, and after wrapping a rasher of bacon around his neck, and under his wings, as ladies wear a scarf, you incline him to the fire, turning the spit in the ground, and you will have a result such as Soyer* might be proud of."[17]

To Make Tough Meat Tender

"Cut the steaks the day before they are required into slices about 2 inches thick. Rub the surfaces with a little baking-soda. Next morning

*Soyer was a Frenchman who spent his life in England, inventing cooking apparatus, packaged foods and writing cook-books.

wash off the soda; cut the meat into the shape and thickness desired, and cook it to taste."[16]

Desserts
Coloring to Stain Jellies, Ices, or Cakes
"For a beautiful red, boil fifteen grains of cochineal, powdered with a drachm and a half of cream of tartar, in half a pint of water, for one hour. Add, in boiling, a bit of alum, the size of a pea; or, beet root, sliced, with some liquor poured over it. For yellow, yolks of eggs, or a bit of saffron, steeped in the liquor, and squeezed. For green, pound spinach, or beet leaves; express the juice, and boil it in a teacup; set it in a saucepan of water to take off the rawness."[14]

(Early jellies were made from calves' feet and from isinglass — a gelatine extracted from the bladders of fish. Both these jellying agents imparted a slight meat or fish flavour to the elaborately moulded jellies. However, since jellies were coloured not only with the above ingredients but with indigo for blue and violet juice for mauve, there was additional competition of flavours. Most of these early jellied desserts were meant as decoration for formal dinner tables. The most popular enjoyed such names as "Solomon's Temple", "Hens and Chickens", "Fish Pond" and

"Moonshine"; to name only a few. Jellies to be eaten were usually simply flavoured with wine.)

Iced Jelly
"Make calves' feet jelly in the usual way. Then put it into a freezer, and freeze it as you would ice-cream. Serve it up in a glass bowl or in jelly-glasses. You cannot mould it this way: but the taste of jelly when broken up is more lively than when moulded; also it sparkles and looks handsome."[18]

(The following ice-cream appears in a number of books and manuscripts with slight variations from its original, which came from *The Complete Confectioner*, Frederick Nutt, London, 1806.)

Plain Ice Cream
"Put one pint of cream into a freezing pot in a little ice, whisk it about till it hangs about the whisk; then take the whisk out and put as much powdered sugar as will lay on half a crown; stir and scrape it about with your ice scraper till you find it all frozen; put it in your mould, and put in your ice to take the shape.

"Brown Bread Ice Cream: Only when you have frozen it, rasp two handfuls of brown bread and put it in before you put it into your moulds."

(Ice-cream had been known in Europe but was perfected and made popular through all classes in North America. It was helped by the invention of the mechanical ice cutter and the above-ground ice house owned by so many homes, as well as by the early use of refrigerators. Early ice-cream moulds were made of pewter.)

Common Syllabub

"Half a pint of currant,* the same of port or white wine, half a grated nutmeg, and the peel of a lemon; sweeten well with pounded loaf or good brown sugar, and mix it together in a china bowl, and when the sugar dissolves, milk upon it three or four pints of milk. Serve it when cold."[13]

(Known in the previous century as Syllabub Under the Cow.)

Snow Balls

"Boil some rice in milk till it be swelled and soft; pare and carefully scoop out the core of five or six good-sized apples; put into each a little grated lemon-peel and cinnamon; place as much of the rice upon a bit of linen as will entirely cover an apple, and tie each closely. Boil them two hours, and serve them with melted butter, sweetened with sugar."[13]

Thunder and Lightning

"Have maple syrup and place on top Devonshire cream (scald cream), and serve."[9]

Mince Meat

"Three bowls of meat; 5 bowls of apples; 1 bowl of molasses; 1 of vinegar; 1 of cider; 1 of suet or butter; 2 of raisins; 5 of sugar; 1 bottle of brandy, or, if you prefer, leave out the brandy and add more cider; 2 tablespoonfuls each of cinnamon, nutmeg and cloves; 1 tablespoonful each of salt and black pepper; 3 lemons — grate outside and squeeze the juice. This makes a large quantity, but it is very nice and keeps well. If I dared, I'd say put in a teacup of brandy when you are ready to bake."[4]

*A homemade wine.

Hen's Nest

"Make blancmange and set it to cool in three or four egg-shells. Next cut some orange or lemon peel in strips the size of a straw, boil it in syrup till perfectly clear. Make a nice custard and put in a glass dish. On this place the preserved peel in the form of a nest, in which place the blancmange after having taken off the shell. It is a very handsome dish for dessert."[11]

Puddings and Pies
Quebec Macaroni Pudding

"Boil eight ounces of macaroni in a quart of milk, till quite tender; line your dish with a thick paste;* put it in, and add half a pint of milk with a little fresh butter; cover with a paste, and bake about forty-five minutes."[7]

Eve's Pudding

"Six apples, pared and chopped fine; six ounces of bread, crumbed fine; six eggs, six ounces sugar; one-half pound raisins; heaping teaspoonful salt; small teaspoonful cloves; one-half nutmeg; one cup milk. Boil two hours, without any flutter; Adam wouldn't eat it without wine and butter."[2]

*The old word for pie pastry.

189

Half-Pay Pudding

"Four ounces each of the following ingredients, viz., flour, suet, currants, raisins, bread crumbs, two tablespoonfuls of treacle, half a pint of milk, all of which must be well mixed together and boiled three hours in a mould."[11]

Toronto Pie

"One cup of sugar, three eggs, one and one-half cups of flour, one teaspoon of baking powder; flavour to taste; bake as for jelly cake in layers, and spread between the layers raspberry jam."[19]

Centennial Apple Pie

"Peel one dozen and a half of good apples, take out the cores, cut them small, put into a stewpan that will just hold them with a little water, a little cinnamon, two cloves, the rind of a lemon; stew over a slow fire until quite soft, then sweeten them, pass it through a hair sieve, add the yolks of four eggs and one white, quarter of a pound of good butter, half a nutmeg, the peel of a lemon grated, and the juice of one lemon; beat all well together; line the inside of the pie dish with good puff paste; put in the pie and bake half an hour."[19]

(See note after *Centennial Cake,* p. 193.

Plum Pudding

"Forty-eight groat biscuits; six quarts of milk; forty-five eggs; two pounds of butter; four tea-spoonfuls of cloves; four tea-spoonfuls of mace; six of cinnamon; eight nutmegs; five quarts raisins; four gills of rose water; eighteen cups of sugar; four glasses of brandy; citron if you choose. Scald the bread and butter with the milk. Those who are fond of cold plum pudding will find this a very nice recipe."[14]

Rennet Pudding

"If your husband brings home company when you are unprepared, rennet pudding may be made at five minutes' notice; provided you keep a piece of calf's rennet ready prepared soaking in a bottle of wine. One glass of this wine to one quart of milk will make a sort of cold custard. Sweetened with white sugar, and spiced with nutmeg, it is very good. It should be eaten immediately; in a few hours, it begins to curdle."[15]

Chicken Pie

"Fill up the pie with chicken, oysters, and eggs boiled hard and sliced. Strain the liquor; cover the pie, and bake it. If the pie is not to be eaten the day it is baked, the eggs had better be omitted; they give an unpleasant flavor."[14]

Vinegar Pie

"Four tablespoons vinegar; two tea-spoons vanilla; three eggs, two tea-cups sugar; butter size of the eggs. Beat well together. Whites of two eggs spread over the top. This makes two pies."[20]

Partridge and Pigeon Pies

"Some people, in both pigeon and partridge pie, stick the feet of the birds (nicely cleaned) in a hole in the top crust, to mark the kind of pies."[14]

Thatched-Roof Pie

"Rub the inside of a deep-round shape with butter and spread over it two ounces of vermicelli. Lay a thick puff paste in the shape, and put into it three or four pigeons properly seasoned, with a lump of butter in each, and their breasts down. Cover and bake it in a moderate oven. When fired, turn it out on a dish; raise the vermicelli up with a pin, and it will then appear like what it takes its name from."[21]

A Sea Pie

"Four pounds flour, one pound and a half butter rolled in paste, wet with cold water, line the pot there-with, lay in one dozen split pigeons, cover with slices of pork, salt, pep-per, and dust on flour, doing thus till the pot is full, or your ingre-dients expended, add three pints water, cover tight with paste, and stew moderately two hours and a half."[9]

Peach Pie

"Take mellow, juicy peaches—wash and put them in a deep pie plate, lined with pie crust. Sprinkle a thick layer of sugar on each layer of peaches, put in about a table-spoon-ful of water, and sprinkle a little flour over the top — cover it with a thick crust, and bake the pie fifty to sixty minutes. Pies made in this manner are much better than with the stones taken out, as the prussic acid of the stone gives the pie a fine flavor."[22]

Cakes and Cookies

If "a moderate degree of experi-ence is brought to bear upon the following recipes, I have no fears of failure; and those who have not been instructed as they should have been by their mothers, or those having the care of them in their minority, and now find it necessary to make cake for themselves and their husbands must begin with the cookies, and other smaller plainer cakes, lest a failure should too great-ly discourage them; and should they fail a few times, take the mottoes 'don't give up the ship' but 'try, try again' and ultimate success must follow."[23]

Nice Cookies That Will Keep Good Three Months

"Nine cups flour, three and a half of butter, five of sugar, large coffee cup of water, with a heaping tea-spoonful of pearlash dissolved in it; rub your butter and sugar into the flour, great spoonful of caraway."[9]

"For superior kinds of cake, the best of everything must be used, the flour sifted, the sugar pounded or rolled fine and sifted also, and the butter have the salt washed from it in cold water and be pressed dry. Nutmeg is always lighter grated, but other spices must be pounded fine. A hickory spatula should be used for working the butter and sugar to a creamy consistency, though in cold weather many nice cooks use the hand. Beat the eggs when every other preparation has been made. Rods or egg-whisks are considered preferable to anything else for beating eggs. Break each egg in a saucer by itself."[6]

1, 2, 3, 4 Cake

"Cup cake is about as good as pound cake, and is cheaper. One cup of butter, two cups of sugar, three cups of flour, and four eggs, well beat together, and baked in pans or cups. Bake twenty minutes, and no more."[15]

Strawberry Cake

"Mix a quart of flour with a teaspoonful of salt, four beaten eggs, and a tea-cup of thick cream or melted butter. Add sufficient milk to enable you to roll it out — roll it out thin, line a shallow cake pan with part of it, then put in a thick layer of nice ripe strawberries, strew on sufficient white sugar to sweeten the strawberries, cover them with a thin layer of the crust, then add another layer of strawberries and sugar — cover the whole with another layer of crust, and bake it in a quick oven about twenty-five minutes."[22]

(The earliest reference to a strawberry shortcake.)

Methodist Cake

"Two eggs, one cupful sugar, one cupful sweet milk, half cupful butter, two teaspoonfuls cream of tartar, one teaspoonful soda, two cupfuls flour. Bake in three layers. Put raisins, currants and spices in the middle layer; put frosting between one layer and jelly between the other, and frosting on top."[24]

Scripture Cake

Judges 5:25	1 cup butter
I Kings 4:22	3½ cups flour
Jeremiah 6:20	2 cups sugar
I Samuel 30:12	2 cups raisins
I Samuel 30:12	2 cups figs
Genesis 24:17	1 cup water
Genesis 43:11	1 cup almonds
Isaiah 10:14	6 eggs
Leviticus 2:13	little salt
Exodus 16:31	1 large tablespoon honey
I Kings 10:2	sweet spices to taste

"Follow Solomon's advice for making good boys (Proverbs 23:14) and you will have a good cake."[25]

Hydropathic Oatmeal Cake

"Mix fine oatmeal into a stiff dough with milk-warm water; roll it to the thinness almost of a wafer; bake on a griddle or iron plate placed over a slow fire for three or four minutes; then place on edge before the fire to harden. This will be good for months, if kept in a dry place. It is an excellent article to exercise too sedentary teeth upon."[26]

Centennial Cake

"Five eggs, three cups of powdered sugar, one cup of cream or milk, one cup of butter, four cups of flour, the rind and part of juice of one lemon, and a little baking powder, or use prepared flour."

This cake with the up-to-date title was first printed in the Home Cook Book, 1876-1877. Perhaps it commemorates the Revolutionary War.

Pickles and Preserves
Pickled Lily
"Mix equal quantities of chopped tomatoes and cabbage with a few green peppers; turn over it a moderately salty brine and let it stand twenty-four hours, drain thoroughly; take sufficient strong vinegar to cover nicely; and add to it cinnamon, cloves, and allspice, to suit taste, heat and pour over the cabbage mixture."[27]

Pickle for Meat
"For every gal. of water take 7 lbs salt, 3½ lbs brownest sugar, and 1 oz of salt petre (*sic*). Let come to a boil, skim and cover meat when cold — cut up pork when cold and rub lightly with salt and put on a slanting board to drain out all bloody parts away then pack in barrel or crocks and cover with pickle. If it gets slimy boil the pickle over again and skim. You need not cut out the bones and if you can't get sugar, black strap will do. This will keep meat perfectly if followed closely. You want to let it drain untill (*sic*) any cirplus (*sic*) blood or juices are drained off. We let ours lay on board till second day. I hope you have success with it."[25]

Apple Sass
"Take to 3 gallons of cider, 5 pounds of white sugar; 1½ bushels of apples. First boil and skim your cider. Let it boil ½ an hour. Stew your apples in a portion of the cider. When your sauce is thick and glossy, add the cider and sugar. Season with cloves, etc."[9]

A Very Good Sauce
"Especially to hide the bad colour of Fowls. Cut the livers, slices of lemon in dice, scalded parsley, and hard eggs; add salt and mix them with butter; boil them up, and pour over the fowls. This will do for roast rabbit."[28]

Citron Preserves
"Take the rind of a large water melon, cut it in small pieces, allow loaf sugar pound for pound, make a sirup of the sugar, boil two hours slowly, put into pots for use."[9]

Artificial Honey
"Mix together ten pounds white sugar, two pounds clear bees' honey, one quart of hot water, half an ounce cream of tartar; when cool flavour with two or three drops otto roses (*sic*) and sprinkle in a handful of clear yellow honey comb broken up. This will deceive the best judges, and is perfectly healthy "[19]

Left Overs
Bubble and Squeak
"Slice under-done cold roast or boiled beef, with fat to fry it a nice

light brown; take care that it is not done hard. Mince some cooked cabbage, and fry it with pepper and salt, without burning; lay some in the dish, and lay in the meat, and cover it nicely with the rest, garnishing with fried beet-root, eggs or apples. This is an excellent dish if well made, but very bad if ill done."[8]

Save-All Pie

"In every family there are pieces of fresh meat left of roasted meats: these take from the bones, boil and season, put in butter and flour; make a paste and place in a deep dish, put your meat in, cover it and bake one hour. All meats can be used in this way and with good paste and seasoning make a clever dinner."[9]

Crum Cake

"Keep a bowl or pitcher with sour milk in it; and, from time to time, throw in the crums (*sic*) of bread which break off when it is sliced; and also the dry pieces left from the table. When you next want some griddle cakes, take this mixture and break up all the pieces with your hand; add an egg, salt, and saleratus, and a few spoonfuls of flour."[14]

Beverages
Raspberry Vinegar

"Lay a few quarts of raspberries in a dish, with about a pint of white-wine vinegar on them. After they have stood eight or nine days, strain off the liquor, and to every pint add a pound of loaf sugar. Boil it to a syrup. When cold bottle and cork it."[29]

Instantaneous Beer

"Put to a pint and a half of water four tea-spoonsful of ginger, a table-spoonful of lemon juice — sweeten it to the taste with syrup of white sugar, and turn it into a junk bottle. Have ready a cork to fit the bottle, a string of wire to tie it down, and a mallet to drive in the cork. Then put into the bottle a heaping tea-spoonful of the super-carbonate of soda, cork it immediately, tie it down, then shake the whole up well, cut the string, and the cork will fly out. Turn it out, and drink immediately."[22]

Rum Punch
One sour (lemon)
Two sweet (sugar)
Four strong (rum)
Eight weak (water)[29]

Process for Making Rum Shrub

"To effect this, take 65 or 70 gallons of rum, from 7 to 8 gallons of lemon-juice, 6 or 7 gallons of orange-juice, (both fresh expressed from the fruit,) orange-wine 30 gallons, 2 pounds of the rind of fresh lemon-peel, 1 pound of the rind of fresh orange-peel, (both pared off as thin as possible and previously steeped a few days in the rum,) and 100 pounds of loaf-sugar. Fill up the cask, of 120 or 130 gallons, with pure spring water; rouse them well together. If not sweet enough, sweeten to suit you; if too sweet, add more lemon juice."[30]

Sham-Champagne

"A Purely Temperance Drink — Tartaric acid, one ounce; one good sized lemon; ginger root, one ounce; white sugar, one and one-half pounds; water, two and one-half gallons; yeast, one gill.

"Slice the lemon and bruise the ginger, mix all, except the yeast, boil the water and pour it upon them, and let it stand until cooled to blood heat; then add the yeast and let it stand in the sun through the day; at night bottle, tieing the corks, and in two days it will be fit to use. Be sure not to drink over three or four bottles at one times."[1]

Canadian Cobbler

"Half fill a soda-water glass with pounded ice, and add half a small lemon sliced, a dessert-spoonful of sugar and two glasses of sherry. Mix well together, and drink through a straw. Time to make, a few minutes. Probable cost, 3d., exclusive of the sherry. Sufficient for one person."[31]

Beer from Green Pea Shells

"No production of this country abounds so much with saccharine matter as the shells of green peas. A strong decoction of them much resembles malt wort, in odor and taste, as to deceive a brewer. This decoction, rendered slightly bitter with the wood sage, and afterwards fermented with yeast; affords a very excellent beverage for the table. It is prepared as follows:— Take green shells of peas and put them into a suitable vessel, pour on water sufficient to cover them to about an inch above the top, and simmer them for 3 hours. Then strain off the liquor and add a strong decoction of the wood sage, or the hop, so as to render it pleasantly bitter and then ferment in the usual manner."[32]

Fruits and Vegetables
Asparagus

"A Substitute: the young stalks of the milkweed, which grow by the roadside, if cut when about as high as asparagus would be, and boiled like it, and served with toast, in the same manner, makes a delicious substitute for asparagus. It is exceedingly delicate, and tastes like string beans. The plant will shoot up like asparagus after being cut."[14]

Potatoes

"In Canada, they cut the skin all off, and put them in pans to be cooked over a stove, by steam. Those who have eaten them say, they are mealy and white, looking like large snow-balls when brought upon the table. It is said that a bit of unslacked lime, about as big as a robin's egg, thrown among old,

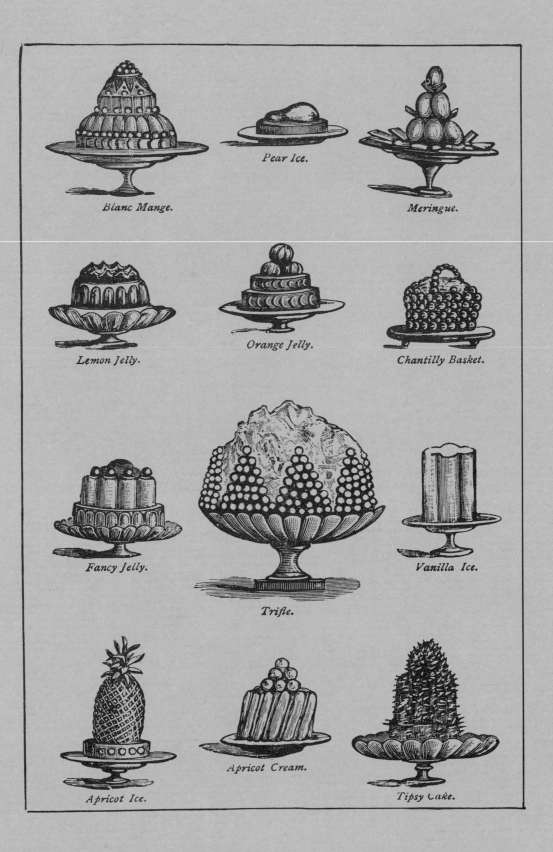

Blanc Mange.

Pear Ice.

Meringue.

Lemon Jelly.

Orange Jelly.

Chantilly Basket.

Fancy Jelly.

Trifle.

Vanilla Ice.

Apricot Ice.

Apricot Cream.

Tipsy Cake.

watery potatoes, while they are boiling, will tend to make them mealy. I never saw the experiment tried."[15]

Time for Boiling Vegetables

Green Peas	1/2	hour
String Beans	3	hours
Asparagus	20	minutes
Cabbage	2	hours
Turnips	1 1/2	hours
Parsnips	1 1/2	hours
Carrots	2	hours
Beets	4	hours
Shelled Beans	1	hour
Spinach	1 1/2	hours[24]

Orange Salad

"Cut one dozen fine ripe oranges into slices without peeling. Sprinkle over them one teaspoonful of pounded cinnamon, and a quarter of a pound of lump sugar. Pour over this whole one pint Cognac brandy. Set fire to the spirit, and stir as long as it will burn. When the flame expires, help the salad round while hot. Let the slices fall as you cut them either into a silver punch-bowl or a porcelain one that will stand fire."[11]

Weddings
Wedding Cake

"Ten pounds of flour, ten pounds of sugar, eight pounds of butter, twenty-five pounds of currants, two ounces of mace, two ounces of nutmeg, half a pint of brandy, half a pint of rosewater, four pounds of citron, ninety eggs. Make a paste for pans, and bake in plumcake pans from three to four hours."[11]

Frosting for the Above

"The whites of nineteen eggs beaten to a froth, a little rosewater, the juice of one lemon; thicken this with the finest pulverized loaf-sugar till a spoon will stand in it. Scrape the cake, and wet it with gumwater before you frost it. Dry it gradually."[11]

A Bride's Pie

"Boil two calves feet, take the meat from the bones, and chop it very small; take a pound of beef suet and a pound of apples shred small; clean and pick a pound of currants, stone and chop a quarter of a pound of raisins, a quarter of an ounce of cinnamon, the same of mace and nutmeg, two ounces of candied citron, the same of lemon peel cut thin, a glass of brandy and champagne; cover a round loose-bottomed pan with puff paste, and put the meat into it, roll out the lid, ornament it with paste leaves, flowers, figures and a ring."[21]

The Mock Dishes

One of the most curious aspects of Canadian gastronomy is the number of "mock" dishes featured in books, leaflets, notebooks and almanacs from the very earliest times. Obviously some were to provide a meal when supplies were low, but they run the gamut from Mock Cherry which was a mixture of cranberries and raisins to Mock Goose, which follows:

Mock Goose

"Pare and cut in two lengthwise a good sized vegetable marrow and remove the seeds. Rub this over inside and out with salt, and leave for an hour to drain. Have ready some onions boiled and chopped, with a little sage, add to them pepper, salt and a little butter, and

197

fill up the halves of the marrow with the mixture. Close up and tie over with tape. Butter a pie dish, place the goose upon it, and bake in a moderate oven till it is browned and tender. Serve warm with a little white sauce."[9]

Mock Mince Pie
"Six soda crackers rolled fine; 1 cup hot water; 1 cup molasses; ¼ cup brown sugar; ½ cup vinegar; ½ cup melted butter; 1 cup raisins chopped; 1 teaspoon each of cinnamon, cloves, allspice and nutmeg. Measure in a coffee-cup."[19]

Mock Duck
"Take the round of beefsteak, salt and pepper either side, prepare bread or crackers with oysters or without, as for stuffing turkey, lay your stuffing on the meat; sew up and roast about an hour; and if you do not see the wings and legs you will think you have roast duck."[9]

Mock Lobster
"Take some cold veal (either boiled or roasted), cut it in small pieces, season with salt, pepper, mustard, vinegar and sweet oil. If preferred hot, leave out the mustard and oil, and put in a piece of butter instead. Put all together in a sauce-pan, place it on the fire, and let it get hot; then serve it immediately. This makes a fine relish for tea or breakfast."[14]

The Royal Family and Their Friends

The Regent's or George IV's Punch
"Pare as thin as possible the rinds of two China oranges, of two lemons, and of one Seville orange, and infuse them for an hour in half a pint of thin cold syrup; then add to them the juice of the fruit. Make a pint of strong green tea, sweeten it well with fine sugar, and when it is quite cold, add it to the fruit and syrup, with a glass of the best old Jamaica rum, a glass of brandy, one of arrack, one of pine-apple syrup, and two bottles of champagne; pass the whole through a fine lawn sieve until it is perfectly clear, then bottle, and put it into ice until dinner is served.

"We are indebted for this receipt to a person who made the punch daily for the prince's table, at Carlton palace, for six months; it has been in our possession some years, and may be relied on."[33]

Prince Albert Pudding
"Pour one pint of cream on twelve ounces of Savoy or sponge cake, then add the yolks of six eggs and whites of two, the rind of a lemon rubbed on sugar, four ounces of sugar, and a little salt. Mix well together, and pour into a mould spread with butter, and steam the pudding one hour and a quarter."[11]

Soupe à la Reine
"Pound, in a marble mortar, the white meat of three cold roasted fowls, and half a pound of sweet almonds blanched; add a little cream whilst pounding. Boil this with four quarts of well-seasoned veal stock, then strain it, and just before serving, stir in a pint of cream. Potage à la Reine is so called from its having been said to be the favourite soup at the table of Queen Victoria."[33]

Berry Charlotte

"Have slices of bread buttered. Stew raspberries, blackberries, or any other kind, and place between the buttered bread, or use, if you like, the uncooked berries in the same way."[11]

(It is said that the Charlotte dishes were named in honour of the wife of George III. Some writers have suggested that Câreme, who was in England for a short time, named and invented the first recipe. Others say that "Charlyt" is the old word for custard.)

Royal Nursery Pudding

"Pour scalding milk upon sliced white bread; let it stand till well soaked, then beat it well with four eggs, a little sugar, and pounded orange-peel. Boil two hours in a nicely floured pudding-bag. Tie up tight."[11]

Gateau de Princess Louise

"Bake a sponge drop mixture or feather cake or snow cake in jelly cake tins. Cut the centre from one cake, leaving a rim one inch and a half wide. Put jelly on the remaining cake, lay the rim on the edge, and fill the centre with Bavarian cream. Garnish with candied fruit. Frost the rim if you prefer."[34]

(Princess Louise was a daughter of Queen Victoria, who was married to the Marquis of Lorne, later the Duke of Argyll. She came to Canada when her husband was appointed Governor-General.)

Prince of Wales' Soup

"Ingredients: 12 turnips, 1 lump of sugar, 2 spoonfuls of strong veal stock, salt and white pepper to taste, 2 quarts of very bright stock.

"Mode — Peel the turnips, and with a cutter cut them in balls as round as possible, but very small. Put them in the stock, which must be very bright, and simmer till tender. Add the veal stock and seasoning. Have little pieces of bread cut round, about the size of a shilling; moisten them with stock; put them into a tureen and pour the soup over without shaking, for fear of crumbling the bread, which would spoil the appearance of the soup, and make it look thick.

"This soup was invented by a philanthropic friend of the Editress, to be distributed among the poor of a considerable village, when the Prince of Wales attained his majority, on the 9th November, 1859."[35]

Poor Knights of Windsor

"Cut some slices of bread, about half an inch thick, and lay them in white wine and sugar; when they have soaked a while, take them out and dip them one by one in the yolk of cast* eggs. Have some fresh butter boiling in a frying-pan; put the bread into it, and fry it a fine brown on both sides; then dish it, and strew sugar and beat cinnamon over it."[21]

Jenny Lind Cake

"One quart flour, two teaspoonfuls of cream of tartar put dry into the flour, about one third of a teaspoon-

*Cast is an old word for beaten eggs.

199

ful of soda, dissolved in a third of a cup of boiling water, a large teacupful of milk, half a teacupful of sugar, and three eggs. Mix all well together. Do not vary the receipt."[11]

Earl Grey Pudding
"Three eggs weight in butter and sugar, weight of two eggs in flour. Beat the butter to a cream and whisk the eggs very light, and pound the sugar, and beat all three together until it is in a froth. Then add the flour gradually and the peel of one lemon grated, a little nutmeg and six bitter almonds bruised. Beat the whole well, fill the mould and boil gently two and a half hours."[24]

Bills of Fare
For a family of six; average 78 cents per day, or 13 cents per person.

Breakfast
Flour Pancakes with Sugar Syrup
Coffee

Dinner
Bread Soup
Beef Neck Stew
Noodles

Supper
Browned Flour Soup with
Fried Bread
Toast and Cheese

For a family of six; average $1.38 per day, or 23 cents per person.

Breakfast
Egg Omelet on Toast
Boiled Rice with Milk and Sugar
Coffee

Dinner
Beef Soup with Egg Sponge
Macaroni with Cheese
Dandelion Greens
Bread

Supper
Sour Cream Soup
Meat Croquettes (of soup meat)
Graham Bread and Butter
Tea   Cake[36]

REFERENCES

[1] *Mother Hubbard's Cupboard or the Canadian Cook Book*, Hamilton, Ontario, 1881.
[2] *The Cook's Friend Cook Book*, Toronto, 1881.
[3] *A New System of Domestic Cookery*, Rundle, London, 1813.
[4] *The Home Guide or a Book by 500 Ladies*, Elgin, Ill., 1877.
[5] *The Family Recipe Book*, Toronto, 1878.
[6] *The New Cook Book*, Philadelphia, 1856.
[7] *The New England Economical Housekeeper*, Howland, Montpellier, 1845.
[8] *The Ladies' New Book of Cookery*, Hale, New York, 1852.
[9] *The Cook Not Mad*, Kingston, Ontario, 1831.
[10] *Manuscript Book*, London, Ontario, n.d.
[11] *Home Cookery*, Chadwick, Boston, 1853.
[12] *Warne's Model Cookery*, Jewry, London, 1868.
[13] *Cook's Own Book*, Boston, 1832.
[14] *The Practical American Cook Book*, New York, 1866.
[15] *The American Frugal Housewife*, Child, New York, 1838.
[16] *Good Living*, Brugière, New York, 1890 .
[17] *The Curiosities of Food*, Simmonds, London, 1856.
[18] *The Lady's Receipt Book*, Leslie, Philadelphia, 1847.
[19] *The Home Cook Book*, Toronto, 1877.
[20] *Manuscript Cook Book*, Cobourg, Ontario, 1870.
[21] *The Practice of Cookery, Pastry and Confectionery*, Frazer, Edinburgh, 1820.
[22] *The American Housewife*, New York, 1839.
[23] *Dr. Chase's Recipes*, A. W. Chase, London, Ontario, 1868.
[24] *The Peerless Cook Book*, Montreal, c. 1890.
[25] *Manuscript Book*, Agincourt, Ontario, 1891.
[26] *The New Hydropathic Cook-Book*, Trall, New York, 1869.
[27] *Almanac*, Buffalo, N.Y., 1881.
[28] *The American Experienced Housekeeper*, New York, 1823.
[29] *The Invalid's Own Book*, Cust, New York, 1853.
[30] *The Complete Practical Distiller*, Byrn, Philadelphia, 1853.
[31] *The Dictionary of Cookery*, London, c. 1870.
[32] *Wrigley's Practical Receipts*, Wrigley, Toronto, 1870.
[33] *Modern Cookery*, Acton, London, 1853.
[34] *Boston Cook Book*, Lincoln, Boston, 1883.
[35] *Household Management*, Beeton, London, 1861.
[36] *The Household Guide*, Jefferis, Toronto, 1894.

Youth's
Miscellany

CHAPTER SIXTEEN

The science of pediatrics belongs to the twentieth century. That the previous hundred years had areas of ignorance concerning infant and child care is, to say the least, an understatement. Many widely-held misconceptions and superstitions had changed but little over several hundred years. So widespread was the lack of knowledge, and so ineffective the treatments, that it makes for fascinating reading.

It was felt that the time of conception and the thoughts of the contracting parties were extremely important as were other prenatal influences. "During pregnancy the mother should take time for self improvement and cultivate an interest for admiring beautiful pictures or engravings which represent cheerful and beautiful figures. Secure a few good books illustrating art, with some fine representations of statues, and other attractive pictures. The purchase of several illustrated art journals might answer the purpose. Pregnant mothers should avoid thinking of ugly people, or those marked by any deformity or disease; avoid injury, fright and disease of any kind. Also avoid ungraceful position and awkward attitude, but cultivate grace and beauty in herself. Avoid difficulty with neighbours or other trouble".[1]

The child is born, and immediately there is concern, action and treatment. The growth of the Temperance movement is reflected in this advice: "The first thing to be done ordinarily is to give the little stranger a bath by using soap and warm water. The application of brandy or liquor is entirely unnecessary, and generally does more injury than good".[1]

However, from the earliest times it was customary to bath a baby in wine to give strength and vitality, a talisman important in times of high infant mortality. "New born infants should be wrapped in soft flannel as soon as born. The navel should be dressed with mutton tallow warmed, and spread on soft fine linen, with a dust of nutmeg grated finely over the tallow".[2]

It was necessary to have the christening as soon as possible and to let all the friends and relatives know of this event. "Upon announcement of the birth of a child, the lady friends of the mother send her their cards, with inquiries after her health. As soon as she is strong enough to permit, the mother returns her own card to all from whom she received cards and inquiries, with 'thanks for kind inquiries'. Her lady friends then make personal visits, but gentlemen do not call upon the mother on these occasions. If they wish, they may pay their respects to the father and inquire after the health of the mother and child".[3]

A day was chosen for the christening ceremony and, if the religion permitted, it was performed at home, in which case "a carriage must be sent for the clergyman and retained to convey him back again after the ceremony is concluded".[3] The christening was sometimes followed by a luncheon, "though a collation of cake and wine will fill all the requirements of etiquette".[3]

The choice of sponsors or godparents was important. "Young persons should not stand as sponsors to infants; and none should offer to act unless their superior position warrants them in so doing".[3] The godfather had the duty of proposing the health of the infant and was required to give a gift; suggestions included a silver mug, a knife, spoon and fork, a handsomely bound Bible. The godmother often provided the robe and cap for the ceremony or a piece of "costly lace or embroidery suitable for infant's wear".[3] All who came remembered the baby, the men with silver and the women with something of their own manufacture.

"The plan of reviving the old Saxon names has been adopted by some, it has been claimed that the names of Edgar, Edwin, Arthur, Alfred, Ethel, Maud, Edith, Theresa and many others of the Saxon names are pleasant sounding and strong, and a desirable contrast to the Fannies, Minnies, Lizzies, Sadies and other petty diminutives which have taken the place of better sounding stronger names".[3] But there are always other opinions, and in Chapter XVII there is a selected list given by Mrs. Clarke, a Toronto cooking authority.

Swaddling clothes had disappeared by the turn of the nineteenth century but babies were still very much over-dressed. The many layers of clothing did not alter very much throughout the hundred years. In the 1840's a baby was put in a shirt, a petticoat of fine flannel (two or three inches longer than its feet). Then came a dimity top or bodice-coat which tied behind, and over this the robe or frock, again to fasten behind and "not much longer than the child's feet, that his motions may be strictly observed".[4] The dress for the night was a shirt, a blanket to tie on and a gown to cover all this. "Caps may be worn till the hair is sufficiently grown, but by no means till the child has got most of its teeth".[4]

In the 1890's, apart from the flannel skirts, slips, and shirt, the "modern approved styles for dressing infants included long cashmere stockings pinned

to the diapers so that the little feet were free to kick without the outmoded pinning blankets to still the naturally active healthy child".[1]

Perhaps the most extraordinary dressing took place within half an hour of birth, just after the nutmeg was dusted on. "The first article put on, after a napkin, should be a flannel band from four to four and a half inches wide; pin it snugly, but not tight enough to bind, the little shirt is the next article of dress; this should be open at the front, and folded smoothly, so as to leave no wrinkles; the pinner comes next; lay the infant on its stomach, fold the shirt smoothly on its back, fasten the shirt and pinner together with a small pin, leaving the point covered, so as to prick neither child nor nurse; wrap its feet in the pinner, and pin it as close as possible without cramping its limbs; then take the flannel skirt, draw it into place, fold the skirt over and fasten shirt, band, pinner and skirt together with two pins".[2] A slip laundered without starch was added, then a dress and "then the little one is ready for presentation to the new mother".[2]

In 1829, it was thought that tossing a young child about and exercising it in the open air was good for it. But for the new born this was recommended: "A child when it comes into the world, should be laid (for the first month) upon a thin mattress, rather longer than itself, which the nurse may sometimes keep upon her lap, that the child may always lie straight, and only sit up as the nurse slants the mattress. To set a child upright before the end of the first month, is hurtful. Afterwards, the nurse may begin to set it up and dance it by degrees: and it must be kept as dry as possible".[5]

Children were to be encouraged to creep and mothers were told that if a long slip or apron was put over the child's dress there need be no fear for soiled clothes. Once infancy was passed children were generally dressed in small size versions of adult dress. In many cases it was an adult's old garment cut down to size. Mrs. Lydia Child suggested that small boys and girls wore stockings cut down from larger worn ones. Old pantaloons were suitable for clothes for small boys while little girls could wear "pelisses made from cheap cotton cloth".[6]

Babies sometimes slept in the same beds as their mothers, some in bureau drawers, others in wooden cradles that varied in style from region to region. Some cradles had rockers, others were built to swing. Some had hoods and quite a few had wooden pegs over which cords were laced to keep the baby in place. Some cradles were open at the foot so that when drawn up to the fire the baby's feet could be warmed. Pillows were allowed but not too many, "because if the head is too warm the nervous irritability increases".[4]

Children were assets, in a pioneering agricultural country, but it is only necessary to look in an old cemetery or glance at early church records to realize how many died before the fifth year.

When children became ill they were usually dosed with one of the many patent or home brewed medicines. The general theory regarding "physic" was that the more bitter the medicine the better the effect. Crying babies were quietened with soothing syrups mostly containing laudanum, an opium derivative, or with catnip tea.

In the 1860's the most famous syrup was Mrs. Winslow's, which she advertised, giving grateful mothers almanacs filled with household hints, recipes and information on other patent medicines. This was by no means the only soothing syrup in a lucrative field. Many so-called nurses to the crowned heads and nobility were bottling nostrums. "Madam La Monte presents to the public the result of more than twenty years' experience as nurse and physician, both in France and the United States, in the form and under the name of *Baby Cordial for Children Teething* which greatly facilitates the process of teething by softening the gums, reducing inflammation and will allay all pain and spasmodic action and is sure to regulate the bowels. Mothers! it will give relief and health to your infants and joy and satisfaction to yourselves".[7]

Apart from lavish doses of laudanum, teething was assisted with the application of leeches behind the ears. Sometimes the gums were lanced.

"A sharp pen-knife and a steady hand making an incision to touch the rising tooth will cause no more pain than a single scratch of the gum, and usually will give speedy relief".[8] Or, "make a necklace of the bean called Job's tears, and let the child wear it around the neck".[9]

Although experts were beginning to write about the need for fresh air, exercise, sunlight and a well-balanced diet, these needs were generally disregarded and remained so until the twentieth century. There was no understanding of the dietetic values of different foods. Sunshine was often avoided because it coloured the skin. The night air was shunned; the old fable that it was dangerous persisted until the twentieth century and even now it has not been completely abandoned.

Children were mostly carried about. The perambulator or baby carriage was invented in the 1840's, and was made more popular when Queen Victoria purchased one. But these carriages were for wealthy families only. Many delightful ones have come down to us complete with elegant silk parasols for summer outings.

The lack of a balanced diet helped contribute to the ills of childhood and so did the primitive sanitation system. Severe constipation was still known by the fifteenth century designation of "straining of the fundament" and there were mighty purges to try and cure it. Dropsy was common and "cured" by applying leeches to the temples and giving powerful cathartics. For the deficiency disease, rickets, there was absolute fatalism: "death often closes the scene".[9] There were decimating outbreaks of measles, scarlet fever, diphtheria and whooping cough.

The changes of seasons were greeted with purges of sulphur and molasses. Worming was frequent, with additional purges. One could say that the philosophy was spare the purge and spoil the child. Some writers vainly tried to halt this continual dosing: "Never give medicine to a very young child. Many have thus lost darling children. It will, if not murdered be permanently injured. If medicine must be given at all, give it to the nurse".[9]

Hair was usually long, presenting obvious problems. "Expel nameless intruders from children's heads. Steep larkspur in water, rub the liquor a few times into the child's hair, and the business of destruction is done. This is an effectual remedy. Does it not make your head itch?"[10]

Pioneer children, too, had toys, even though these might be simple home-made playthings. Indulgent fathers whittled wooden dolls, trains and wagons. Rocking and hobby horses were home-made, and most boys made their own whistles. On butchering day, the pig's bladder was saved to make a football. Other balls were made from ravelling out old hand-knit stockings. There were wooden sleds and skates with wood platforms and iron runners. Some fortunate children had railroad trains and imported wax dolls with elaborate wardrobes. By the end of the nineteenth century many children played with model stores, doll houses, cooking stoves, miniature baby carriages, and steam engines. Children saved their money in elaborate clock-work iron banks. There were many puzzle and card games. Such games were sometimes allowed on a Sunday if they were based on a bibical theme and if not strictly forbidden by the religious sect. Noah's Ark, filled with hand-

PUZZLE PROVERBS.

18.

19.

20.

21.

22.

23.

24.

whittled animals, was a popular plaything. Because of its biblical origin, it, too, was a permissible Sabbath toy.

Purchased playthings were frowned on by the child care authorities. They felt that children should be encouraged to collect stones and rocks in order to take an interest in nature. Small boys were to be given simple tools and little girls were to cut and sew their own dolls' dresses.

There were many simple games. Some of them still linger, including "catch" and "hide-and-go-seek". Children played with tops, iron or wood hoops, marbles or alleys, and household string was saved to play "scratch-cradle" or "cat's-cradle". Small children played and sang about the things and people they knew. Songs about the miller, the blacksmith, the hunter and the farmer were popular.

All the founding peoples brought their own songs and nursery rhymes. No matter the origin, there is a distinct affinity between all of them both in words and music. Michael Sherck in *Pen Pictures of Upper Canada* mentions that in the early nineteenth century, "Patty Cake; Hush my Baby; Trot, Trot to Boston; Bah, Bah Black Sheep; Once there was a Little Boy; Shoe the Horse" were all well known.

Nursery rhymes are handed down from one generation to another. Their history is ancient and often lost in time. The play-song:

> *Shoe the horse, and shoe the mare,*
> *Let the little colt go bare*

was played by English adults at Christmas festivities in the time of Elizabeth I. It is also very similar to a song known to German-Canadian children who brought it to Canada from Pennsylvania and New York State. Other rhymes of American origin known in Canada include:

> *Hush-a-bye, baby, on the tree top,*
> *When the wind blows the cradle will rock.*

It is traditionally sung to the tune of "Lilliburlero" and the author is said to have been a Pilgrim who first saw the Indian mothers hanging their papooses from a tree branch. Another childhood favourite, "Mary had a little lamb" was written by Mrs. Sara Hale in the 1830's and is supposed to describe a true incident.

Political satire, doggerel and comment find their way into the nursery. Children happily sing and play about events of which they are unaware. The Duke of York, for whom Toronto was originally named, is commemorated in a dancing-singing game. Occasionally heard now, but very well known a hundred years ago, it runs

> *Oh, the brave old Duke of York,*
> *He had ten thousand men;*
> *He marched them up to the top of the hill,*
> *And he marched them down again.*

Loyalist children on their way to haven in Canada heard their American neighbours singing:

> As we were marching to Quebec
> The drums were loudly beating;
> The Americans have won the day,
> The British are retreating,
> March! march! march! march!

Young children were kept busy helping around the house and in the fields. In many pioneer settlements small boys were sent to collect punk, a fungus growth on decayed trees, which was dried to make kindling. Another chore for small boys, and one they hated, was to help cool freshly dipped candles. Wax for dipped candles has to be gradually built up, layer by layer. To this end a boy had to stand in the yard or a cold room with a rod of fresh "dips". When they started to harden, he returned to the warm dipping room and took another set outside.

Older boys were sent to round up the cattle. Frequently the cows were belled and turned free and it could be hard work to locate a herd. In *Adventures in Canada* the writer remembers a sly cow who always lifted her bell to rest on the top fence rail and waited silently for the boy to miss her. As soon as settlements increased in size, this free-and-easy way of dealing

209

with cattle was brought to an end and fences were the order of the day. They were important both in order to keep good neighbours and to improve the stock. Some of the earliest Quebec ordinances made it an offence to turn cattle loose.

Girls learned to spin and weave. They also sewed, knitted and took charge of younger brothers and sisters. It was a job of the girls to help with the "geese-picking". This took place in some areas about three or four times a year, from June onwards. Geese were raised primarily for their feathers and down. "Geese-picking" was a cruel business because feathers and quills were plucked from living geese. In some areas it was the occasion for a bee, but mostly it was a family affair. The girls caught the bird and the mother pulled an old stocking over its head so it would not bite. The feathers were used for bedding and the quills were cured to make pens, the nib being cut with the special "pen-knife".

Girls also had to cut the hard sugar cones with special nippers to make "company" lump sugar. They also grated the salt and helped clean the candlesticks and snuffers. They helped clean the knives, using a slicked board and special abrasives and stain removers.

Brothers and sisters helped clean the boots. They were sent to collect and help wash the eggs. (Unwashed eggs arriving at the market in the 1890's were known as "western dirties".) Children spent time tearing old clothes and rags into strips that were later braided by the adults into floor coverings.

"Provided brothers and sisters go together, and are not allowed to go with bad children, it is a great deal better for the boys and girls on a farm to be picking blackberries at six cents a quart, then to be wearing out their clothes in useless play. They enjoy themselves just as well and they are are earning something to buy clothes, at the same time they are tearing them.

"In the country, where grain is raised it is a good plan to teach children to prepare the braid straw for their own bonnets, and their brothers' hats. Where turkeys and geese are kept, handsome feather fans may as well be made by the younger members of a family, as to be bought.

"The sooner children are taught to turn their faculties to some account, the better for them and their parents.

"In this country, we are apt to let children romp away their existence, till they get to be thirteen or fourteen. This is not well. It is not well for the purses and patience of parents; and it has a still worse effect on the morals and habits of the children.

"Begin early is the great maxim for everything in education. A child of six years old can be made useful; and should be taught to consider every day lost on which some little thing has not been done to assist others. Children can very early be taught to take all the care of their own clothes. They can knit garters, suspenders, and stockings; they can make patchwork and braid straw; they can make mats for the table, and mats for the floor; they can weed the garden, and pick cranberries from the meadow, to be carried to market."[6]

In newly settled and remote areas schooling often took place at home, provided the mother was capable of teaching her children and had the time. Books were scarce and extremely expensive. Some early children's books survive with the pages varnished for extra strength. In wealthy families, the sons were often sent to the schoolmaster in the nearest town. There the boys resided as members of the family for the length of the school term. In other areas, girls and small boys were taught in the Canadian equivalent of "dame" schools, where a young and educated girl would take a few pupils for their early lessons. The various orders of Catholic Sisters taught children from the earliest times.

But generally, education was sporadic in the early years of the century. British visitors as late as 1874 were rather scathing about the system. "Whether the absence of a school is a disadvantage, depends on the social status of the parents. National schools, such as one finds in the back townships of Canada and the United States, are in every way adapted to the requirements of the ordinary run of settlers, but they are not precisely the kind of academies to which a gentleman would like to send his children. It is doubtless very amusing to read of the rough-and-ready way in which instruction is imparted by the American skulemarm. The man who had any real regard for his children would much prefer to instruct them himself, and he could do that in the woods. The only accomplishments that girls would be likely to acquire in a back settlement would be singing, or the nasal harmony which passes muster for it, quilting, and patchwork; and if they were very smart indeed, they might possibly attain to cross-stitch, and achieve a kettle-holder or a marker for the family Bible. In the large towns

there are excellent schools where boys are prepared for the learned professions, and where girls are taught everything, from sewing on a button to bravura singing and water-colour drawing. But hamlets are not towns, and in back settlements educational advantages in a liberal sense there are none".[11]

Some writers, particularly Miss Beecher, campaigned for more domestic education for girls. This authority felt that female education should have "less intellectual excitements and more domestic pursuits".[4] All her life she varied not a jot from her stand that women needed no rights, only homes. But she did feel that neat and cheerful kitchens would help girls grow up with good domestic habits. No matter what the circumstances of the family might be, she felt that the sweeping, dusting, care of furniture and beds as well as the starching and fancy cooking should all be done by daughters and not by hired help.

No one underestimated the need for fluent reading and many books were published specially for children. Of course, these were privileged children. To our eyes many of the earlier books are heavy on theology, and verbose, with dull stories and duller illustrations. There were of course some remarkable exceptions that were outstanding publishing achievements. Towards the end of the century more lighter reading became available, notably adventure stories, collections of tales called "annuals", which appeared around Christmas, and some stories without a heavy moral tone for young children. Kate Greenaway pioneered the charming tale with illustrations to match. R. L. Stevenson's poems were written for small children. There were also delightful step-by-step cook-books for the very young. Most of these were imported from Europe or the United States.

Once a child could read, he could, said Mrs. Wright in 1881 — "be much entertained with home readings, especially when these are well selected: not expecting the young to be always satisfied with mouthing Bolingbroke, or Pitt, or Burke, or Clay, or Pope — though they will be willing to use these with livelier works. Among pleasant readings for the home circle we will find: Macaulay's Lays of Ancient Rome; Lamb's Essays of Elia; Hood's Lost Heir; Tennyson's Poems, Thackeray's Four Georges".[12]

The Bible and Pilgrim's Progress were also highly recommended, particularly if these were illustrated editions. As an educational influence for Sundays, Mrs. Hale mentions the need for a melodeon so that all could enjoy sacred music and the children could sing hymns on Sunday evenings.

Reading was all very well, but there were dangers of which the parent should be forewarned and prepared. "Much of the evil literature is sold in nickel and dime novels, of which constitutes the principal part of the contents of such papers as the Police Gazette, the Police News and a large proportion of the sensational story books which flood the land. You might better place a coal of fire or a live viper in your bosom, then allow yourself to read such a book. Many of the papers and magazines sold at our news stands, and eagerly sought after by young men and boys, are better suited for the parlours of a house of ill-fame than for the eyes of pure-minded youth. When the devil determines to take charge of a young soul, he often employs a very ingenious method. He slyly hands a little novel filled with 'voluptuous forms', 'reclining on bosoms', 'languishing eyes' etc. For years there has been a great craze after the nude in art, and the realistic in literature. Many art galleries abound in pictures and statuary which cannot fail to fan the fires of sensualism, unless the thoughts of the visitor are trained in the strictest purity. Why should artists and sculptors persist in shocking the finer sensibilities of old and young of both sexes by crowding upon their view representations of naked human forms in attitudes of luxurious abandon?".[1]

Like us, parents were confused by the experts who said chastise the child and make him obedient, and those who felt that love and kindness work wonders. In many ways the later years of the nineteenth century saw the dawn of a new understanding of children. Parents have always complained about their young, but up to the middle of the nineteenth century there was always complete obedience. However, frontier society with the accent on youth began to alter this attitude. Obedience covered all phases of life and behaviour and included advice on dress, friends, manners, directions on choice of marriage partner, profession and finances. This concern did not

end on a child's majority or on marriage but persisted, quite often, as long as the parent lived. In the early years of the century it was still quite usual for children, even those of middle age, to stand in the presence of a parent. In the early days of settlement in New England, children used to stand to eat when with parents. Even upper class Loyalist children naturally started the day with a deep bow on first seeing their mother or father.

Mrs. Moodie mentions in *Life in the Clearings* that "age in Canada is seldom honoured. You would imagine it almost a crime for any one to grow old — such slighting, cold indifference are the aged treated by the young and strong".[14] There was also the age-old question of children speaking to their parents in a too familiar tone. Nevertheless, children in Canada were still considered by all visitors to be less bold than those across the border.

Although life for everyone was often hard, children were definitely an asset and were loved and cosseted to the best of their parents' ability. Mrs. Moodie remarks on the "large parties given to very young children, which are so common in this country, are very pernicious in the way in which they generally operate upon youthful minds. They foster the passions of vanity and envy, and produce a love of dress and display which is very repulsive in the character of a child".[14]

At these many parties, little girls were often dressed in rather fancy clothes. (Fancy and ostentatious perhaps by Mrs. Moodie's standards of class.) But regardless of censure, the young guests enjoyed the welcome break from tedious routine, the chance to wear fancy clothes and to play such games as "Hunt the Slipper", "Blind Man's Buff" and "Puss in the Corner".

Adolescent sex worried mothers during the second half of the century. The household writers certainly dealt with it frequently though obliquely. Called at that time the "nameless sin", it was perpetrated, they said, by the devil who encouraged idle hands.

"But few mothers are sufficiently aware of the dreadful penalties which often result from indulged impurity of thought. If children, in future life, can be preserved from licentious associates, it is supposed that their safety is secured. But the records of our insane retreats, and the pages of medical writers, teach that even in solitude, and without being aware of the sin — or the danger, children may inflict evils on themselves, which not unfrequently terminate in disease, delirium, and death. Every mother and every teacher, therefore, carefully avoiding all explanation of the mystery, should teach the young, that the indulgence of impure thoughts and actions, is visited by the most awful and terrific penalties. Disclosing the details of vice, in order to awaken dread of its penalties, is a most dangerous experiment, and often leads to the very evils feared".[8]

What did children eat? The cook-books are full of recipes for "A plain pudding for children" or "A cheap cake for children"; and in an age when the adults ate hot bread and suffered dyspepsia, the young were saved by being fed stale bread. This period, so close to our own, is interesting because in many ways dietetic knowledge had not really changed for decades. But in the second half of the century, Pasteur, Liebig and the first discoverers of vitamins played an immeasurable part in giving children a chance to live.

The nineteenth century also saw the decline of the age-old wet nurse and the increase of feeding babies by artificial means. The numbers of children successfully raised in this century increased with the passing of years even though infant mortality was still horrifyingly high. Until condensed milk was introduced, the substitute for mother's milk was generally a mixture of cow's milk and water or skimmed milk and barley water. The great danger with artificial feeding was the ignorance of hygiene. Absolutely nothing was known about sterilization. The bottle and nipple were death traps. Early nipples were of wash leather and even parchment, but rubber ones became available around the 1860's.

By the 1860's there were many attempts at providing infant foods, artificial milk and ready-made foods. Time was spent on chemical analysis of infant nourishment. However, the deductions of the various scientists involved no longer tally with our findings.

Canned and pre-cooked infant foods were known soon after the middle of the century and were in common use by the last quarter. Most of the foods were canned pre-cooked starches. These were added to milk, or in more luring advertisements, to water. The selling message was that baby could have anywhere from one hundred meals upwards for one dollar. One of the earliest pioneers in this field was the German Baron Liebig, who used a patented mixture of wheat flour, milk, malt flour and bicarbonate of potash. His rivals made a canned mixture of cooked flour and sugar and omitted the milk.

"It cannot be said that starch is unfit for the nourishment of infants, but it is nevertheless true that its transformation into sugar in the stomach imposes useless labour on the organization of the suckling. This is spared by first converting the starch into sugar, or soluble dextrine, which consideration accounts for my use of sprouted barley or malt in my preparation. It is also important that the consistency of the mixture should be such that it can be administered by the suckling bottle. The preparation of the artificial milk thus described: Sixteen grammes or about five ounces of flour are boiled in about ten times its weight of skimmed milk, until the mixture is perfectly homogeneous. It is then removed from the fire and immediately afterwards is added to it about five ounces of barley ground in a coffee mill and mixed with twice its weight of water, and one ounce of a solution of bi-carbonate of potash, consisting of 11 parts of water to 2 parts of salt. After the addition of the barley and the bi-carbonate of potash, the vessel is placed either in warm water or in a warm position until the mixture shall have lost its thickness and assumed the consistency of cream. At the end of fifteen or twenty minutes the vessel is again placed on the fire and allowed to boil for a few seconds after which the milk is passed through a close linen or hair sieve or strainer, in order to clear it of the fibrous substances of the barley. Before giving this milk to the child, it should be allowed to stand at rest for a few minutes so that the fibrous matter still held in suspension may subside. Milk prepared by this method contains exactly the same flesh-making and heat-giving substances as normal woman's milk. . . ."[15]

Children were usually fed a diet of milk, starches and occasional eggs or meat juice, until they were either two or three years old. It depended on the authority the mother happened to favour.

"The rational course seems to be, to feed infants, till about three years old, chiefly with milk and mild farinaceous vegetable preparations; a large proportion of good bread, light, well-baked, and cold should be given them; after that period, proportion their solid food to the amount of exercise they are able to take."[16]

There was an interesting custom concerning children's milk. Many town families insisted that it should come from the one cow. Some even owned a cow that was pastured locally. Farmers, dairies and good neighbours would co-operate and someone from the house would go daily to either milk the cow or take the pitcher home. There was, of course, no sterilization of dairy equipment, no pasteurization and no examination of the animals; yet there was an awareness and fear of typhoid.

In most homes milk was kept in the cold room, or on ice. Sometimes jugs were lowered into the well or set out in the nearby spring. But at the first sign of a summer storm all the milk would be boiled to help prevent the souring.

"Oatmeal, where it agrees with the stomach, is much better for children being a fine opener as well as cleanser; fine flour in every shape is the reverse. Where biscuit powder is in use, let it be made at home; this, at all events, will prevent them getting the sweepings of the baker's counters, boxes, and baskets."[16]

"Vegetables for children — their vegetables so well cooked as to make them require little butter, and less digestion; their eggs boiled slow and soft. The boiling of their milk ought to be directed by the state of their bowels; if flatulent or bilious a very little curry powder may be given in their vegetables with good effect."[16]

"Fruits that have seeds are much healthier than the stone fruits, except perhaps peaches. But all fruits are better, for very young children, if baked or cooked in some manner, and eaten with bread."[16]

"Flour gruel: Put into boiling water half a pint of wheat flour, tied in a thick cloth, and continue boiling three hours. Then remove the cloth, placing the lump where it will become quite dry. When used, with a dessert spoonful of it grated, and wet with cold water, thicken two gills of milk, adding a little salt. Excellent food for invalid children."[17]

(This flour gruel is identical with those used in the eighteenth century and the recipe continued unchanged until well into the 1920's when it was still being reprinted in Canadian cook-books.)

"Children's Cheap Cake: take a pint of molasses and half a pint of milk warmed together, a spoonful of ginger, a teaspoonful of cloves, a little butter, and a teaspoonful of saleratus dissolved in a little of the milk. Mix all with flour enough to make a dough, and let it stand for an hour. Roll out, cut in shapes, and bake."[6]

"The average healthy child of 14 months and upward is better for a carefully chosen variety in its diet. The following bills of fare will answer for any healthy child of from 14 months up to 2½ years of age.
1. Milk to drink. Half a saucer of oatmeal with a little butter and salt. A few teaspoonfuls of prune juice.
2. Thoroughly mashed potato with a little butter, cream and salt. A thick strip of rare beefsteak to suck (should be allowed the juice only), a few teaspoonfuls of scraped apple.
3. A teaspoonful of breast of turkey or chicken minced very fine. Toast and milk. Small lump of sugar for dessert.
4. Half a slice buttered toast without crust. Bread and milk. Taste of custard, wine jelly or melted vanilla or chocolate ice cream."[18]

"How to Give Castor Oil: 1 cup milk, 1 cup molasses, ½ cup sugar, ½ cup castor oil, 1 teaspoon soda, 2 teaspoons ginger, a little salt and enough flour

217

to make a stiff paste. Roll out and cut in shapes, bake in a quick oven: one or two are as good as a dose of oil."[19]

"Children should not be prohibited from laughing and talking at the table. Joyousness promotes the circulation of the blood, enlivens and invigorates it, and sends it to all parts of the system, carrying with it animation, vigour and life."[3]

Where Did the Baby Come From?

Where did you come from, baby dear?
Out of the everywhere into here.

Where did you get the eyes so blue?
Out of the sky as I came through.

Where did you get that little tear?
I found it waiting when I got here.

What makes your forehead so smooth and high?
A soft hand stroked it as I went by.

What makes your cheek like a warm, white rose?
I saw something better than anyone knows.

Whence that three-cornered smile of bliss?
Three angels gave me at once a kiss.

Where did you get this pretty ear?
God spoke, and it came out to hear.

Where did you get those arms and hands?
Love made itself into hooks and bands.

Feet, whence did you come, you darling things?
From the same box as the cherub's wings.

How did they all come just to be you?
God thought of me, and so I grew.

But how did you come to us, you dear?
God thought about you, and so I am here.

George MacDonald, n.d.

218

(This poem was repeated frequently in child-care books, cook-books, home etiquette and amusement books, and it was suggested as suitable for evening recitations. It appeared in the junior readers of only sixty years ago.)

REFERENCES
1 *Search Lights on Health*, Jefferis, Toronto, 1894.
2 *The Housekeeper's Encyclopedia*, Haskell, New York, 1869.
3 *Our Deportment*, Young, Paris, Ontario, 1883.
4 *A Treatise on Domestic Economy*, Beecher, New York, 1849.
5 *Mackenzie's Five Thousand Receipts*, Anonymous, Philadelphia, 1829.
6 *The American Frugal Housewife*, Child, New York, 1838.
7 *Mother Hubbard's Cupboard*, Anonymous, Hamilton, 1881.
8 *The American Woman's Home*, Beecher, New York, 1869.
9 *Ladies' Indispensable Assistant*, Anonymous, New York, 1851.
10 *The Cook Not Mad*, Anonymous, Kingston, Ontario, 1831.
11 *The Gentleman Immigrant*, Stamer, London, 1874.
12 *Practical Life*, Wright, Brantford, Ontario, 1881.
13 *Manners*, Hale, Boston, 1868.
14 *Life in the Clearings*, Moodie, London, 1853.
15 *Wrigley's Practical Receipts*, Wrigley, Toronto, 1870.
16 *The Ladies' New Book of Cookery*, Hale, New York, 1852.
17 *The Improved Housewife*, Webster, Boston, 1856.
18 *Breakfast, Dinner and Supper*, Cooke, Brantford, Ontario, 1897.
19 *The Reliable Cook Book*, Anonymous, Alvinston, Ontario, 1902.

Omnium-Gatherum

CHAPTER SEVENTEEN

What to Eat
"At the earnest request of numerous young housekeepers, the author has been induced to offer the following hints for the selection of suitable articles in preparing breakfasts, dinners, and suppers. They, of course, may be varied according to convenience, taste, and the size and circumstances of the family.

Breakfast for Spring and Summer:
Mutton chops; omelet; boiled potatoes — Rice batter cakes, muffins. Pickled salmon; broiled chickens; eggs — Indian cakes; milk toast. In warm weather fresh fruit (thoroughly ripe, and eaten with sugar) is an agreeable wholesome addition to the breakfast table. Fruit-jam, marmalade, and honey may be introduced at any season.

Autumn and Winter breakfasts:
Oysters stewed or fried; broiled ham with poached eggs — toast; rolls. Venison steaks; potatoes; eggs — Indian batter cakes; rolls. In cold weather, small hominy, boiled, is often introduced at breakfast tables — also Indian mush, to be eaten with butter and molasses."[1]

"Breakfast parties: black tea; green tea; coffee; chocolate; hot cakes of various sorts; omelets; birds; game; oysters, stewed, fried and pickled; cold tongue; cold ham; biscuit sandwiches; boned turkey; cold, potted or pickled lobster; raised French pie; pigeon, partridge or moorfowl pie; mushrooms fried, broiled, or stewed; jellies; marmalade; honey; fresh fruit, or sweetmeats, according to the season; a large almond sponge-cake. The table decorated with flowers."[1]

Canadian Menus

Breakfast

Fine Hominy   Buttered Toast
Beefsteak
French Rolls   Potatoes à la Crème
Buckwheat Cakes
Tea Coffee Chocolate[2]

Lunch Party

Beef Tea,
served in small porcelain cups
Cold Chicken and Oyster and other
forms of Croquettes
Chicken Salad Escalloped Oysters
Minced Ham Sandwiches
Tutti Fruiti Chocolate Cream
Cake Basket of Mixed Cake
Mulled Chocolate
Mixed Pickles Biscuits, etc.
Ice Cream and Charlottes can either
be added or substituted[2]

Dinners

First Course
        Raw Oysters
        White and Brown Soup
Second Course
        Broiled White Fish with Sauce
                and Sliced Lemon
Third Course
        Roast Beef
Fourth Course
        Roast Turkey
        Ducks
        Vegetables in Season
Croquettes of Rice or Hominy
Cranberry Sauce Currant Jelly
Cream Custard Lemon Pie
        Fruit Nuts
        Coffee[2]

Luncheon

Cold Roast Pork
Lobster Salad
Baked Sweet Potatoes
German Bread
Doughnuts Apple Sauce
Chocolate[3]

Miss Fannie Merritt Farmer, of the Boston School of Cooking fame, wrote a book dedicated to Canadian women and the holidays celebrated in this country.

Victoria Day Spread

Chicken Timbales Salad Rolls
Chaufroid of Salmon
Fairmont Sandwiches
Almond Cream Peanut Drops
Victoria Maple Leaves
Fruit Punch[4]

(The sandwiches were thin layers of finely chopped red and green peppers moistened with mayonnaise. The Maple Leaves were shortbreads cut in leaf shape, brushed with egg yolk and decorated with a candied half-cherry.)

The Canadian Kitchen 1877

Kitchen equipment was extensive and the reasonably prosperous housewife had plenty to choose from. The type of utensils varied according to the circumstances of the family and the development of the area. For instance, earlier or more primitive kitchen lists would have included more iron pots as well as kettles, and skillets with legs to stand among the coals. Lids would have had troughs to hold additional hot cinders to speed up cooking. Towards the end of the century, most town homes had dispensed with candle-making moulds, brass kettles for soap boiling and portable laundry furnaces. Reflector ovens to roast meats and to bake pies in front of the open hearth were all but a memory. Most homes had forgotten about the butter-making churns and the filtering jars to purify the drinking water.

Necessary for the Kitchen of a Small Family

"*Wooden ware*: wash bench, wash tubs (three sizes), wash board, skirt board, bosom board, bread board, towel roll, potato masher, wooden spoons, clothes stick, flour barrel cover, flour sieve, chopping bowl, soap bowl, pails, lemon squeezer, clothes wringer, clothes bars, clothes pins, clothes baskets, mop, wood boxes (nests).
Tin ware: one boiler for clothes, one boiler for ham, one bread pan, two dish pans, one preserving pan, four milk pans, two quart basins, two pint basins, two quart covered tin pails, one 4 quart covered tin pail, sauce pans with covers, two sizes. Two tin cups with handles, four jelly moulds (half pint), two pint

moulds for rice, blancmange, etc., one skimmer, two dippers, different sizes; two funnels, (one for jug and one for cruets), one quart measure, also pint, half pint and gill measures —they should be broad and low, as they are more easily kept clean — three scoops, bread pans, two round jelly cake pans and two long pie pans, one coffee pot, one tea steeper, one colander, one steamer, one horse-radish grater, one nutmeg grater, one small salt sieve, one hair sieve for straining jelly, one Dover's egg beater, one cake turner, one cake cutter, one apple corer, one potato cutter, one dozen muffin rings, one soap shaker, one ice filter, flour dredge, tea canister, coffee canister, cake, bread, cracker and cheese boxes, crumb tray, dust pans.

Iron ware: range, one pot with steamer to fit, one soup kettle, preserving kettle (porcelain), tea kettle, large and small frying pans, dripping pans, gem pans, iron spoons of different sizes, one gridiron, one griddle, one waffle iron, toasting rack, meat fork, jagging iron, can opener, coffee mill, flat irons, hammer, tack hammer, screw driver, ice pick.

Stone ware: crocks of various sizes. Bowls holding six quarts, four quarts, two quarts and pint bowls. Six earthern baking dishes of different sizes.

Brushes: table brush, two dust brooms, two scrub brushes, one blacking brush for stove, shoe brush, hearth brush, brooms."[2]

An Accessory for Boating Parties
"To make an Aquatic Life Hat. The upper part of the crown of the hat is made air-tight and water-proof, so that in the event of the wearer falling into water, it will save him by its buoyancy from being drowned, if he only holds it in his hand. It is to be fastened by a small ribband to the button-hole of the wearer's coat, in aquatic expeditions, &c. In order to render the hat more efficacious and enable it to save more lives than one, the lining

---

The Art of Letter Writing
On receiving a favourable answer:

October 16th, 18——

"Dearest Miss (or use Christian name) —
Words cannot express my delight in finding your note on my table last night. The toils of the day were over, but how delightful was it to find a letter — and *such* a letter! — from one whom I may now hope to hail as the companion of my whole future life! The weight taken off my mind by the candid and gentle confession of one whose love seemed too great a happiness to hope for is beyond description. Tomorrow I shall hasten to the presence of her from whom I hope I may never henceforth be parted, but I could not retire to rest without making one feeble attempt to express my delight at finding that hopes so flattering have not been in vain.

"Believe me, dearest,
"Your devoted and happy lover,[5]

is formed so as to be capable of being pulled out and inflated by the breath, and then closed at the extremity; in which state it will save several persons in the water."[6]

What to Name the Baby

(This list is abbreviated but still gives an idea of what was fashionable and current.)

"Our dear Baby, what shall we call it? Consult the following list, and select the prettiest name you can find. This dictionary has been prepared at great expense and trouble, and is made as complete as possible; but no surnames, that are sometime used as Christian names, such as Sydney, &c, are included."[7]

For Boys

Abiathar	Father of plenty
Adolphus	Noble hero
Albert	Illustrious
Algernon	With whiskers
Ambrose	Divine
Baldwin	Bold
Beriah	In calamity
Cadwallader	Battle arranger
Caleb	A dog
Cecil	Dim-sighted
Claude	Lame
Crispin	Having curly hair
Dennis	The God of Wine
Ebenezer	The stone of help
Elmer	Noble
Ephraim	Very fruitful
Felix	Happy
Hannibal	Grace of Baal
Ichabod	The glory has departed
Jabez	He will cause pain
James	A supplanter
Julius	Soft-haired
Lancelot	A little angel
Marmaduke	A mighty noble
Napoleon	Lion of the forest dell
Obadiah	Mouth of brass
Phineas	Servant of the Lord
Rupert	Bright in fame
Silas	Living in the Wood
Thaddeus	The wise
Uriah	Light of the Lord

For Girls

Abigail	My father's joy
Azubah	Deserted
Cassandra	She who inflames with love
Clementine	Mild
Deborah	A bee
Eliza	Worshipper of God
Emma	Industrious
Eulalia	Fair speech
Fanny	Free
Gertrude	Spear-maiden
Hortensia	A lady gardener
Inez	Pure
Jemima	A dove
Letitia	Happiness
Maria	Bitter
Ophelia	Serpent
Priscilla	Somewhat old
Rosamond	Horse protection
Selina	Parsley
Sophia	Wisdom
Tabitha	A gazelle
Theresa	Carrying corn ears
Ursula	She-bear
Zenobia	Having life from Jupiter

Herbs

As soon as a patch of land was cleared for a garden many women grew both culinary and medicinal herbs. Rare was the settlement where there was no access to these healing plants. Immigrants brought cuttings and the age-old lore from their homelands, adding new knowledge gained from local Indians, who were adept at this type of curing.

The following list of medicinal

herbs includes only those more commonly used. It is culled from a number of books including *The American Frugal Housewife*, written by Mrs. Child and published in 1838. This was consulted by Mrs. Traill, and her own *Wild Flowers of Canada*, 1869 mentions a number of herbal and Indian cures. Another source is *Search Lights on Health*, Toronto, 1894.

A Table of Popular Herbs

"*Blackberries*: are extremely useful in cases of dysentery. Tea made of the roots and leaves is beneficial; and a syrup of the berries is still better. Blackberries have sometimes effected a cure when physicians despaired. Blackberry root is a sure remedy for canker in the mouth."

"*Burdock*: warmed in vinegar is soothing applied to the feet."

"*Black snakeroot*: it is an astringent, promotes urinary evacuations, and general healthy actions."

"*Blue flag root*: has effected wonderful cures in aggravated rheumatic complaints. Extract from the bark makes a mild cathartic like rhubarb. The hard seeds have been used as a coffee substitute."

"*Buttercup*: it is good for drawing blisters and corns on the feet, and made into tea is excellent in cases of asthma."

"*Carrots*: boiled in milk and water and applied as a poultice to old sores is excellent."

"*Catnip*: steeped and sweetened with loaf sugar is good for sore throats and good for crying babies."

"*Costmary*: in salads sometimes preferred to mint." (Traditionally a dried leaf was placed in the prayer book as a restorative in too long sermons.)

"*Currants*: tea made of the leaves is good for dropsical complaints."

"*Fever root*: useful in fever especially typhus."

"*Elder*: bark and berries for scurvy."

"*Foxglove*: said to be of use in cases of convulsion fits."

"*Fir balsam*: good for sore nipples and weakness of the stomach."

"*Flaxseed*: a remedy for coughs, colds and disorders of the bowels."

"*Golden Rod*: for the head-ache."

"*Garlic*: draughts applied to the feet at night are good to remove feverish symptoms. Good for whooping cough, colds, asthma, worms."

"*Horseradish*: promotes appetite and excellent in cases of the ague."

"*Hops*: tonic, good in dysentery, nervous tremors and weakness and tremors of inebriates."

"*Hoarhound*: strengthens the lungs."

"*Juniper Bush*: its berries very excellent counter-poison, and also a great resister of pestilence."

"*Liverwort*: the root is excellent in all diseases of the liver, yellow jaundice, will check the spread of ring-worm."

"*Mosses*: will ease all inflammation and pain caused by heat."

"*Mouse Ear or Chickweed*: one of the best things for dysentery."

"*Mustard*: promotes digestion, creates appetite, removes pain from the stomach and bowels."

"*Mandrake or May Apple*: a stimulant and a laxative."

"*Plantain*: if poisoned by dogwood boil plantain strong, and wash in the tea; if poisoned by ivy do the same; if you have an old sore do the same. Plantain and house-leek boiled in cream, and strained before it is put away to cool, makes a very cooling, soothing ointment."

"*Pitcher Plant*: a decoction of the root and leaves lessens the more violent symptoms of smallpox."

"*Poplar*: a sovereign remedy for the toothache."

"*Red Clover*: a salve of them is good for cancer, old sores, sore lips."

"*Sumach*: the bark, root and berries are good for canker in the mouth or throat."

"*Violet*: makes a slimy tea, which is excellent for the canker. Leaves and blossoms are both good. Those who have families should take some pains to dry these flowers."

"*Wintergreen*: called by Indian herbalists the rheumatism weed."

"*Windflower or Canadian Snowflower*: used as a mild tonic in fevers and disorders of the liver."

The Family Medicine Chest
"*Borax* is one of the most powerful, if not indeed the most powerful antiseptic known. Good for gumboil."[8]

"*Turpentine* is good for rheumatism."[8]

"*Malt Beer*, or malt in any way, is said to be a preservative against fevers."[9]

"*Saltpetre* is a remedy for inflammatory rheumatism, sore throat, dysentery, gravel and skin diseases."[10]

"*Cayenne* prevents flatulence and increases digestive powers of weak stomachs."[10]

"*Alum* stops bleeding."[10]

Vegetables Cures
In the days before nutrition was a science and when vitamins were almost unknown, it was felt that somehow fruits and vegetables could contribute to health.

Never Sign a Paper for a Stranger.

"*Watercress* is a remedy for scurvy; *Carrots* for those suffering from asthma; *Asparagus* is used to induce perspiration and purges the blood; *Turnips* for nervous disorders and scurvy; *Spinach* is useful for those suffering from insomnia; *Cranberries* for erysipelas externally as well as internally; *Walnuts* give nerve or brain food, muscle, heat and waste; *Apples* supply the high nerve and muscle food, but do not give stay; *Oranges* are refreshing and feeding, but are not good if the liver is out of order; *Dried Figs* contain nerve and muscle food, heat and waste, but are bad for the liver; *Prunes* afford the highest nerve or brain food; supply heat and waste, but are not muscle-feeding. They should be avoided by those who suffer from the liver. *Pieplant** is wholesome and aperient; *Celery* is invaluable as a food for those suffering from any form of dyspepsia."[11]

Household Hints
For Cough and Hoarseness
"A piece of anchovy will almost instantly restore the just tone of voice to any one who has become hoarse by public speaking."[12]

To Test Mushrooms
"Rub the upper skin with a gold ring or any piece of gold: the part rubbed will turn yellow if it is a poisonous fungus."[12]

Singularly Useful Properties of Garlic
"The smell of garlic, which is formidable to many ladies, is, perhaps, the most infallible remedy in the world against the vapours, and all the nervous disorders to which women are subject."[12]

To Destroy Rats and Other Vermin
"Sponge, if cut in small pieces, fried or dipped in honey, and given to vermin, distends their intestines, and effectually destroys them.

"Mix flour of malt with some butter; add thereto a drop or two of oil of anise seeds; make it up into balls, and bait your traps therewith. If you have thousands, by this means you may take them all."[12]

After-dinner Accomplishments
The Passenger to Boulogne
"The requirements for this touching picture are an orange, a pocket-handkerchief or soft table-napkin, and a wineglass. The orange is first prepared by cutting in the rind with a penknife the best ears, nose, and mouth which the skill of the artist can compass, a couple of raisin-pips supplying the place of eyes. A pocket handkerchief is stretched lightly over the glass, and the prepared orange laid thereon, as in the annexed illustration.

"The pocket handkerchief is then moved gently backwards and forwards over the top of the glass, imparting to the orange a rolling motion, and affording a laughable but striking caricature of the agonies of a sea-sick passenger.

"We have seen the performance terminated by draping the pocket-handkerchief hood-fashion over the supposed head, and squeezing the orange into the glass. This last scene, however, is disagreeably realistic, and we venture to think is much better omitted."[13]

Speech: The Canadian Way
Time, place and circumstances change language. So it was in Canada. Those coming from the British

226

*rhubarb

Isles, particularly the educated people, thought they had an advantage in speaking English. They could not have been more wrong. Many had a rude shock. The language was English but the usage differed. Some of the new meanings and many of the phrases have persisted to this day. English-speaking immigrants felt that the same manners, customs and etiquette would prevail in Canada. Again they could not have been more wrong.

Life in Western Ontario
"We were struck, as every new comer is, by the new meanings put by Canadians on words, the new connections in which they used them, and the extraordinary way in which some were pronounced. Of course, we heard people 'guessing' at every turn, and whatever any one intended doing, he spoke of as 'fixing'. You would hear a man say, that his wagon, or his chimney, or his gun, must be 'fixed'; a girl would be ready to take a walk with you, as soon as she had 'fixed herself'; and the baby was always 'fixed' in the morning, when washed and dressed for the day. 'Catherine', said a husband one day to his wife, in my hearing pronouncing the last syllable of her name, so as to rhyme with line, 'I calculate that them apples'll want regulatin', referring to some that were drying in the sun. They 'reckon' at every third sentence. A well-informed man is said to be 'well posted up' in some particular subject. Instead of 'what', they commonly say 'how', in asking questions. A pony was praised to me as being 'as fat as mud'. In place of our exclama-

tions of surprise at the communication of any new fact, the listener will exclaim, 'I want to know'. Any log, or trunk of a tree, or other single piece of timber, is invariably a 'stick', even if it is long enough for a mast. All the stock of a timberyard is alike, 'lumber'. An ewer is 'a pitcher'; a tinpail is 'a kettle'; a servant is 'a help'; an employer is 'a boss'; a church pew is 'a slip'; a platform at a meeting is 'a stage'; children are 'juveniles'; and a baby is 'a babe'. In pronouncing if you would imitate a Canadian, you would need to open your mouth very wide, and makes as much of each sound as you can. Of course, I speak only of the country folks, native born."[14]

How to Take on Local Colour
"Our gentleman settler is wont to give himself airs, and to treat his illiterate neighbours with a certain degree of arrogance. It won't do. If he desire to lead a peaceful life, he must put his pride in his pocket. To secure good will and kind offices of his neighbours, not only must he be courteous, he must be familiar. He must not be shocked when the wife of his bosom is inquired after as 'the woman'. 'How's the woman?', is a very common question in the backwoods. Instead of frigidly responding, 'Mrs. Greene is tolerably well, I thank you', the answer should be, 'Spry, thank'ee, how's yourn?'. We are, of course, speaking of one's intercourse with the neighbouring farmers."[15]

REFERENCES
1 *The Lady's Receipt-Book*, Leslie, Philadelphia, 1847.
2 *The Home Cook Book*, Anonymous, Toronto, 1877.
3 *The White House Cook Book*, Zieman and Gillette, Toronto, 1899.
4 *Catering for Special Occasions*, Farmer, Toronto, n.d.
5 *Chesterfield's Art of Letter-Writing Simplified*, Anonymous, New York, 1857.
6 *The American Receipt Book*, Anonymous, Halifax, Yorks., c. 1840.
7 *Mrs. Clarke's Cookery Book*, Clarke, Toronto, 1883.
8 *Search Lights on Health*, Jefferis, Toronto, 1894.
9 *The American Frugal Housewife*, Child, New York, 1838.
10 *Ladies' Indispensable Assistant*, Anonymous, New York, 1851.
11 *The Household Guide*, Jefferis, Toronto, 1897.
12 *New Household Receipt Book*, Hale, London, 1854.
13 *Parlour Amusements*, Hoffmann, London, c. 1860.
14 *Adventures in Canada*, Geikie, Philadelphia, n.d.
15 *The Gentleman Immigrant*, Stamer, London, 1874.

Bibliography

The collecting of domestic books is much like a detective story. Slowly, step by step, the past is recreated. Where once it was possible only to guess at food, home organization and etiquette, now there is assurance that this is the way things were done.

At present no bibliography of Canadian domestic books exists. There is good reason for this. Little original work found a publisher. The majority of books were imported from Britain, France and the United States. Enterprising printers copied or adapted from foreign books for the home market, occasionally using a different title, sometimes adding their own names to the title page, but leaving the book basically unchanged. This led to such Canadian curiosities as *The White House Cook Book*[1] with the dedication reading:

TO THE
WIVES OF OUR PRESIDENTS
THOSE NOBLE WOMEN WHO HAVE GRACED THE
WHITE HOUSE
AND WHOSE NAMES AND MEMORIES ARE
DEAR TO ALL AMERICANS
THIS VOLUME
IS AFFECTIONATELY DEDICATED
BY THE AUTHOR

Another instance: *Breakfast, Dinner and Supper Selected by Celebrated Chefs*[2] is identical with *The 20th Century Cook Book* as issued at the same time in the United States. It was against so much of this importing that William Lyon Mackenzie published a broadsheet in 1827, warning the citizens against, "Yankee wooden clock pedlars, wooden nutmeg gentry, lottery ticket vendors, pretended hawkers of the lives of La Fayette and Washington. . . ."

The rare Canadian cook-book with the odd title *The Cook Not Mad* is the earliest known cook-book printed in Canada. It was published in Kingston, Ontario, 1831, yet it is almost identical with a book of the same name published in 1831 in Watertown, New York.

It took many years for Canadian and American books to reflect the new foods in common use such as rye flour, corn, pumpkin and the plentiful game from venison to squirrel. *The Cook Not Mad* is such a book. In general, a book devoted to the new way of life is rare; most North American domestic books owe a great debt to the writers of Great Britain and France. Many books came with settlers' effects but the information written for European kitchens had to be adapted.

Of course, the greater part of the population needed no book. Women managed their provisions as best they could. But the educated demanded books. If books were not available in Canada, then imported ones were purchased. One way or another these women managed to adapt what was modish in the larger centres of civilization regardless of whether it was food, fashion, manners or housekeeping.

What were the books in use in this country, where pioneer life in the early years of the nineteenth century was rugged and where provisions were sometimes scarce? Travellers' tales and diaries mention books by Mrs. Child,[3] Mrs. Dalgairns[4] and Mrs. Frazer.[5] The English-speaking Loyalists were familiar with both Mrs. H. Glasse[6] and E(liza) Smith.[7] Their books were known and even reprinted in the American colonies.

It is possible to trace other influences because women gave credit to the source when copying recipes into notebooks. Such famous nineteenth century food authorities as Dr. Kitchiner,[8] Alexis Soyer[9] and Mrs. Isabella Beeton[10] were also household names in Canada.

The lax copyright laws of the period enabled printers to publish foreign books as soon as they arrived, but this trade went both ways. The British were receptive to new ideas from across the Atlantic where the many appliances and the use of corn gave a touch of the exotic. The French showed where their sympathies lay during the Revolutionary War by adapting, as a novelty, such North American foods as turkey and Indian pudding. These dishes assumed a sophistication in France unknown to their originators.

As a group, cook-book writers have never hesitated to borrow from each other, sometimes with acknowledgment, often without. This simplifies the tracing of recipes back in time. The dependence of writers on each other is illustrated with Miss Eliza Acton's *Modern Cookery In All Its Branches Reduced To A System Of Easy Practice*, published in London, England in 1845 because her publisher preferred her cooking to her poetry. (Later, when the cook-book was successful, he did publish her poetry, which was not.) Miss Acton set the stage for Mrs. Isabella Beeton who wrote the monumental *Household Management* in 1861. Miss Acton's book was "edited" for North America by Mrs. Sara Hale, herself a writer of note whose books on food and household economy flooded into Canada and were published in both England and the United States. Similarly, Miss Catherine Beecher acknowledged her debt to Mrs. William Parkes' *Domestic Duties*.[11]

It should not be thought that all Canadian books were imported or loosely adapted. Many original books appeared towards the end of the century. Possibly a larger population together with easier communication made publishing less speculative. One of the most popular, judging by the number of copies still existing, was *The Home Cook Book*, first published in Toronto in the 1870's to raise money to help establish the Hospital for Sick Children. Edition after edition followed, and the later ones have a title page giving credit to the "Ladies of Toronto and Chief Cities and Towns in Canada" for their "tried, tested and proven recipes".

Mrs. Anne Clarke[12] gave her name to a cook-book in 1883. But this book returns in 1899 as *The Dominion Cook Book*.[13] As a sign of changing times the later book drops the tips on butter-making at home and the complete section on wines and spirits.

Church women still raise money with cook-books. The ladies of St. James Methodist Church in Montreal were no different. When they moved in 1890 to a new building on St. Catharine Street they published *The Peerless Cook Book — A Compilation of Tested Recipes.*

In an effort to supply the growing demand for information during the closing years of the century, books, pamphlets and leaflets were issued by manufacturers of baking powder, flour, chocolate and patent medicine, to name only a few of the sponsors. Such ephemera as almanacs, trade cards, calendars and pocket books printed recipes. It was also common for newspapers and department stores to give cook-books as premiums.

Throughout this book where reference is made to specific books the date listed is the edition used and is not necessarily the first printing.

REFERENCES
1 *The White House Cook Book,* Zieman and Gillette, Toronto, 1899.
2 *Breakfast, Dinner and Supper,* Cooke, Brantford, Ontario, 1897.
3 *The American Frugal Housewife,* Child, New York, 1838.
4 *The Practice of Cookery,* Dalgairns, Edinburgh, 1845.
5 *The Practice of Cookery, Pastry and Confectionary,* Frazer, Edinburgh, 1820.
6 *The Art of Cookery Made Plain and Easy,* Glasse, London, 1765.
7 *The Complete Housewife,* Smith, London, 1750.
8 *The Cook's Oracle,* Kitchiner, New York, 1838.
9 *The Modern Housewife,* Soyer, London, 1853.
10 *Household Management,* Beeton, London, 1861.
11 *Domestic Duties,* Parkes, London, 1841.
12 *Mrs. Clarke's Cookery Book,* Clarke, Toronto, 1883.
13 *The Dominion Cook Book,* Clarke, Toronto, 1899.

Index

Agricultural Fairs, 22, 37.
Ailments, 8, 10, 47, 56, 58, 167.
Albums, 137.
Almanacs, 21.
Animals, 22, 31, 42, 143, 210.
Balls, 27.
Bathing, 126.
Bazaars, 22.
Beauty, 6, 126.
Bees, 30, 41, 123.
Camp Meetings, 41.
Charivari, 14, 17.
Cheese, 37, 179.
Children, 57, 114, 202, 223.
Chores, 84, 104, 209.
Church, 15, 21, 203, 206.
Clothing and Fashion, 27, 87, 90, 108, 110, 134, 203, 214, 222.
Cosmetics, 126, 130, 132.
Courting, 14, 123.
Dances, 16, 27.
Drunkenness, 8.
Dyes, 102.
Education, 210.
Etiquette, 12, 26, 29, 35, 144, 148, 155, 158, 175, 203.
Fans, 148.
Fishing, 43.
Flowers, 81, 140, 157.
Food, 12, 24, 31, 34, 43, 46, 56, 64, 72, 88, 103, 130, 152, 155, 162, 169, 174, 206, 214, 220.
Furnishings, 81, 91, 205.
Funerals, 18, 21, 124, 139.
Games, 39, 148, 227.
Gardening, 82.
General Store, 38.
Hair, 127, 130.
Heating, 69, 85, 163.
Herbs, 46, 223.
Hobbies, 137, 142.
Holidays, 22.
Household Equipment, 72, 74, 163, 167, 221.
Household Hints, 87, 89, 91, 101, 108, 110, 116, 226.

Housekeeping, 7, 84, 88, 90.
Humour, 45, 137.
Hunting, 42.
Kitchens, 72, 74, 85, 221.
Laundry, 99.
Letter writing, 148, 222.
Lighting, 43, 96, 209.
Maple, 39, 179.
Marriage, 4, 16.
Medicine, 46, 205.
Menus, 25, 35, 88, 200, 220.
Milling, 177.
Music, 147.
Names, 203, 223.
Needlework, 138.
Nursery Rhymes, 208.
Plumbing, 68, 127.
Poultry, 106, 210.
Recipes, 168, 173, 177, 182.
Remedies, 9, 12, 48, 58, 129, 204, 225.
Servants, 73, 109, 127, 157.
Sex, 5, 10.
Shoes, 116.
Singing, 38.
Soapmaking, 21, 99.
Social Events, 9, 16, 36, 39, 41, 45, 152, 155, 214.
Songs, 38, 208.
Speech, 226.
Spinning and Weaving, 102, 121, 210.
Storerooms, 78.
Stoves, 69.
Superstitions, 20.
Table Setting, 156.
Taverns, 18, 36.
Teeth, 132.
Temperance, 8, 31, 41, 202.
Toys, 206.
Transgressors, 18.
Travelling, 34.
Vermin, 90, 92, 226.
Visiting, 34.
Weddings, 15, 123.
Wigs, 118.
Wines and Liquors, 36, 158, 168.

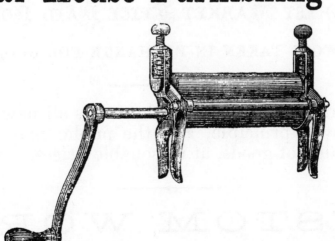

J. W. FARRAND,

Woollen Manufacturer,

CAMPBELLFORD WOOLLEN MILLS.

CAMPBELLFORD, NEAR BRIGHTON, ONT.

MANUFACTURER OF

FANCY TWEED CLOTHS,

PLAIN AND FANCY WOOLLENS,

Flannels, Blankets, &c.,

The Highest Market Price Paid For Wool

OR WOOL TAKEN IN EXCHANGE FOR GOODS.

The machinery of this establishment is all new and on the most improved principle, and the public may rely on a superior quality of goods, at reasonable prices.

CUSTOM WORK

PROMPTLY EXECUTED IN A SATISFACTORY MANNER, AT REASONABLE PRICES.

Cloth
Columbia Millbank Linen

Jacket Stock
70 lb. Georgian Offset Matte

Text Stock
60 lb. Byronic Text White Wove
70 lb. Byronic Text Laid — Egyptian Red

Text Type
11 on 12 Baskerville

Headings
Kennerly Oldstyle — Roman and Italic

Design
Howard Pain

Printed and Bound by
McCorquodale & Blades Printers Limited,
Toronto, Canada